PEREMPTORY INTERNATIONAL LAW – *JUS COGENS*

Robert Kolb, one of the leading international scholars of his generation, offers a seminal survey of the question of peremptory international law. The author analyses and systemises different questions, such as: the typology of peremptory norms beyond the Vienna Convention on the Law of Treaties; here he distinguishes between 'public order' *jus cogens* and mere 'public utility' *jus cogens*. Furthermore, what about relative *jus cogens*, for example regional *jus cogens* norms or conventional *jus cogens* norms? What about some consequences of *jus cogens* breaches in the law of State responsibility: are they themselves *jus cogens*? Thus, can individual war reparations be renounced by lump-sum agreements? What happens if different *jus cogens* norms are in conflict? Is there a difference between the scope of *jus cogens* in inter-State relations and its scope for other subjects of law, such as the UN and its Security Council? Is *jus cogens* necessarily predicated on the concept of a hierarchy of norms? What is the exact extent of the peremptory nature of some rules? Sometimes, only the core of a principle is peremptory, while its normative periphery is not. Also, in the use of force, the peremptory character of the provision is compatible with agreements falling under the recognised exceptions, such as collective self-defence. These and other unusual questions are discussed in the present book.

Peremptory International Law – *Jus Cogens*

A General Inventory

Robert Kolb

·HART·
PUBLISHING
OXFORD AND PORTLAND, OREGON
2017

Hart Publishing
An imprint of Bloomsbury Publishing Plc

Hart Publishing Ltd
Kemp House
Chawley Park
Cumnor Hill
Oxford OX2 9PH
UK

Bloomsbury Publishing Plc
50 Bedford Square
London
WC1B 3DP
UK

www.hartpub.co.uk
www.bloomsbury.com

Published in North America (US and Canada) by
Hart Publishing
c/o International Specialized Book Services
920 NE 58th Avenue, Suite 300
Portland, OR 97213-3786
USA

www.isbs.com

HART PUBLISHING, the Hart/Stag logo, BLOOMSBURY and the Diana logo are trademarks of Bloomsbury Publishing Plc

First published in hardback, 2015
Paperback edition, 2017

British Library Cataloguing-in-Publication Data
A catalogue record for this book is available from the British Library.

ISBN: PB: 978-1-50991-781-5
HB: 978-1-78225-727-1

Typeset by Compuscript Ltd, Shannon
Printed and bound in Great Britain by
Lightning Source UK Ltd

PREFACE

Yet another monograph on international peremptory norms (*jus cogens*)? What could possibly be added to the rich and seminal literature on this subject that has thrived so much over the last 40 years? And would a full account of all the matters discussed under the flag of *jus cogens* not just prompt yet another of these lengthy and serious studies, where the reader has to fight through the jungle of many hundreds of highly learned pages?

There is at least one reason why I hope I might be forgiven for venturing once again into the domain of peremptory norms. Much of the existing literature is ancient, dating back to the time of the adoption of the Vienna Convention on the Law of Treaties (VCLT) in 1969. These works are only partial, in the sense that they naturally omit more recent manifestations of the *jus cogens* concept, which has spread Big Bang-like beyond the law of treaties. Such works are often quite theoretical in nature. Some more recent works concentrate on giving a fairly non-technical, and certainly non-heroic, account of the subject. The case law is reviewed and several questions are treated, but authors concentrate on the 'value-orientedness' of peremptory laws and on the fundamental interests of the international community. Yet other modern works are bluntly excessively ideological in nature, with authors arrogating to themselves the role of law-giver by largely erasing any distinction between *lex lata* and *lex ferenda* in the name of progress and values. *Jus cogens* is moreover a concept that is often misunderstood and poorly marshalled from a technical point of view. It attracts the attention of many non-lawyers who are poorly equipped to understand the true functioning of such a concept within the four corners of the legal order.

The present monograph seeks to fill two gaps that have resulted from such mainstream treatment of the concept. First, it aims to match a 'value-oriented approach', which is not simply or barely rejected by the present author,[1] with the proper underlying legal construction. It is not sufficient for a lawyer to speak about fundamental values; he must proceed to give these values and the legal constructs that carry them a precise setting in legal technique. Only then can the mapping

[1] This is not always understood, as shown by A Bianchi, 'Human Rights and the Magic of *Jus Cogens*' (2008) 19 *European Journal of International Law* 495. As well as the fact that I do not limit *jus cogens* to 'procedural norms', I also do not reject the idea of public order or of values in international law. My point is simply that reference to such concepts is not sufficient and that legal technique has to follow in order to give a proper meaning to such possibly lofty constructions in view of the concrete functioning of the legal order. My criticism of the 'messianic dimension' is essentially that this dimension often remains too isolated and is not sustained by adequate legal clothing.

of the concept of *jus cogens* be said to be complete. In my opinion, this does not seem to have been adequately achieved to this day, and efforts in this direction are thus necessary—which the present contribution purports to make. Second, the current literature on *jus cogens* limits the concept to so-called 'public-order' norms, namely those embodying the fundamental interests of a given society. By doing so, the analysis of *jus cogens* is at best limited to Articles 53 and 64 VCLT. These provisions are thus taken as the exclusive *sedes materiae* of peremptory phenomena in international law. This has always seemed to me to be utterly narrow and therefore imprecise. In municipal law, *jus cogens* is not limited to public order norms, but spreads its tentacles across the entire—and huge—area of public law (*jus publicum*).[2] It is quite natural that the legislation of the State cannot normally be contracted away by private actors.

By the same token, there are many examples of 'non-derogability' of norms in international law, which all come close to the very concept of peremptoriness. Thus, a second objective of this monograph is to give a full account of peremptory norms in international law beyond the usually described public order phenomena rooted in the VCLT. It is true that by doing so, I will disturb many deeply entrenched positions such that the reader may at first sight fail to find himself or herself at ease. I would simply ask the reader to try to rid himself of various preconceptions for a short time; such preconceptions are, after all, nourished only by the sheer repetition in the literature rather than by incontestable scientific truth. He may then judge the extent to which the conception I present here fulfils a useful function in capturing the full spectrum of 'peremptoriness' in international law and to what extent differences which may legitimately remain are more a matter of words than substance.

It may be added that I have always been sympathetic to the *jus cogens* phenomenon in international law, since the technique of peremptoriness is for me an ordinary and indispensable tool of any mature legal order. By going beyond the public order limb, the conception of *jus cogens* to be presented is indeed fairly broad (hence the subtitle of this work, 'A General Inventory'). At the same time, I have attempted to limit the concept so that it remains compatible with the legal certainty necessary for the proper functioning of a legal order (especially the rather chaotic international legal order). Efforts have also been made to avoid presenting my personal legal wishes as an expression of standing positive law. Hopefully, the treatment of *jus cogens* in this study will appear on the whole balanced between a broad range

[2] For one of the many authors overlooking this aspect, see eg J Verhoeven, 'Sur les "bons" et les "mauvais" emplois du *jus cogens*' (2008) 5 *Anuario Brasileiro de Direito Internacional* 133ff. The author sees any enlargement of *jus cogens* enquiries beyond the realm of public order norms as pushing the concept too far and as a legal mistake. To me, this just reveals dogmatic preconceptions, which by the way also contradict municipal law experiences, and which therefore should have a sort of presumption against them. Precise legal argument should be offered to rebut such a larger concept entrenched in legal experience, an *ipse dixit* ('that has nothing to do with *jus cogens*') being hardly sufficient, if not arrogant, even taking account of the great distinction of the Belgian author.

of peremptory phenomena and a narrow treatment of the effects and reach of peremptoriness.

In view of the aim of the present study, as set out above, it is a short work. There is hardly any necessity to repeat what has already been uttered many times or what appears to be irrelevant to my self-tailored purpose. The plan while writing was to remain within the bounds of 100 manuscript pages, which required significant limitations and selection in terms of the subject matter analysed. Therefore the reader should not expect a fully fledged treatment of the question; this is a book for reflection, not for acquiring encyclopaedic or even basic knowledge. I will also be somewhat sparing in the footnotes. The reader interested in more detailed development of certain questions treated here, and in the literature referring to them, may consult my *Théorie du jus cogens international* (Paris, 2001). The present monograph is a sort of follow-up to this French study, 15 years after its writing. I have remained faithful to my main construction of *jus cogens*, but I have also gone further on some aspects and abandoned one or two specific views. Moreover, there are some matters I did not treat in 2001, but which now demand to be developed in view of the important legal developments of the last 15 years. Overall, I hope that this journey through international *jus cogens* will be as interesting for the reader as might a magnificent landscape high in the mountains, with its reduction to essence and at the same time its many violently unexpected details, often surrounded by the stern sound of cascading waters.

CONTENTS

Preface v
Table of Cases xiii
Table of Legislation xv

1. Definition and Functions of *Jus Cogens* 1
I. Definitional Issues 1
A. Concept 1
B. Opinions 7
C. Definitions 10
II. Functions of *Jus Cogens* 12

2. Negationism: The Adversaries of *Jus Cogens* 15
I. An Institutional Critique: *Jus Cogens* Supposes a Centralised Legal Order 16
II. A Structural Argument: *Jus Cogens* Supposes a Clear Distinction Between the Creators and the Subjects of the Law, and Between Objective Law and Contractual Engagements 18
III. A Second Structural Argument: *Jus Cogens* Supposes a Hierarchy or Differentiation of Norms Unknown to International Law 21
IV. A Positive Law Argument: *Jus Cogens* is Not Recognised in the International Legal Order 23
V. A Pragmatic Argument: *Jus Cogens* is Useless 23
VI. A Political Argument: *Jus Cogens* is Dangerous for International Law and is a Tool for Political Manipulation 25
VII. A Multicoloured Bouquet of Arguments Against *Jus Cogens*: M Glennon 27

3. Theories of *Jus Cogens* 30
I. *Jus Cogens* as an Expression of Natural Law 30
II. *Jus Cogens* as the Public Order of the International Community, Giving Rise to Hierarchically Superior Norms (Rules of Vertical Collision) 32
III. *Jus Cogens* as Rules of International Constitutional Law (Fundamental General Principles, Minimum Necessary for the Existence of an International Legal Order) 38

IV. *Jus Cogens* as a Legal Technique Inherent in Law: Defining *Jus Cogens* by Its Effect (Non-Derogability) 39
V. *Jus Cogens* as a Specific Rule for Conflict of Successive Treaties (Rules of Horizontal Collision) 40
VI. The Theories of Cançado Trindade, Chaumont and Wengler 42
A. Cançado Trindade 42
B. Chaumont 43
C. Wengler 43

4. Legal Construction of International *Jus Cogens* 45
I. Relativity of *Jus Cogens* 45
II. Types of *Jus Cogens* 46
A. Public Order *Jus Cogens* 46
B. Public Utility (or Public Law) *Jus Cogens* 49
C. Logical *Jus Cogens* 56
III. The Extension of *Jus Cogens*: What Legal Acts and Facts are Covered by the Notion? 58
A. Agreements 60
B. Unilateral Legal Acts 61
C. Customary International Law? 64
D. General Principles of Law? 72
IV. Some Special Issues 73
A. Extent of Peremptoriness 73
(i) The Non-Use of Force Rule (Hereinafter NUFR) 73
(ii) Provisions of International Humanitarian Law (Law of Armed Conflict) Containing a 'Military Necessity' Clause 75
B. Human Rights Law and So-Called 'Derogation' Clauses 77
C. International Humanitarian Law, in Particular Articles 6/6/6/7 of Geneva Conventions (GC) I–IV 81
D. Differentiation of *Jus Cogens* According to Legal Subjects? 85
E. Definition of the Proper Normative Conflict 86

5. Sources of *Jus Cogens* 89
I. The General Issue 89
II. Regional *Jus Cogens*? Bilateral *Jus Cogens*? 97
III. Modification of *Jus Cogens* Norms 100
A. Modification 101
B. Parallelism of Form 103

6. Effects of *Jus Cogens* 104
I. An Extension of Possible Effects: From Nullity of Legal Acts to Consequences of Breach, to Potentially Unlimited Effects 104
A. Nullity 104
B. Responsibility 106
C. Boundlessness? 108

II. Secondary Rules as *Jus Cogens*? 109
III. What Effects Flow from *Jus Cogens*? 113

7. A Blind Spot: Conflicts Between *Jus Cogens* Norms 116
I. Conflicts Between Public Order *Jus Cogens* and Public Utility *Jus Cogens* 118
II. Conflicts Between Public Utility *Jus Cogens* Norms 119
III. Conflicts Between Public Order *Jus Cogens* Norms 121
A. 'Humanitarian Intervention'/'Responsibility to Protect' 121
B. Non-Recognition of Territorial Situations Obtained by Force and Self-Determination of Peoples 124

8. Conclusion 127

Select Bibliography 130
Index 138

TABLE OF CASES

A c Seco, arrêt du Tribunal fédéral suisse du 22 avril 2008 120
Al-Adsani (2001) 123 ILR 32 (ECtHR) 37, 65, 66
Aloeboetoe v Suriname (1993) 116 ILR 278 (Inter-American Ct of Human Rights) 18, 61, 105
Armed Activities case (DRC v Rwanda) [2006] ICJ Rep 31–32 66
Armed Activities case (DRC v Uganda) [2006] ICJ Rep 91 65
Arrest Warrant case [2002] ICJ Rep 98 110
Bouzari v Iran (2002) 124 ILR 442 (Canada, Ontario Superior Ct of Justice) 33, 65, 90
Certain Expenses, advisory opinion [1962] ICJ Rep 167 121
Certain German Interests in Polish Upper Silesia (1925) PCIJ series A no 6, p 21 53
Continental Shelf case (Tunisia/Libya, 1982) 53
East Timor case [1995] ICJ Rep 102 118
Exchange of Greek and Turkish Populations opinion (1925) PCIJ series B no 10, p 21 7
Ferrini (2004) 128 ILR 668–69 (Italian Ct of Cassation) 65, 108
Free Zones case (1929) PCIJ series A no 22, pp 48–49 .... 50, 52–54
Furundzija case (1998) 121 ILR 260–62 (International Criminal Tribunal for the Former Yugoslavia) 33, 65, 80, 108
Genocide case, provisional measures [1993] ICJ Rep 440 65
Genocide case [1996-II] ICJ Rep 754 62
Interhandel case [1959] ICJ Rep 101 51
Interpretation of the Greco-Bulgarian Agreement of 9 December 1927 (Caphandaris-Molloff Agreement (1932) PCIJ series A/B no 45, p 87 53
Judicial Guarantees in Times of Emergency, advisory opinion (1987) series A, no 9, 92 ILR 405 (Inter-American Ct of Human Rights) 79
Jurisdiction Immunities (3 February 2012) (ICJ) 14, 37, 66, 87, 115
Kadi (2005) 149 ILR 297–97 (Ct of First Instance of the EC) 63, 85, 120
Kaunda case (2004) 136 ILR 463 (SA Constitutional Ct) 109
Kosovo opinion [2010-II] ICJ Rep 608–09 73
Krupp case 15 ILR 626–27 (US Military Tribunal at Nurembourg) 60, 82
Military and Paramilitary Activities in and against Nicaragua, merits [1986] ICJ Rep 39 51
Nada c Seco, arrêt du Tribunal fédéral suisse du 14 novembre 2007 120
Northern Cameroons case [1963] ICJ Rep 29 51
Norwegian Loans case [1957] ICJ Rep 69 51
Nottebohm case, preliminary objection [1953] ICJ Rep 122 .... 50, 51
Nuclear Weapons, opinion (1996) (ICJ) 24

Prefecture of Voioitia (2011) 150 ILR 720–21 (Italy, Ct of Cassation) 65
Right of Passage, merits [1960] ICJ Rep 39 99
Sam Hinga Norman case (2003) case no 2003-08-PT
(Special Ct for Sierra Leone) 79
Serbian Loans case, PCIJ series A no 20/21, p 65 50
Siderman de Blake case (1992) 103 ILR 472 (US Ct of Appeals) 65
Tadic (1999) 124 ILR 181 (UN Security Council Appeals Chamber) 63
US v Matta-Ballesteros (1995) 107 ILR 435
(US Ct of Appeals, 9th Circuit) 12, 33
Wimbledon case, PCIJ series A, no 1, p 25 7
Yusuf and Barakaat (2005) 149 ILR 237 (Ct of First Instance
of the EC) 63, 85, 120

TABLE OF LEGISLATION

International

Additional Protocol I to the Geneva Conventions 1977 82
Art 48 81
Art 51(6) 81
Additional Protocol II to the Geneva Conventions 1977 82
Art 11(1) 81
Aegidian Constitutions 1357 56
African Charter on Human and Peoples' Rights 1981 77
Arab Charter on Human Rights 2004
Art 4 77
Camp David Israel/Egypt Peace Treaty 1979 46
Cyprus Guarantee Treaty 1960 46
Dayton Agreement 1995 ....25, 27
European Convention on Human Rights 1950 78
Art 15 77
European Social Charter 1961
Art 30 77
General Assembly Resolution 92(I) of 7 December 1946 55
Geneva Convention I 1949 ....93, 99, 115
Art 1 120
Art 3 ....81, 120
(3) 81
Art 6 ....6, 81–85, 94, 106, 108, 119
Art 7 83
Art 15 81
Art 50 83
Geneva Convention II 1949 ....93, 99, 115
Art 1 120
Art 3 ....81, 120
(3) 81
Art 6 ....6, 81–85, 94, 106, 108, 119
Art 7 83
Art 51 83
Geneva Convention III on Prisoners of War 1949 ....93, 99, 115
Art 1 120
Art 3 ....81, 120
(3) 81
Art 6 ....6, 60, 81–85, 94, 106, 108, 119
Art 7 83

Art 12 ... 83
Art 13 ... 81
Art 22 ... 84
Art 52(1) ... 84
Art 71 ... 83
Art 109(2) ... 81
Art 118(1) ... 83
Art 130 ... 83
Geneva Convention IV 1949 ... 93, 99, 115
Art 1 ... 120
Art 3 ... 81, 120
(3) ... 81
Art 6(3) ... 79
Art 7 ... 6, 79, 81–85, 94, 106, 108, 119
Art 8 ... 83
Art 18 ... 81
Art 47 ... 124
Art 147 ... 83
Geneva Convention on Prisoners of War 1929 ... 60
Genocide Convention 1948 ... 93
Hague Regulations 1907
Art 23g ... 76
Inter-American Convention on Human Rights 1969
Art 27 ... 77
International Covenant on Children's and Peoples Rights (ICCPR) ... 77–79
Art 11 ... 79
Art 14(5) ... 79
Art 18(3) ... 78
International Covenant on Civil and Political Rights 1966
Art 4 ... 48, 77
International Law Commission (ILC) Articles
on State Responsibility (ASR) 2001 ... 106, 107
Art 26 ... 6, 74, 107
Art 40(1) ... 107
Arts 40–41 ... 6, 106, 107
Art 41(1) ... 106
(2) ... 106
Art 50(1)(d) ... 107
NATO Charter ... 29
Oslo Agreements (Palestine/Israel) ... 124
Resolution 242 of the UN Security Council ... 25, 27
Resolution 377 of the UN Security Council ... 123
Rules of the International Court of Justice ... 52
Statute of the International Court of Justice ... 6, 49–52, 54, 93, 103, 106, 118
Art 30 ... 51
Art 32 (now 101) ... 52
Art 36 ... 118
(2) ... 51, 113
(6) ... 51

Art 38 89
(1)(b) 99
Art 38b 89
Art 54(2) 52
(3) 52
Art 58 52
Arts 65–68 52
Swiss Constitution 36
Art 139(3) 108
Treaty between Russia and Persia 1921 46
UN Charter (UNC) 89, 119
Ch VII 74, 85, 119, 120, 122
Art 42 85
Art 43 74
Art 51 74
Art 96 52
Art 103 ....38, 86, 95, 117, 119
Vienna Convention on the Law of Treaties
(VCLT) 1969 ....10, 11, 16, 23, 41, 60, 73, 91, 93, 101, 103
Art 30 ....49, 58
Art 41 82
(1)(b) 42, 49, 82
Art 44(3) 61
(5) 121
Art 53 ....1, 7, 8–10, 12, 13, 15, 20, 23, 31–34, 37, 41, 57, 58, 60, 62, 65, 69, 71, 72, 78, 82, 89, 92, 93, 99–101, 103, 105, 107, 113, 115
Art 60(2)(c) 42
Art 64 ....7, 8, 23, 60, 61, 72, 92, 99, 107, 113
Art 65 105
Art 71 115
Western Sahara Treaty 1975 46

1

Definition and Functions of *Jus Cogens*

I. Definitional Issues

It may not be out of order to start with a short definition of *jus cogens*[1] (or 'peremptory norms',[2] sometimes 'imperative law' or sometimes 'compelling law',[3] the latter being however an imprecise expression, since all binding[4] legal norms are compelling—not only *jus cogens* norms, but also their counterpart norms, *jus dispositivum*). This is all the more true when we take account of the fact that we will depart from the mainstream classification. However, the definition will be nothing more than a sort of starting hypothesis for our work. Its justification will hopefully follow from the substantive developments provided in the following chapters.

So, then, what is to be considered *jus cogens* or legal peremptoriness, either in general or specifically in international law?

A. Concept

There is a fundamental distinction in all municipal legal orders between peremptory and non-peremptory laws—that is, between laws whose normative injunction

[1] The term can be expressed as either *jus cogens* or *ius cogens*. The latter is correct in classical Latin style (but note that the term *jus cogens* emerged only in the 19th century); the former is the modern version. The 'j' was developed in the context of styled first letters of a chapter in printed books after the invention of the Gutenberg press. In the past I used to write '*ius*', perhaps in order to show that I had studied Roman Law. I may be forgiven, when approaching the age of 50, for not finding it necessary to prove such a pedigree.

[2] See, eg, Art 53 VCLT; A Orakhelashvili, *Peremptory Norms in International Law* (Oxford, 2006). The term 'peremptory norms' is the proper and correct legal translation of *jus cogens* into legal language.

[3] See, eg, MW Janis, 'The Nature of *Jus Cogens*' in L May and J Brown (eds), *Philosophy of Law: Classic and Contemporary Readings* (Chichester, 2010) 184.

[4] Conversely, there are also non-binding legal norms or subjective situations, the first mainly in the form of soft law (eg recommendations), the second mainly in the form of simple entitlements which may be exercised or not. In the latter case, such subjective optional entitlements will flow from a legal norm, either of *jus dispositivum* or even possibly of *jus cogens* (for example, judicial action based on an enhanced standing—obligations *erga omnes*—may be exercised or not). But these are not in themselves 'binding', ie not compelling norms. On the other hand, soft law norms are in themselves neither *jus cogens* nor *jus dispositivum*, as they are not binding legal norms at all. In other words, *jus cogens* supposes a binding legal norm; but not all binding legal norms are *jus cogens*.

can be derogated from by the parties to a legal relationship, and laws whose normative injunction cannot be contracted out of or contracted away. The former are called non-peremptory (*jus dispositivum*), the latter peremptory (*jus cogens*). The key term for the classical understanding of *jus cogens* is therefore 'derogability'. In other words, *jus cogens* is defined by a particular quality of the norm at stake, that is, the legal fact that it does not allow derogation. Derogation is to be carefully distinguished from abrogation (even if in the literature confusion is not infrequent).[5] Abrogation refers to the termination of a legal norm as regards all its addressees. The result is that the norm is no longer in force as from a certain date. It does not bind any legal subject from that date onwards; it is no longer applicable. Concretely, the norm is terminated by repealing legislation, by replacement with a new law, or by obsolescence (desuetude). Derogation, on the other hand, leaves the norm at stake intact. It remains in force and thus continues to be applicable. However, if that norm is not peremptory, the subjects of the law may contract out of it through the creation of special legal rules that these subjects want to apply in their mutual relations. In other words, the general legal regime is replaced by a specific contractual one and becomes applicable *inter se* on the basis of the *lex specialis* rule. As between the subjects that have contracted out, the special legal regime they have provided for will apply; conversely, in relations between these derogating subjects and third party non-derogating subjects (all these subjects being parties to the general legal regime), this general legal regime will apply. There is thus a split in legal relationships according to the subjects at stake: one *inter se* (derogatory regime) and one *erga tertios* (ordinary regime). The legal order allows this 'choice of law' in all matters where there is no public concern to maintain the unity of the original legal regime. The legislator here wishes to allow the parties to tailor their own regimes according to their needs, while providing a network of subsidiary legal solutions where the parties have not provided for a *lex specialis*.

Now, if a rule is *jus cogens*, what has been said in the preceding lines will not apply. In such cases, there is an interest, imposed by the legislator or ruled by tribunals, in keeping a legal regime entire and binding on all subjects by allowing no contracting out.[6] The reasons for this choice are manifold: the wish to protect the weaker party to a contract (such as the imposition of minimum wages notwithstanding contrary stipulations); the wish for public security in the control of electricity installations; the necessity of collecting taxes based on the principle of

[5] The confusion may also be exacerbated by maxims such as '*lex posterior derogat legi priori*', where, if there is identity of the parties to the legal act, what is indeed at stake is abrogation/modification and not derogation/priority of application. See, eg, H Kelsen, *The Law of the United Nations* (London, 1951) 112.

[6] As has previously been stated by the present author: see R Kolb, 'Théorie du ius cogens international' (2003) 36 *Revue belge de droit international* 9: '[L]e *ius cogens* est une technique juridique qui vise à maintenir l'unité et l'intégrité d'un régime juridique en ne permettant pas sa fragmentation en régimes juridiques plus particuliers qui seraient autrement applicables prioritairement en vertu de la *lex specialis*, dans tous les cas où il existe un intérêt public à cet effet. Le *ius cogens* constitue donc une limitation du *law-making power* eu égard à l'intégrité de régimes normatifs.'

equality, which does not allow for bargaining with taxpayers, etc. These legal norms are thus said to be 'non-derogable', that is, not replaceable by special legal regimes applicable as *leges speciales* between some parties. This is the proper domain of *jus cogens*. Hence, in municipal legal orders, *jus cogens* is a legal technique which attaches to a series of norms to confer on them a particular resistance to derogation. In other words, *jus cogens* is a legal technique whereby the unity of a legal regime is maintained *ratione personae* by denying the application of the rule *lex specialis derogat generali* in order to satisfy a collectively held interest in the equal application of a legal regime to all parties.[7] *Jus cogens* is a legal technique which protects against fragmentation of the law into a plurality of separately applicable legal regimes under the guise of private autonomy. Or still in other words, by *jus cogens* the rule *lex specialis derogat generali* is replaced by the opposite rule *lex specialis non derogat generali cogentis*. Peremptoriness is the counterpart to the *lex specialis* rule. It therefore relates to one aspect of the relationship between the general and the particular law, that is, to an issue of conflict of norms. Its aim is to provide a specific solution to this conflict by giving specific precedence to the general norm over the special one, in reversal of the ordinary rule of *lex specialis*. This specific preference is grounded, in principle, in the nullity or voidness of the contrary particular rule. This is quite a radical legal mechanism: it legally erases the conflict at its root, since the particular norm conflicting with the peremptory general one is voided. The following points should be borne in mind.

First, such municipal *jus cogens* is not limited to public policy norms embodying fundamental values. It is linked rather to public legislation not admitting derogation. *Second*, there is no question of hierarchy of norms here. The public legislation at stake can be situated at any level of the normativity, from the constitution to the barest administrative regulation.[8] *Third*, *jus cogens* is here not so much a norm in itself, as a legal quality that certain norms possess: they are either peremptory or not, according to the type of legal interest protected. *Jus cogens* is a quality of a norm, not a norm in itself. It is a legal technique, not a substantive provision or a source of law in itself. The 'jus' refers not just to substance, but to the legal characteristics of a norm, that is, the applicability or otherwise of the *lex specialis* principle. *Fourth*, the concept of *jus cogens* is intrinsically linked to the principle of *lex specialis*: when the latter applies, the norm is dispositive; when the latter does not apply, the norm is peremptory. In other words, as already stressed, peremptoriness is the other side of the coin of the *lex specialis* principle. *Fifth*, the effect of such *jus cogens* is the voiding of contrary legal acts, such as contracts or unilateral acts. If municipal '*ordre public*' (public policy) has a series of legal

[7] On this notion, see eg G Arzt, *Einführung in die Rechtswissenschaft* (Basel/Frankfurt, 1987) 36ff. Professor Arzt expressly notices, quite correctly, that *jus cogens* does not limit itself to questions of fundamental importance, but encompasses a series of detailed administrative regulations (at 37). See, to the same effect, P Forstmoser and H-U Vogt, *Einführung in das Recht*, 5th edn (Bern, 2012) 127; H Seiler, *Einführung in das Recht*, 3rd edn (Zurich/Basel/Geneva, 2009) 92.

[8] See Arzt (n 7).

effects, particularly in the realm of private international law, *jus cogens* is limited to the voiding effect with regard to legal acts. This voidness does not extend to factual acts, such as the act of murder (where there is nothing to void, but only an appraisal of legality or illegality and the consequences arising therefrom); nor does it extend to objective legal facts (because the voiding effect is directed to the subjective normative acts of the subjects of law, not to the objective norms of the legal order itself). *Sixth*, the peremptory status of a norm entails a significant limitation on the law-making power (or better: legal act-making power) of the subjects bound by that norm.[9] Any stipulations or legal acts they perform that are contrary to the imperative norm are voided. Moreover, their stipulation can give rise to other legal consequences, such as criminal law suits. Whether in international law that is an effect of *jus cogens* or of other norms of general international law must await analysis in a later chapter (as we will see, this is an effect situated outside the bounds of *jus cogens*). *Finally*, the categories of *jus cogens* and *jus dispositivum* are exhaustive and related: any norm has either the one legal or the other legal quality; *tertium non datur*.[10] A legal proposition can either be derogated from or it cannot; it can be derogated from in part or totally, or it cannot be derogated from in part or totally. Derogation is a quality which is not one of degree but one of kind. The fact that certain aspects of normative content can be derogated from and not others does not prove the contrary, but extends only to the *extent* to which derogation is allowed. The concept of derogation itself remains binary.[11]

To what extent can these aspects of municipal law be taken as applying analogously in international law? Is international *jus cogens* of the same type as its municipal counterpart,[12] or does it have a peculiar and divergent meaning?[13]

[9] See, eg, GA Christenson, '*Jus Cogens*: Guarding Interests Fundamental to International Society' (1988) 28 *Virginia Journal of International Law* 585, 632, 646, 648; A Cassese, 'An Enhanced Role of *Jus Cogens*' in A Cassese (ed), *Realizing Utopia: The Future of International Law* (Oxford, 2012) 160. Thus, the normative competence of States is limited: C Rozakis, *The Concept of Jus Cogens in the Law of Treaties* (Amsterdam/New York/Oxford, 1976) 14ff, 27.

[10] See U Linderfalk, 'What is So Special about *Jus Cogens*? On the Difference between the Ordinary and the Peremptory International Law' (2012) 14 *International Community Law Review* 5.

[11] On this point the arguments of Linderfalk, ibid, 12ff are imprecise. He claims that the 'defeasibility' of a norm is a relative concept which reflects relative normativity in international law: thus a *jus cogens* norm is not necessarily protected against all types of exception (eg military necessity for international humanitarian law norms). The matter then becomes one of degree and not one of kind; hence the *jus cogens* concept is inherently imprecise; it suggests absolute protection where there is none. The error in this chain of argument is that its premises are wrong. The claim that *jus cogens* is based in any case on 'absolute' norms protected against any type of exception or inroad is indeed wrong, and on this point Linderfalk is right. But his point does not prove that derogability is not a binary concept (which it is); it only shows that self-defined 'defeasibility' is not such a binary concept. To the extent that *jus cogens* is centred on the notion of non-derogability, and not 'non-defeasibility', which is not a legal term of art at all, it is precisely not fuzzy, at least on this account; but it may be fuzzy in the definition of the norms which possess such a quality, which is another matter, of a substantive nature.

[12] For a brief overview of the most salient features of municipal legislation regarding the public order aspect of *jus cogens*, see Orakhelashvili (n 2) 11ff.

[13] There are different views on this issue. For some authors, the two types of *jus cogens* have more differences than similarities: see eg I Diaconu, *Contribution à une étude sur les norms imperatives en*

We may note already at this juncture that there are at least three arguments on the basis of which a particular concept of *jus cogens* has been justified as regards the international legal order, departing from the municipal law experience.

First, there is the argument relating to the decentralised or 'decentral'[14] nature of international society. In short, the argument goes to the lack of a superior public authority, namely the lack of a centralised legislature, integrated executive and regular judiciary. It goes on to state that the application of 'public order' norms supposes a capacity to legislate to define such common interest norms and also the presence of a judge to impose them in case of recalcitrance.[15] This is possible in centralised municipal law; it is not in international law. Hence, so the argument goes, the structure of international *jus cogens* must be different from its internal counterpart. This argument is mainly situated at a conceptual and abstract level. In this regard, however, it must be recalled that all concepts of international law are to be seen in the context of this particular facet of international society. It would be wrong to conclude therefrom that municipal law analogies or similarities are always impossible in all situations.[16] After all, if that were true, there could be no 'law' at all in international society (a conclusion which has indeed been defended by some authors).[17] The extent to which the analogy is unwarranted for *jus cogens* norms, in view of their 'public' function, must first be ascertained. Much will depend on the definition of *jus cogens*: the more it is restricted to public order norms, the more the argument will have weight;[18] the less it is equated with public order norms, the less the argument will appear convincing.

Second, there is the argument that international *jus cogens*, contrary to its domestic counterpart, spreads far beyond the bounds of the voidness of contrary legal acts.[19] *Jus cogens* norms in international law are said to have a series of other

droit international (jus cogens) (Geneva/Bucharest, 1971) 21ff. For others, the similarities between the two notions are stronger than the differences: see eg H Mosler, 'Ius Cogens im Völkerrecht' (1968) 25 *Annuaire suisse de droit international* 25. The best answer will be that there are a series of similarities but also some differences between the two notions. The question is essentially a matter of degree and depends also on the evolution of the concept of international *jus cogens*, which, compared with its municipal counterpart, is still in its infancy.

[14] Decentralisation is strictly speaking an incorrect notion, since it implies that there is or there was a central entity, from which power was then devolved to peripheral subjects. This is not the case in international society, which is not and was never centralised (apart from the *jus publicum europaeum*, which developed in the Middle Ages after the demise of the Roman Empire).

[15] See, eg, J Sztucki, *Jus Cogens and the Vienna Convention on the Law of Treaties: A Critical Appraisal* (Vienna/New York, 1974) 8–9.

[16] As is known, there are many differing views on municipal law analogies (or even more limitedly private law analogies), between on the one hand the enthusiasts (H Lauterpacht, *Private Law Sources and Analogies of International Law* (London, 1927)) and the sceptics (eg E Raftopoulos, *The Inadequacy of the Contractual Analogy in the Law of Treaties* (Athens, 1990)).

[17] See, eg, GA Walz, *Wesen des Völkerrechts und Kritik der Völkerrechtsleugner* (Stuttgart, 1930).

[18] It was thus rightly recalled in that particular context by K Zemanek, 'The Metamorphosis of *Jus Cogens*: From an Institution of Treaty Law to the Bedrock of the International Legal Order?' in E Cannizzaro (ed), *The Law of Treaties Beyond the Vienna Convention* (Oxford, 2010) 385.

[19] See G Gaja, '*Jus Cogens* beyond the Vienna Convention' (1981-III) 172 *Recueil des cours de l'Académie de droit international de La Haye* 271ff.

effects than the mere voiding of legal acts, such as in the law of State responsibility (Articles 26 and 40–41 of the International Law Commission (ILC) Articles on State Responsibility (2001)). In municipal law, there is indeed a difference between substantive public order norms and constitutional norms of fundamental importance on the one hand, and *jus cogens* on the other. The latter in principle applies only in the context of contractual freedom/private autonomy—that is, in what would be in international law the domain of treaties and normative unilateral acts. It must be conceded that in the last 15 years (that is, only very recently), international *jus cogens* has spread in many different directions beyond the law of treaties. This is certainly a difference with municipal law. However, it does not prove that in the traditional core area of *jus cogens* (that is, the voidness of legal acts) there can be no meaningful analogy or even identity of functioning. It shows merely that the coextension of the concepts is only partial. In other words, differences will appear in certain areas, but that does not mean that differences must exist in every area. Moreover, it is not yet certain that all the aforementioned supplementary effects are conducible to the concept of *jus cogens*. It must first be analysed to what extent a given effect—such as the claimed non-applicability of State immunity in case of *jus cogens* violations—is an accepted norm of general international law. As will be seen in a later chapter, most of these further effects are not recognised under international law as it stands today.

Third, it has been argued that *jus cogens* limits in a sensitive way the freedom of States to contract and to undertake legal acts, and that such a limitation can only have a minimum effect in international law because of the pervasive role of sovereignty.[20] Thus, international *jus cogens* can only be linked to the dimension of public order norms—that is, norms that are fundamental to the survival and development of the international community. But this argument too is far from entirely convincing. There are different phenomena of imperativeness in international law; imperativeness is a common and wholly proper legal tool used to achieve certain legitimate ends. If States desire to protect the unity of a legal regime against fragmentation, they are free to set up a *jus cogens* regime. Thus, Articles 6/6/6/7 of the four Geneva Conventions on humanitarian law of 1949 prohibit the lessening of protections for 'protected persons' by special agreements between States. Or, to give another example, the States parties to the Statute of the International Court of Justice (ICJ) do not want the work at the ICJ to be split into procedures *à la carte*, where different parties to a contentious case could impose on the Court a *lex specialis* regime as to composition of the bench, the unfolding of procedure or the effect of a decision. After all, by crafting such regimes, States are exercising their sovereignty. There is no reason to consider that this is contrary to that very sovereignty. As the Permanent Court of International Justice recalled as early as 1923, outside the context of *jus cogens*:

> The Court declines to see in the conclusion of any Treaty by which a State undertakes to perform or refrain from performing a particular act an abandonment of its sovereignty.

[20] See H Waldock in [1963-I] *Yearbook of the ILC*, 685th meeting, § 48.

> No doubt any convention creating an obligation of this kind places a restriction upon the exercise of the sovereign rights of the State, in the sense that it requires them to be exercised in a certain way. But the right of entering into international engagements is an attribute of State sovereignty.[21]

This is true also when States enact legal regimes founded on the rule *lex specialis non derogat legi generali cogentis.*

Overall, then, there remains some room for thinking that international *jus cogens* can work at least partially in a similar way to municipal *jus cogens*. The two notions need not be identical or coextensive; but they may perfectly well have a common core. The extent to which this is or is not the case will be ascertained later.

B. Opinions

When considering mainstream legal writings on the definition of international *jus cogens*, two salient aspects can immediately be noted. *First*, there is a significant amount of disagreement and multiplicity in the various approaches to the notion of *jus cogens*. Doctrinal debates range from those denying the existence of the concept to those offering definitions of various kinds and degrees of robustness. If it is therefore not wrong to affirm that there is much agreement regarding the existence of the concept in the international legal order,[22] more than regarding its actual content, it is also true that there is a greater amount of uncertainty in the context of *jus cogens* than in almost any other cardinal concept of the legal order—with the exception, perhaps, of sovereignty.

Second, the mainstream definitions of *jus cogens* are at once narrower and also broader than the provisional one proffered by the present author. They are narrower in the sense that *jus cogens* is most often limited to the 'fundamental' norms of international law, that is, to a small number of norms of international public policy (hence the examples of non-use of force, peaceful settlement of disputes, self-determination, prohibition of genocide or torture, etc). By contrast, the present study seeks to encompass in the analysis the whole spectrum of peremptoriness in international law—that is, the very concept of imperative law even beyond Articles 53 and 64 of the Vienna Convention on the Law of Treaties (VCLT). There is indeed no *a priori* reason why the legislator cannot devise a regime of non-fragmentation of the law—that is, the putting aside of the *lex specialis* rule—in contexts other than public policy. This can happen every time the legislator considers that a given community has a public or collective interest in the unity

[21] *Wimbledon* case, PCIJ series A no 1, p 25. See also, to the same effect, *Exchange of Greek and Turkish Populations* opinion (1925), PCIJ series B no 10, p 21.

[22] See P Tavernier, 'L'identification des règles fondamentales: un problème résolu?' in C Tomuschat and JM Thouvenin (eds), *The Fundamental Rules of the International Legal Order: Jus Cogens and Obligations Erga Omnes* (Leiden/Boston, 2006) 1.

of a legal regime. This can be of any complexion *ratione personarum* and in any subject-matter. At the end of the day, whether one wants to call these phenomena *jus cogens* or not is a matter of taste and definition. It is certainly clear that this form of *jus cogens* is not fully the one of Article 53 VCLT. But nowhere is it written that Article 53 is exhaustive of all *jus cogens* phenomena in international law. It could well be that Article 53 codifies or develops just one notion or facet of *jus cogens*, which is the most relevant for the voidance of treaties, while leaving other phenomena untouched. True, by subsuming all these extended phenomena under *jus cogens* there might be some danger of confusion. There are, however, also benefits arising from such a global approach. It is useful in that it unveils the common legal core and legal technique mechanism uniting all these phenomena. If indeed the root of *jus cogens* is viewed in terms of 'non-derogability', then the broader approach is justified. If, conversely, the core element of *jus cogens* is seen in its public order-relatedness, then the narrower approach becomes necessary, that is, only *jus cogens* under Articles 53 and 64 VCLT will be termed as peremptory. Other non-derogability phenomena will fall to be qualified by other words, such as 'integral obligations', 'non-derogable obligations', 'absolute obligations', etc. The disadvantage of such a course is to insist on the differences between the legal phenomena (which is welcome) but to veil the common aspects between them (which is unwelcome). Moreover, the terminology will quickly become bewildering and excessively abundant. In the opinion of the present author, it is better to use the common core terminology (*jus cogens*) as it stems from the municipal tradition, and then to specify which type of *jus cogens* is at stake in a particular context: for example 'public order *jus cogens*' (which on this view is not a pleonasm), 'public interest *jus cogens*', and the like. With such a course, the differences are upheld while sight is not lost of the important commonalities. At the end of the day, there is no thoroughly ideal way to deal with these definitional issues. The essential point is that the use of terms is made clear and coherent. This is the case here, since the common root of *jus cogens* phenomena is—in the eyes of the present author—the non-derogability issue.

As was mentioned above, the current mainstream definitions of *jus cogens* are also broader than that used in the present monograph. Here, *jus cogens* is centred upon non-derogability. It is therefore not a matter of seeing *jus cogens* as a sort of new constitutional legal order of the international community, or as a series of substantive norms of international law of fundamental importance to the collectivity.[23] This latter aspect is one of 'public policy' norms. According to

[23] This is undoubtedly the mainstream view on the matter; see eg Z Drnas de Clément, 'Las normas imperativas de derecho internacional general (*jus cogens*): dimension sustancial' in Z Drnas de Clément (ed), *Estudios de derecho internacional en homenja al professor EJ Rey Caro*, vol I (Cordoba, 2002) 647ff. For a very strong view in this direction, see AA Cançado Trindade, 'International Law for Humankind: Towards a New *Jus Gentium*' (2005) 316 *Recueil des cours de l'Académie de droit international de La Haye* 336ff.

our definition above, there is however a difference between public policy and *jus cogens*. The former is only one of the material sources—that is, one of the reasons for the existence of *jus cogens* norms. In other words, if there is, and to the extent that there is, such a public policy norm, it will give rise, as *one* of its legal constituents, to *jus cogens*. More precisely, the public policy norm will have as *one* of its qualities non-derogability by legal acts. It will also give rise to a series of other consequences, such as various aggravated consequences under the limb of State responsibility. But since *jus cogens* is not simply public policy, but merely one consequence of it, and moreover not an exclusive consequence of such norms, the tendency to conflate the two notions is rejected. *Jus cogens* is thus on the present reading not a class of norms of international law with specific qualities, such as being 'superior' in a hierarchy or centred on concerns of the international community. *Jus cogens* is not a series of substantive norms; it is a *quality* of certain legal norms, a quality engrafted upon them in order not to allow the operation of the *lex specialis* principle in respect of them. In other words, *jus cogens* (contrary to what the word 'jus' conveys) is nothing but a legal technique engrafted by the legislator onto a certain number of international norms in order to protect them from fragmentation into particular legal acts enjoying priority application *inter partes* because of the *lex specialis* principle. This quality is conferred on public order norms of international law (whose existence is not at all negated); but it is also conferred on some other types of norms.

True, Article 53 VCLT contains the words 'peremptory norm', which may convey the idea that *jus cogens* consists of a series of special substantive norms. But the text then goes on to insist that this is a norm 'of general international law accepted and recognized by the international community of States as a whole', showing that the issue here is one of how the norm at stake emerges in the system of sources, that is, the process of creation of the norm (not its definition, *differentia specifica*). The main process of creation envisaged seems to be that of customary international law, perhaps also that of generally applicable treaties. Only then comes the core definitional point of peremptoriness: 'as a norm from which no derogation is permitted'. *Jus cogens* is thus a norm of general international law (that is the underlying substantive norm, for the purposes of Article 53 a public policy norm) which, because of its public policy character and its recognition by States, has a peremptory quality—that is, cannot be derogated from. The definition of the term 'peremptory' is thus directly linked to non-derogability. To take the point further: the VCLT defines *jus cogens* essentially by its effect—non-derogability.[24] The missing link in Article 53 is the public policy element, which is not explicated. This latter aspect belongs to the underlying 'norm' of customary law; peremptoriness is an addition, an aspect of legal technique: non-derogability.

[24] A Pellet, 'The Normative Dilemma: Will and Consent in International Law-Making' (1992) 12 *Australian Yearbook of International Law* 38.

However that may be, we may notice that our definition is on this account much narrower than that of the mainstream school. Instead of viewing *jus cogens* as a number of highly cherished constitutional or international community-centred rules of law (with an unlimited number of miraculous legal consequences in the form of super-norms), the present view limits *jus cogens* to a legal technique against the fragmentation of a unitarian legal regime: *lex specialis non derogat legi generali cogentis* (an inversion of the generally applicable rule: *lex specialis derogat legi generali dispositiva*).

C. Definitions

We may now briefly and selectively consider some definitions of *jus cogens* that go beyond the reproduction of the wording of Article 53 of the VCLT.[25] There are two main groups of definitions. The first tend more towards the formal side of the spectrum, while the second tend towards the material side of it.

(a) In a first class of definitions we may put those that remain close to the *criterion of non-derogability*. The reasons for non-derogability are however slightly different. The main conception links non-derogability with public policy. This view is held by, amongst others, Hannikainen.[26] For this author, peremptory norms are those imbued with a limitation on the right of the subjects of law to conclude agreements *inter se*, in view of the general values and interests considered indispensable by a society at a given time. The aim of *jus cogens* is thus to protect the overriding interests and values of the international community.[27] We may note in passing that the non-derogability element is here completely identified with public order norms, at whose

[25] A series of definitions limit themselves to reproducing the terms of Art 53 VCLT: see eg JA Frowein, 'Ius Cogens' in R Wolfrum (ed), *The Max Planck Encyclopedia of Public International Law*, vol VI (Oxford, 2012) 443; J Salmon (ed), *Dictionnaire de droit international public* (Brussels, 2001) 631. Several authors have worked on the conditions that must be fulfilled for a norm to qualify as *jus cogens* (mainly from the vantage point of Art 53 VCLT). Thus, it has been argued (ME Villiger, 'The 1969 Vienna Convention on the Law of Treaties: 40 Years After' (2009) 344 *Recueil des cours de l'Académie de droit international de La Haye* 138; R Nieto-Navia, 'International Peremptory Norms (*Jus Cogens*) and International Humanitarian Law' in LC Vorah (ed), *Man's Inhumanity to Man: Essays in Honour of A Cassese* (The Hague/London/New York, 2003) 610ff) that four elements are constitutive for a *jus cogens* norm: (i) it must be a norm of general international law; (ii) no derogation from it may be permitted; (iii) it must be accepted as such by the international community of States as a whole; and (iv) it must be modifiable only through a norm of the same character (parallelism of form). These criteria analytically reflect the content of Art 53 VCLT. But they say nothing on the notion of *jus cogens* beyond the VCLT. It would be too short-sighted to assume that all forms of *jus cogens* must have the complexion of peremptory norms for voidance of treaties. In a certain sense, therefore, such criteria are but a regional ontology of the concept, albeit they purport to map the most important province of peremptory norms. The criterion for a general theory of *jus cogens* has been presented above: it is non-derogability in the sense of inverting the *lex specialis* principle.

[26] L Hannikainen, *Peremptory Norms (Jus Cogens) in International Law: Historical Development, Criteria, Present Status* (Helsinki, 1988) 1–2.

[27] ibid, 4.

exclusive service *jus cogens* is put. This definition is shared by many other authors, sometimes with reference to the public policy aspect, sometimes without such a reference (in which case only the non-derogation aspect is mentioned).[28] Some authors link the non-derogation aspect with the proper functioning of the legal system rather than with public policy values: some rules are fundamental to the legal system and thus cannot be contracted out of.[29] There may not be a great difference between public policy schools and these intra-systemic legal considerations. But we may note that public policy is rooted in the substantive values of a community, whereas the necessities of a legal system are of a more abstract and structural nature. Still other authors stress the moral aspect: a 'hard core of norms that are founded on considerations of morality and general well-being'.[30] This class of definitions is based on the non-derogability criterion, but offers different reasons as to why such non-derogability is posited by the legal order.

(b) Falling into a second class of definitions are those authors who insist that *jus cogens* is a series of *substantive rules of hierarchically superior status* and forming a sort of constitution of the international community. This conception, which is very widespread today,[31] can be traced back to the years after the codification of the VCLT.[32] Thus, Yasseen, a member of the ILC, ventured to define *jus cogens* in the following way:

> Une norme impérative internationale peut à notre sens être définie comme étant une norme de droit international général, supérieure dans la hiérarchie des règles dans l'ordre juridique international, étant donné son importance pour la communauté internationale.[33] [A peremptory norm of international law may be defined as a norm of general international law which is hierarchically superior to other rules of international law in view of its importance for the international community.]

Sometimes, conceptions rooted in this class lead to quite encompassing but equally quite vague definitions. Thus, it has been said that *jus cogens* norms are those from

[28] See, eg, Diaconu (n 13) 1ff.

[29] See E Suy, 'The Concept of *Jus Cogens* in Public International Law' in Lagonissi Conference, Carnegie Endowment for International Peace (ed), *The Concept of Jus Cogens in Public International Law: Papers and Proceedings* (Geneva, 1967) 18: 'Body of general rules of law whose non-observance may affect the very essence of a legal system to which they belong to such an extent that the subjects of the law may not, under pain of absolute nullity, depart from them in virtue of particular agreements'. See similarly J Martensen, '*Ius Cogens* im Völkerrecht—Gibt es bindende Normen des Völkerrechts die durch völkerrechtliche Verträge nicht aufgehoben warden können?', PhD thesis (Hamburg, 1971) 23.

[30] See, eg, V Nageswar Rao, '*Jus Cogens* and the Vienna Convention on the Law of Treaties' (1974) 14 *Indian Journal of International Law* 368.

[31] See, eg, Orakhelashvili (n 2) 1, 5ff. See also ME O'Connell, '*Jus Cogens*: International Law's Higher Ethical Norms' in DE Childress (ed), *The Role of Ethics in International Law* (Cambridge, 2012) 79, 84, 97.

[32] See, eg, GJH Van Hoof, *Rethinking the Sources of International Law* (Antwerp/Boston/Frankfurt/London, 1983) 151–54.

[33] MK Yasseen, 'Réflexions sur la détermination du "*jus cogens*"' in Société française pour le droit international, *L'élaboration du droit international* (Paris, 1975) 206. Translation by this author.

which States are not allowed 'to depart under any circumstances'.[34] Such a formulation conveys the idea of absolute obligation. However, *jus cogens* may be much more relative than the purported divinity of peremptory norms appears to allow. Overall, this class is not centred on a formal criterion such as non-derogability. True, this technical aspect does not disappear. But the main issue here is the material constitution of the community and its superior norms.

II. Functions of *Jus Cogens*

Various legal writings have presented the main functions that *jus cogens* is called upon to perform within the legal order. These functions overlap to some extent with definitional issues, but to a significant degree they are placed beyond that pale. They are not limited to the technical legal aspects discussed above, but plunge into policy aspects, considering in what contexts *jus cogens* is mobilised, by whom and to what ends.

(a) At one end of the spectrum,[35] some authors deny *jus cogens* any distinctive role in positive law. Its various specific effects flow from autonomous norms of customary international law, such as those providing for the nullity of some legal acts, for the existence of universal jurisdiction, for the non-availability of some circumstances precluding wrongfulness, for the special consequences of State responsibility, etc. While the concept is thus of no use in positive law, it nevertheless has a role to play in the context of legislation. It is therefore an argument in the context of the dynamics of international law, where it plays a promotional role: to try to persuade legal operators to bring into existence a new and different international law for the future, along the lines of *jus cogens* requirements. Thus, *jus cogens* essentially attempts to educate State practice to the better and to mobilise pressure groups for legal reform.

[34] S Knuchel, 'General Principles: The Surest Path for the Formation of *Jus Cogens*?' in S Besson and P Pichonnaz (eds), *Les principes en droit européen* (Paris/Geneva, 2011) 128. Other judicial definitions, rooted in the same ground, are not fully satisfactory. Thus, in *US v Matta-Ballesteros* (1995), the US Court of Appeals (9th Circuit) defined *jus cogens* as a set of 'norms [that] are inderogable and peremptory, enjoy the highest status within customary international law, are binding on all nations, and cannot be preempted by treaty' (107 ILR 435 fn 5). In standard language, the terms 'inderogable' and 'peremeptory' are synonymous; thus their cumulative mention is but a repetition; the sentence as formulated however opens up a question as to the distinction made by the Court between the two terms, presuming an *effet utile*. The criterion of being 'binding on all nations' is certainly correct from the standpoint of Art 53 VCLT *jus cogens*. But its formulation may convey the wrong idea that only *jus cogens* norms of customary international law are truly binding. However, norms of dispositive law are just as binding as norms of *jus cogens*; any confusion on this point reveals a grave legal misconception.

[35] C Focarelli, 'Promotional *Jus Cogens*: A Critical Appraisal of *Jus Cogens*' Legal Effects' (2008) 77 *Nordic Journal of International Law* 455.

(b) In the middle of the spectrum there are authors providing a political background analysis, and others limiting themselves to legal considerations. Both identify several distinctive functions of *jus cogens*. In the first class[36] are those who consider that *jus cogens* sometimes plays the role of a shield and sometimes that of a sword. In its shield function, *jus cogens* restricts the power of a State to assume binding obligations by providing for nullity. Thus, at the end of the day, it expands the domain of liberty of States, for it casts off potential international law restraints. States such as China might be interested in such a function of peremptory norms. Conversely, in its sword function *jus cogens* empowers the international community to enforce certain overriding obligations against States regardless of their consent. This is the *jus cogens* of human rights advocates and of hegemonic States. The pendulum of *jus cogens* thus swings in all directions: limiting the impact of international law or favouring the intrusion of international law. How *jus cogens* functions in a specific context depends on context and policy; it depends on how it is used by the various actors. Such a political analysis is useful. It tends to show that 'more' *jus cogens* does not necessarily mean progress. It also shows that *jus cogens*, like any other legal concept, will also be mustered and used according to political contingencies.

In the second class,[37] it has been argued that *jus cogens* mainly displays three recognised and sound legal functions: (i) a contractual *jus cogens*, with the effect of nullifying treaties (Article 53 VCLT); (ii) a judicial *jus cogens*, where peremptory norms act as a standard of control over acts of the Security Council by internal or international tribunals; and (iii) a sanctioning *jus cogens*, setting out specific consequences of State responsibility.

In a third class,[38] we may place mixed political and legal approaches. It has been said that *jus cogens* performs three main functions: (i) to emphasise that States are not valuable in themselves and concomitantly to safeguard human values; (ii) to relativise sovereignty and to limit power; and (iii) to set up a common law immunised against fragmentation. By the same token, it has been said[39] that *jus cogens* makes two valuable contributions: (i) it provides a 'sanction' of nullity for some legal acts; and (ii) it displays a preventive function: States will not dare to indulge in open defiance of *jus cogens* norms, for example by openly concluding immoral treaties.

[36] PB Stephan, 'The Political Economy of *Jus Cogens*' (2011) 44 *Vanderbilt Journal of Transnational Law* 1077–79.

[37] J Verhoeven, 'Sur les "bons" et les "mauvais" emplois du *jus cogens*' (2008) 5 *Anuario brasileiro de direito internacional* 133, 140ff.

[38] A Paulus, '*Jus Cogens* in a Time of Hegemony and Fragmentation' (2005) 74 *Nordic Journal of International Law* 297, 332.

[39] R Puceiro Ripoll, 'Las normas de *jus cogens* en el campo del derecho internacional contemporaneo' in H Arbuet-Vignali and R Puceiro Ripoll (eds), *Derecho internacional publico, Breviarrio*, vol 1 (Montevideo, 2010) 124.

(c) At the other end of the spectrum[40] are those who view *jus cogens* as super-norms of international law, creating a new international legal order for humankind (a new *jus gentium*). *Jus cogens* here manifests the widest range of functions throughout the legal system. Its main role is to rewrite its content in the desired sense by furnishing a legal argument that is 'absolute' in nature. It thus becomes possible to adapt all rules of the legal order to the superior injunctions of the peremptory public order. *Jus cogens* is here not just a promotional element in the context of classical legislative function; it is a strong catalysing element within the positive law, allowing the judge to directly adapt all the rules and situations of the legal order to the superior law as he or she sees it. Through the concept of *jus cogens*, a legislative function has been recognised for the judge and for other operators; *jus cogens* is consequently about the delegation and decentralisation of legislative power. The question is no longer essentially one of not allowing derogation from certain norms; it is centred on norms which abrogate, derogate from, void, take priority over, interpret, etc all other norms of the legal order.

* * *

This short chapter has aimed show that the functions of *jus cogens* are manifold. In particular, lawyers have spotted some functions which may be unexpected and atypical, such as the 'shield function' in order to free oneself from international legal constraints. True, this function has not yet featured prominently in international practice. But with the rise of new international actors and powers, notably in Asia, it is not impossible that some limbs of *jus cogens* will be influenced in this direction, all the more so if one reflects on the high esteem in which the rising States of the former Third World hold sovereignty. It would thus be too short-sighted to think that *jus cogens* will always develop only in the sense of the dominant Western or Latin American conceptions, as many Western authors seem to tacitly presuppose in robust displays of cultural and political self-confidence. A political-legal shift in the construction and in the functions of *jus cogens* is not excluded for the future. All the more reason to be at pains to provide a solid legal framework for the concept in order to forestall excessive quibbling and endless political abuses, which are deeply damaging to the functioning of the international legal system.

[40] Cançado Trindade (n 23) 336ff. See also the Dissenting Opinion of Cançado Trindade in *Jurisdictional Immunities* (International Court of Justice, 2012): www.icj-cij.org.

2

Negationism: The Adversaries of *Jus Cogens*

The aim of chapter one was to lay the first foundations of an understanding of *jus cogens*. The time has now come to consider the arguments of various authors who have contested *jus cogens* either (i) regarding its very existence in positive international law as it stands, (ii) regarding its legal utility in international law, or (iii) regarding its legal possibility in a legal order such as that which governs relations among States. Their arguments must first be considered and then refuted if our enquiry is to continue. It stands to reason that if the arguments of some of the authors in the present class are to be considered solid, and thus *jus cogens* is but a chimera in international law, the question is settled once and for all and our enquiry will have to end. Contrary to the present author's approach in the earlier study *Théorie du ius cogens international* (2001), all the main attacks against *jus cogens* will here be briefly considered—not only those which attach the possibility of the existence of *jus cogens* in view of structural data regarding the international legal order.[1] However, we will not consider those authors who disagree only with some concrete construction of peremptory norms, since they can hardly be classified as deniers of the very concept of *jus cogens*. Nor are the skeptical to be treated here; they cannot be regarded as opponents of the notion of *jus cogens*, limiting themselves as they do to doubting its utility only in some contexts. Thus, for example, we shall not consider in any detail the arguments of those who criticise the definition of *jus cogens* in Article 53 of the Vienna Convention on the Law of Treaties (VCLT) as being too vague and leaving too much room for subjective speculation, which they claim is dangerous for legal certainty;[2] or those who consider that international practice sustaining the concept of peremptory norms

[1] On the arguments of the adversaries of *jus cogens*, see S Kadelbach, *Zwingendes Völkerrecht* (Berlin, 1992) 124–26; EP Nicoloudis, *La nullité de jus cogens et le développement contemporain du droit international public* (Athens, 1974) 144ff; M Schweitzer, 'Ius Cogens im Völkerrecht' (1971) 15 *Archiv des Völkerrechts* 206; L Hannikainen, *Peremptory Norms (Jus Cogens) in International Law: Historical Development, Criteria, Present Status* (Helsinki, 1988) 128ff, 194ff; J Sztucki, *Jus Cogens and the Vienna Convention on the Law of Treaties: A Critical Appraisal* (Vienna/New York, 1974) 54ff; K Zemanek, 'The Metamorphosis of *Jus Cogens*: From an Institution of Treaty Law to the Bedrock of the International Legal Order?' in E Cannizzaro (ed), *The Law of Treaties Beyond the Vienna Convention* (Oxford, 2010) 405ff.

[2] See Sztucki (n 1) 114ff.

is still too sparse, for example at the time of the drafting of the VCLT.[3] Let us now plunge into the subject-matter.

I. An Institutional Critique: *Jus Cogens* Supposes a Centralised Legal Order

This objection was developed with particular force and clarity by the London-based professor of international law, G Schwarzenberger.[4] In brief, it is claimed that public order norms of the type of *jus cogens* suppose a superior authority entrusted with the task of enforcing those norms. Such is the case in municipal law, where the State, as the overriding power, is clothed with the authority to enforce and coerce. In international law, which is a decentralised society of a barely integrated nature and with divergent views on cherished values, there is no public authority able to define authoritatively such a public order, never mind enforce it. To put it bluntly, without centralised organs of governance there is no *jus cogens*. Schwarzenberger, however, considered the possibility of *jus cogens* in conventional law, in the narrow context of organs of international governance (international organisations). Here there are embryonic public organs, which may possibly sustain imperative norms. But, he concluded at the time of writing, these quasi-orders were still too precarious, compared with State sovereignty, to be able to found a set of international peremptory norms.

The argument as presented tends to prove too much. If taken seriously, it goes to the root of the possibility of an international legal order: one knows about the numerous arguments against the legal nature of international law in view of the absence of a regular superior and organised power ('no centralized legislator, no policeman, no regular judge').[5] Moreover, strictly speaking there is no absence of 'public organs' in international law; they are not centralised, but they do exist. Thus, a judge exists: a remedy is not assured in any situation, but the judicial institution

[3] See the references in R Kolb, 'Théorie du ius cogens international' (2003) 36 *Revue belge de droit international* 5, 9, 34.

[4] G Schwarzenberger, 'International *Jus Cogens*?' in Lagonissi Conference, Carnegie Endowment for International Peace (ed), *The Concept of Jus Cogens in Public International Law: Papers and Proceedings* (Geneva, 1967) 117ff, notably 138–40; G Schwarzenberger, 'The Problem of International Public Policy' (1965) 18 *Current Legal Problems* 191ff, notably 212–14. Other authors have taken up the same argument: eg K Marek, 'Contribution à l'étude du *jus cogens* en droit international' in *Essays in Honor of P Guggenheim* (Geneva, 1968) 426ff; J Nisot, 'Le concept de *jus cogens* envisage par rapport au droit international' (1968) 4 *Revue belge de droit international* 1–3; P Weil, 'Le droit international en quête de son identité' (1992) 237 *Recueil des cours de l'Académie de droit international de La Haye* 237; GA Christenson, '*Jus Cogens*: Guarding Interests Fundamental to International Society' (1988) 28 *Virginia Journal of International Law* 585, 598ff.

[5] In a most graphic expression: J de Louter, *Le droit international public positif*, vol I (Oxford, 1920) 58ff.

is there. This state of affairs suggests that *jus cogens* can perhaps be applied only in a fragmentary way (like all the norms of international law); but certainly it does not prove that it cannot be applied at all. As a technique of non-fragmentation of legal regimes, it is difficult to see why *jus cogens* could not operate when the legislator (that is, the various States participating in setting up a legal regime) wants it to operate. Why should it be possible to apply the *lex specialis derogat legi generali* principle in international law but not the parallel principle *lex specialis non derogat legi generali*? Even for the narrower *jus cogens* concept, centred as it is on public order norms, it is not clear why the customary law process should not be able to crystallise such norms. States can perfectly well attach special qualities to the norms they create. Is centralised enforcement necessary for the existence of such norms? This does not seem to be the case: the existence of the norm is solely a matter of sources; the enforcement of the norm is a matter of how, once established, it will be treated. Thus, it may be possible to say that public order norms without public order organs to enforce them make no practical sense (which is a legal policy argument), but it can hardly be said that such norms cannot exist in the first place (which is a positive law argument). Let us, however, ask the question: do such norms make no sense without public order organs? It seems not. Practice shows that public order arguments are used in international intercourse in order to justify certain legal results.[6] True, the operation of *jus cogens* norms may function less well in the context of international law than in the context of certain (really not all!) municipal legal orders; but that is a matter of degree, not of existence. The nugatory argument does not prove, moreover, that international law would fare better if it were devoid of any legal crystallisation of common concerns and interests.

Some authors have claimed that if the international institutional regime were strengthened, this would not require more *jus cogens* (as suggested by Schwarzenberger) but render *jus cogens* less relevant. Indeed, public organs would operate according to their own public law rules; thus *jus cogens* would disappear behind their legally defined domain of competence and action.[7] This argument is regarded by the present author as unconvincing;[8] it is mentioned only in order to show that certain authors turn the matter upside down: a centralised public organ regime would not render *jus cogens* possible but sweep away its necessity.

Overall, it must be conceded that the absence of a State-like organisation casts the peremptory phenomenon into a specific legal environment and imposes on

[6] See the practice of tribunals mentioned in C Maia, 'Le jus cogens dans la jurisprudence de la Cour interaméricaine des droits de l'homme' in L Hennebel and H Tigroudja (eds), *Le particularisme interaméricain des droits de l'homme* (Paris, 2009) 273ff; C Maia, 'Le juge international au cœur du dévoilement du droit impératif: entre nécessité et prudence' (2005) 83 *Revue de droit international, de sciences diplomatiques et politiques* 1ff.

[7] A Paulus, '*Jus Cogens* in a Time of Hegemony and Fragmentation' (2005) 74 *Nordic Journal of International Law* 297, 331.

[8] It is not convincing since the public order regime of these organs would for us reflect a *jus cogens* order of 'public law'. The rules applied by such organs and their own jurisdiction would then be at least non-derogable, ie *jus cogens*.

it a specific way of functioning. But there is no legal impossibility regarding the operation of *jus cogens* in such a context. Evidence of this fact can be found in international practice since 1969. It may be questioned whether all uses of *jus cogens* have been sensible, but the concept has clearly been applied and operated in fact and in law, notably through the international and national judiciary. A classic application of *jus cogens* is the obiter statement of the Inter-American Court of Human Rights as to the voidness of an old treaty providing for the capture and selling of slaves.[9] Why should a tribunal not be able to declare a legal nullity in relation to a treaty? Where are the structural reasons which render that impossible? There are clearly none.

II. A Structural Argument: *Jus Cogens* Supposes a Clear Distinction Between the Creators and the Subjects of the Law, and Between Objective Law and Contractual Engagements

It has been claimed that the identity of law-creators and law-subjected entities in international law, mainly States, renders impossible the construction of an international *jus cogens*.[10] In municipal law, there are various persons entrusted with the making of law. Once they adopt a piece of legislation, this will bind the general constituency—that is, a significant number of other persons. The latter are subject to the norms created by the superior power of the State. It therefore seems sensible to think that the legislator may limit the reach of the will and consent of the subjects (those subject to the law) by defining the extent to which their common intent may derogate or otherwise from the objective norms adopted by the legislator. As a consequence, there is a neat distinction in municipal law between the level of the objective law—the legislative norms of the State, binding all subjects; and the level of subjective engagements—contractual agreements between some subjects binding only themselves and only by virtue of provisions of the superior objective law of the State. The former are laws in the proper sense of the word; the latter are legal acts whose legal effect does not flow out of themselves but depends

[9] *Aloeboetoe v Suriname* (1993) 116 ILR 278 (Inter-American Court of Human Rights).

[10] See, eg, A Cavaglieri, 'Règles générales du droit de la paix' (1929-I) 26 *Recueil des cours de l'Académie de droit international de La Haye* 320–23, 330. See generally E Kaufmann, *Das Wesen des Völkerrechts und die clausula rebus sic stantibus* (Tübingen, 1911) 178ff. For most authors, this argument justifies some influence on international *jus cogens*, but does not imply the impossibility of the notion: see eg Marek (n 4) 435; R Monaco, *Manuale di diritto internazionale pubblico*, 2nd edn (Turin, 1971) 166–69; G Jaenicke, 'Zur Frage des internationalen Ordre Public' in *Berichte der Deutschen Gesellschaft für Völkerrecht*, vol 7 (Karlsruhe, 1967) 88–89.

on objective legal norms. This latter subjective law is subordinate to the objective law of the State. A contract is valid only if it is compatible with the norms of the legal order. Since there is such a subordination, it becomes clear that subjective laws can be voided by the operation of the primary objective laws on which they rest. This qualitative distinction remains true even if the objective laws are adopted by the entire constituency (via a referendum, etc). The body corporate of all voters acts in its capacity as superior legislator; individual subjects and voters remains subordinate to the laws adopted. In such a structural setting, old rules such as *ius publicum privatorum pactis mutari non potest*[11] make sense: there is the level of objective laws (*jus publicum*) and the level of subjective legal acts (*pacta privatorum*).

The position under international law is radically different. There is no similar distinction between legal spheres. There is no general legislator: all States and other actors, when agreeing on something through a treaty, are partial legislators; the legislative function is decentralised. We are therefore always placed at the level of objective laws. There is no level of simple legal acts, at least not if an agreement is concluded. The agreement is a source of international law, a source of objective law, not simply a source of obligations (that is, of legal acts).[12] Thus, there is no room for the nullity of contractual norms. *Jus cogens* operates to void legal acts of a subjective nature; it is not there to void objective norms of the legal system. An international *jus cogens* is thus a misnomer. We may notice that such a conception could leave room for the application of *jus cogens* to normative unilateral acts (legal acts) when entitlement to them is found in a treaty. There is at this subordinate level room for subjective legal acts, such as a reservation under some special treaty regime. But the nullity of the agreement itself is impossible according to this conception.

Once again, this construction is only tenable if the analogy with municipal law is pushed too far. The argument rests on the assumption that if international *jus cogens* does not operate in *exactly the same* legal environment and in precisely the same way as under municipal law, there cannot be any international *jus cogens* at all. But this assumption is not proven; and it cannot be solidly proven. Each legal order has its own concepts and its own parameters. Analogy is allowed in some situations, but it is never conclusive in all respects. Thus, the particular environment of international law means that *jus cogens* functions in a particular manner rather than being altogether impossible. In this regard, the following aspects must be considered.

[11] See M Kaser, 'Ius publicum und ius privatum' (1986) 103 *Zeitschrift der Savigny-Stiftung für Rechtsgeschichte, Romanistische Abteilung* 75ff.

[12] It has been argued that treaties or agreements are simply sources of obligation in international law, but this view has been contested with solid arguments: see GG Fitzmaurice, 'Some Problems regarding the Formal Sources of International Law' in *Essays in Honor of JHW Verzijl* (The Hague, 1958) 153ff, and the criticism by M Mendelson, 'Are Treaties Merely a Source of Obligation?' in WE Butler (ed), *Perestroika and International Law* (Dordrecht/Boston/London, 1990) 81ff.

First, conventional international law (the domain in which *jus cogens* was classically applied, according to Article 53 VCLT) has a double pedigree in international law. It is not only a body of objective law, in the sense discussed above; it is also a legal act. A legal act is an expression of will by a subject of the legal order which produces legal consequences concordant with the will expressed.[13] Under this definition, it becomes apparent that an international agreement does not lose its pedigree as a legal act merely because it also forms part of the objective legal order. Conversely, customary international law is not a legal act but a legal fact. The latter is a fact to which some norm of the legal order attaches specific legal consequences:[14] for example, the peaceful and continuous exercise of State authority over a piece of territory may lead, under certain further conditions, to the acquisition of sovereignty over that territory.[15] In our context, the legal fact lies in the norms governing the production of international law: they prescribe that customary law presupposes some degree of practice and legal opinion; if there is such practice and legal opinion, the norm governing the production of customary international law will attach consequences to the facts of practice and opinion. Now, it is generally admitted that *jus cogens* applies to legal acts, whereas its application to legal facts is much more doubtful. But since an international agreement is not only an objective norm of law but also a legal act, the application of international *jus cogens* to this agreement remains within the four walls of legal orthodoxy.

Second, by the fact that agreements under international law also give rise to norms of objective international law, the notion of international *jus cogens*, contrary to its municipal counterpart, is to some extent linked to the level of objective norms rather than being limited to the validity of subjective legal acts. Since an agreement is at once a norm and a legal act, the operation of *jus cogens* entails greater inroads into the setting of objective norms of the legal order than it does under municipal law, where the two spheres tend to be neatly separated. In the latter system, *jus cogens* will only operate to exclude the subjective regime set up by the parties under their 'private autonomy'. In international law, *jus cogens* will more robustly reach to the nullity of norms of the legal system, at least if these norms are based on a legal act.[16]

Third, it is not completely correct to consider that the identity of law-creating and law-subjected entities entails as a consequence the fact that these entities are not merely subject to the law but also able always to modify it under their power as legislators—whereby the notion of *jus cogens* would lose its sense. There is indeed

[13] See J Salmon (ed), *Dictionnaire de droit international public* (Brussels, 2001) 31.

[14] ibid, 498.

[15] See L Oppenheim, *International Law* (ed RY Jennings and A Watts), 9th edn, vol I pt 2 (London, 1992) 705ff. See also G Distefano, *L'ordre international entre légalité et effectivité* (Paris, 2002) 292ff.

[16] Conversely, *jus cogens* in international law will protect both the non-derogable objective norm and the subjective legal regime emanating from it, against attempts at derogation (whereas in municipal law it is clear that a legal act of some subjects cannot derogate from the objective legislative norm that this aspect is not covered by *jus cogens*): Kolb (n 3) 121.

a functional distinction between States as law-creating and States as law-abiding entities. This distinction is less rigid than in municipal law, but it exists, as it exists in each legal order. The 'international legislator' is a given group of States: for example a plurality of States bound by an agreement, the totality of States bound by a universal customary norm, some States bound by a local custom, etc. The individual States in each group are subject to the rules created. This entails that they cannot liberate themselves unilaterally from the obligations incurred; and they cannot modify these norms by unilateral acts. Modification is also impossible to achieve by means of special agreements *inter se* within sub-groups of States bound by the general norm. Only the legislator—that is, the totality of States bound by the norms—can modify these norms. The foregoing does not mean that the sub-group of States cannot derogate from the general norm if it is not *jus cogens*. But it does show that it is wrong to think that there is an identity of law-maker and subjects bound by the norm in all concrete situations. The identity exists only on the general plane and implies nothing more than the unorganised nature of international society, where there are no institutionalised authorities placed above the subjects of law. This leads us back to the first series of objections, whereby *jus cogens* cannot exist in a decentralised society.

III. A Second Structural Argument: *Jus Cogens* Supposes a Hierarchy or Differentiation of Norms Unknown to International Law

On this view, international law is still normatively too underdeveloped to be able to shoulder refined and demanding concepts such as *jus cogens*.[17] The norms of international law often overlap, and yet there are many gaps in the law; many norms are unclear and uncertain, flowing from complicated political compromises; *leges generales* interact with many *leges speciales*; there are different geometries of obligation, from soft law standards to—at least for the believers—so-called super-norms like *jus cogens*. In such a precarious environment, the introduction of *jus cogens* is an attempt to reorganise international normativity in a vertical sense (hierarchy) around the fictitious concept of the international community; that is, to create the illusion of progress without the reality of progress. Since international law is essentially a legal order founded on the will of States, and since it is consequently inherently non-hierarchical, *jus cogens* cannot but remain incompatible with the most intimate structure and functioning of the international legal order.

[17] See particularly Weil (n 4) 129ff. See also Marek (n 4) 433ff.

We may note four things in this regard. *First*, the criticism is once more premised on the idea of a degree of primitivism of international law: it would therefore be unable to open itself to concepts such as *jus cogens*, which suppose a much more developed legal order. But if international law may develop into a more mature legal order—unless it is bound by some dogmatic profession of faith to perpetuate the claimed primitive nature—the idea of inserting such notions as *jus cogens* might perhaps appear to be a legitimate step. If it were otherwise, the above-presented argument would be nothing more than a political device aimed at forestalling any maturation or adequate development of the international legal order. Moreover, structural arguments should always be considered with some reserve. In particular, they cannot be taken as arguments against legal reform: structures may partially adapt and become novel. In other words, structural arguments should remain descriptive (in the sense of an inventory) but avoid becoming normative. One may regret some structural shifts and adjustments. But this is a question of legal policy and not a question of the possibility of the existence of a certain concept in the complexion of a legal order. To put it briefly, structural arguments cannot be taken as *a priori* reasons for the inadmissibility of a given concept in international law. If a concept exists, it does not depend on the structure of the system but on the positive law of the system. The system reflects the state of the positive law as being the consequence of its sum total; it is not to be taken as a supplementary condition for a rule to become part and parcel of the legal system.

Second, P Weil admits that the concept of *jus cogens* cannot be completely avoided in international law, since it would be preposterous to posit that under the banner of voluntarism States may agree on whatever monstrosity they wish,[18] such as the commission of a genocide. But if that is conceded, the question becomes a matter of degree and the negation of *jus cogens* is far from absolute. One then fails to see the exact scope of the structural arguments presented by the distinguished French author: if some *jus cogens* is necessary also in international law, and therefore does exist in this legal order, then the structural arguments against its existence are deprived of their demonstrative force. The point would then be to caution against an excessive extension of *jus cogens* norms, which is another matter.

Third, Weil's criticism is mainly directed against a certain type and a certain vision of *jus cogens*, that is, public order *jus cogens* supposing a superior hierarchical status and the prevalence of the interests of the international community over the interests of States. However, if there are other types of *jus cogens* than the one described, as is indeed claimed in this monograph, then the arguments presented by the French author cannot be taken as arguments against *jus cogens* in international law, but only as arguments against one type of *jus cogens* in international law. It will be appreciated that the two positions are not identical.

[18] Weil (n 4) 277.

IV. A Positive Law Argument: *Jus Cogens* is Not Recognised in the International Legal Order

Since the adoption of the VCLT in 1969, this argument has become rare because it is exceedingly difficult to sustain. In the past, a series of authors based their arguments on the fact that international practice did not sustain the existence of *jus cogens* as a concept of international law. They then concluded that all norms of international law could be derogated from. This clear-cut statement was sometimes garnished with the caveat that the adoption of derogatory norms can constitute an internationally wrongful act or that such norms could be deprived of legal effect because of legal impossibility (but not of *jus cogens* voidness), such as where a group of States purported to impose an obligation on a non-consenting third State.[19]

This argument can be laid to rest today. Since Articles 53 and 64 VCLT posit *jus cogens*, since almost all States utter the concept in the Sixth Committee of the UN General Assembly, and since international tribunals have regularly mentioned it in the last 20 years,[20] it may be considered that a wholesale denial of a positive law basis for the concept has become impossible. It is indeed no longer found in legal writings, apart from lukewarm comments on the international practice sustaining the notion.

V. A Pragmatic Argument: *Jus Cogens* is Useless

In his general course of international law held at the Hague Academy, S Sur has argued that beyond a series of inherent weaknesses (fuzziness, moral dimension, uncertainty as to the formation and identification of peremptory norms, non-clarity in case of conflict between *jus cogens* norms, etc), the gist of the matter is the uselessness of *jus cogens*.[21] Thus, for example, in international criminal law the concept would not add any value to the recognised bases of jurisdiction for criminal prosecution; notions like *jus cogens* crimes would add nothing to this state of affairs.

19 See, eg, AP Sereni, *Diritto internazionale*, vol I (Milan, 1966) 167–68; Nisot (n 4) 6.

20 See A Orakhelashvili, *Peremptory Norms in International Law* (Oxford, 2006) 131ff.

21 S Sur, 'La créativité du droit international' (2012) 363 *Recueil des cours de l'Académie de droit international de La Haye* 197ff.

First, let us note that Sur is forced to admit a series of other notions linked to non-derogability in order to palliate the absence of the *jus cogens* notion. Thus, he admits that there are some 'intransgressible obligations', according to the dictum of the International Court of Justice in the *Nuclear Weapons* Opinion of 1996, which he quotes with approval.[22] He also admits specific effects of non-derogability elsewhere in his article.[23] Thus, a type of *jus cogens* is reintroduced under the flag of other names, through a discreet backdoor. It seems that, like Weil, Sur dislikes the 'public policy/international community/hierarchy' approach to *jus cogens*, and that he is unable to think of *jus cogens* as being possibly separated and severable from these notions. The legal technique of non-derogability is however admitted by Sur. For us, this is tantamount to the admission of some forms of peremptoriness in international law.

Second, if taken seriously, the argument that *jus cogens* is superfluous is not sustainable. It performs some legal functions which cannot be performed by any other legal concept. Thus, if a slave trade treaty were to be applied today because it is still in force, the claim for *pactum est servandum* advanced by one State could be countered with the desired effect only by *jus cogens*. This example may seem far-fetched, but it is sufficient to replace it with various agreements departing from fundamental norms of international humanitarian law (as occurred between Vichy and the German Occupying Power) to come within the reach of reality. Clearly, it could be argued—as Sur did in an exchange of correspondence with the present author—that when the total number of violations of international humanitarian law during World War Two is considered, the legal fate of various Vichy agreements may seem entirely derisory. But it is certainly not excessive to possess a legal device through which the legalisation of serious breaches of international humanitarian law can be avoided. This device prevents this hideous course of conduct from being treated as covered by a formally valid legal engagement.

Third, it is certainly true that *jus cogens* is used in many contexts where it is superfluous,[24] sometimes simply to signal that a certain norm or obligation is 'important'. To say 'it is *jus cogens*' apparently enhances its status and sounds so incredibly learned. But this is an argument of degree, extent and scope, not one going to the root of the matter, namely the existence or otherwise of *jus cogens* in international law.

[22] ibid, 202.

[23] Thus, it is admitted at 197 (ibid) that certain norms of customary international law are non-derogable, an example being *pacta sunt servanda*. It is certainly a matter of definition whether this non-derogability is called *jus cogens* or given another name. The gist of the matter is that not all norms of international law can be derogated from.

[24] See the examples in R Nigro, 'Lo jus cogens nella prassi internazionale più recente' in C Focarelli (ed), *Le nuove frontiere del diritto internazionale* (Perugia, 2008) 119ff.

VI. A Political Argument: *Jus Cogens* is Dangerous for International Law and is a Tool for Political Manipulation

This argument has been presented in slightly different forms, mainly by authors from the USA. It has thus been noted[25] that *jus cogens* carries with it the danger that some elites, with their own hidden agendas, pretend to speak out for the international community (thereby hiding their interests behind lofty words) and impose their vision of a suitable ideology under the lenitive and permissive guise of peremptory norms. This heavily ideological load of *jus cogens* would make the notion unworkable and ineffective in international affairs (the word 'ineffective' may be surprising here, since if *jus cogens* is the vehicle for imposing a certain ideology of the powerful, it will be very 'effective' albeit unwelcome). These elites might attempt to impose their views by claiming the hierarchical primacy and nullity of contrary norms, under the guise of *jus cogens*. It has been added[26] that *jus cogens* tends to devalue and debilitate ordinary norms of international law by surreptitiously imposing the idea that only *jus cogens* super-norms are truly binding; and that the whole body of international law is thereby ideologised and moralised in the sense of specific values (eg Western), diminishing its advantage of cross-cultural applicability. In this sense, *jus cogens* may accentuate the struggle between States and political systems, rather than advancing the common cause of the international community. Rounding up this chain of arguments, it has been emphasised[27] that behind the values and common interests talk lurks a weapon for partisan politics, for conferring pathos on arguments, or for free-riding inventions of illusionary thought. *Jus cogens* may here serve as a trump card to silence dissent and to foster a reactionary ossification of the law. It is then observed that the notion is used for uncompromising, unequivocal, passionate and even angry attacks. Thus, is it useful to argue that Resolution 242 of the UN Security Council is void since it does not insist on the return of all Palestinian refugees? Could any compromise agreement on such questions be voided by reference to *jus cogens*? How then to explain compromise settlements like the Dayton Agreement of 1995 at the end of the Bosnian War, which was hardly fully in line with *jus cogens* claims?[28] Are all the Arab Charters calling for the destruction of Israel void, since

[25] Christenson (n 4) 601–02, 615.

[26] J Petman, 'Panglossian Views upon the New World Order' (2002) 13 *Finnish Yearbook of International Law* 336ff.

[27] R Barnidge, 'Questioning the Legitimacy of *Jus Cogens* in the Global Legal Order' (2008) 38 *Israel Yearbook on Human Rights* 199ff.

[28] For a critique of *jus cogens* in this context, see AM Weisburd, 'The Emptiness of the Concept of *Jus Cogens*, as Illustrated by the War in Bosnia-Herzegovina' (1995) 17 *Michigan Journal of International Law* 21ff.

they do not respect the self-determination of the Jewish people, a right considered to be *jus cogens*? Nuance and compromise are necessary in such contexts, it is emphasised—not rigid and predetermined consequences flowing from some partisan *jus cogens*. (It may however be added by the present author that even absent *jus cogens* there would be some 'rigid' norms of international law, which politically could not just be done away with easily. A legal order is there to prescribe, not just to accommodate.)[29]

These and similar arguments are not essentially directed to the existence of *jus cogens* in international law. They focus rather on its practical promise, and even more so on its particular dangers. It would be wrong and inadequate to brush aside such critiques as being excessive, one-eyed and reactionary. Indeed, the critics shine a light on very important issues which are too often neglected by the panegyrics of *jus cogens*. The danger of political manipulation of *some versions* of *jus cogens* is indeed far from negligible. If peremptoriness is taken as a highly effective Rambo-tool for dismantling any international normativity which is contrary to the subjective wishes of a legal operator, the concept will indeed do more harm than good. However, some limits to the arguments presented must also be seen and keenly taken account of.

First, the dangers depicted caution for a narrow version of *jus cogens* rather than a triumphant version, and one which is solidly rooted in the practice of States rather than deduced from variable inherent qualities of the concept itself as 'discovered' selectively by any legal operator in exercises of unlimited subjectivism. In particular, we have to reject any version of *jus cogens* where the means to remedy breaches of peremptory norms are themselves considered peremptory. This is the device by which excessive rigidity is imported into the international legal system. But the abovementioned authors would certainly not claim—I guess—that a treaty organising a genocide should be enforced as such by the International Court of Justice or by any other law-applying body. Thus, the question of the propriety of *jus cogens* is one of degree.

Second, the existence and the justification of a legal concept can never depend on the dangers of manipulation, since there is no legal concept at all which cannot be manipulated: *ab abusu ad usum non valet consequentia*. The better approach is to separate legitimate uses from illegitimate ones and to argue the whole point substantively, while insisting as much as necessary on the dangers spotted. This

[29] Thus, the argument of Barnidge (n 27) 212 that for the US invasion of Iraq in 2003 a good argument can be made for legality in international law is unfortunately at best grotesque, and can be forgiven only considering the nationality of the author of the statement. I doubt that he would conclude similarly regarding the annexation of Crimea, where his words would probably be also somewhat 'uncompromising', or at least sharp. I am aware of the fact that he will consider my own words as a proof of 'passionate and angry' pleading, but he may at least note that I do not found myself on *jus cogens*. Passion, however defined, is not exclusive to *jus cogens*. I want to add that his article is in any case worth reading: it is a refreshing and searching piece, reaching far beyond the evergreen views of *jus cogens* enthusiasts.

substantive course is certainly more burdensome than a round and sharp general rejection, but it is to some extent also intellectually more honest. There remains the fact that *jus cogens* may be more prone to political abuses which are heavily destabilising of the international legal system than other legal concepts. To date, such excessive effects of peremptory norms have been claimed by some authors, but they have not found their way into actual international practice. Thus, was the Dayton Agreement voided? Was Resolution 242 voided? And would that agreement or resolution not have been attacked on political or other grounds even if *jus cogens* did not exist in international law? Would such uncompromising arguments, as they are called, not simply be channelled elsewhere? Why should we think that they would disappear, since they express a political reality? Overall, there are certainly good reasons to remain vigilant. There is however no reason to jettison the baby with the bathwater.

VII. A Multicoloured Bouquet of Arguments Against *Jus Cogens*: M Glennon

One last author who deserves to be mentioned in this section on the adversaries of *jus cogens* is M Glennon.[30] His arguments against peremptory norms are so manifold that he must be put in a category of his own. We may list those arguments:

- the concept of *jus cogens* is not compatible with the positivistic foundation of the modern international legal order;[31]
- it creates more problems than it is capable of solving;[32]
- it is an unwelcome attempt to insist on the moralisation of the international legal order;[33]
- it is not sufficiently rooted in the practice of States and is rejected by some important States (USA, France);[34]
- new norms of customary international law cannot develop for peremptory norms, since any new practice would be a derogation from the old norm and thus considered void;[35]
- it is difficult to identify *jus cogens* norms and thus the whole process is heavily prone to subjectivism;[36]

[30] MJ Glennon, 'Peremptory Nonsense' in *Human Rights, Democracy and the Rule of Law: Essays in Honor of L Wildhaber* (Zurich/Baden-Baden, 2007) 1265ff. The same text has been published in French: MJ Glennon, 'De l'absurdité du droit impératif (*Jus cogens*)' (2006) 110 *Revue générale de droit international public* 529ff.

[31] Glennon, 'Peremptory Nonsense' (n 30) 1266.

[32] ibid.

[33] ibid, 1268.

[34] ibid.

[35] ibid, 1269.

[36] ibid, 1270.

— peremptory norms create practical problems: for example, would the NATO treaty be void because of a purportedly unlawful use of force in Kosovo (1999), since the prohibition on the use of force is said to be peremptory?[37]

Overall, it is concluded, certain treaties may shock the conscience, and to reject *jus cogens* is not to condone them, but it remains necessary to admit that these documents are treaties, as shocking as they may be. The world must be treated as it is, not as one wishes it to be.[38]

These criticisms are unimpressive, and some of them bluntly fail to show an elementary understanding of the concept of *jus cogens*. Criticism 1 is far from well founded: a concept of *jus cogens* can perfectly well be adopted and accepted by the legislator—that is, by the common will of States. How that could be incompatible with their … *will*, falls to be explained. Criticism 2 may not be wrong, but it concerns essentially the extension given to *jus cogens*. It hardly militates against restrictive versions of it. Aspect 3 raises the same answer: moralisation is the agenda of some public policy proponents of *jus cogens*, but not of others, which are concerned rather with the legal technique of peremptoriness. The fourth claim is too bold. It is not true that the practice of States does not evidence any place for *jus cogens*: witness the numerous statements in the Sixth Committee of the UN General Assembly. Actual voidness of legal acts is much rarer, but this is so by the nature of things; and it should be welcomed by skeptical authors, since this limited use reduces the scope of the problems raised by the concept. It is also not true that the US is generally against the concept, either in the drafting history or in the aftermath; it would be more correct to say that the US remains measured and cautious, and will use the concept *à géométrie variable*. Argument 5 reveals a not uncommon misunderstanding. The development of a new practice for customary norms is not a 'derogation' from a *jus cogens* norm and is thus not void. Practice is a material act which takes place as a matter of fact and possibly operates in the context of the modification (precisely not derogation)[39] of the old customary norm. A material act is not void; only legal acts can be void in the legal system. What remains is simply that the threshold for modification of the *jus cogens* norm may be notably higher than for an ordinary norm, since the new practice will have to work harder to erode a *jus cogens* norm.[40] Criticism 6 is to be taken seriously and cautions against heroic and bold conceptions of *jus cogens*. If minimum legal certainty must be maintained, subjectivism in the definition and

[37] ibid, 1271.

[38] ibid, 1272.

[39] Derogation is a matter of replacing the general norm with a special legal regime *inter se*— which is not the point here. The modification of a norm has to do with its abrogation and replacement by a new norm. The two things are essentially different.

[40] This is noticed by some authors, eg Y Dinstein, 'The Interaction between Customary International Law and Treaties' (2006) 322 *Recueil des cours de l'Académie de droit international de La Haye* 402–03; MM Magallona, 'The Concept of *Jus Cogens* in the Vienna Convention on the Law of Treaties' in J Scott Davidson (ed), *The Law of Treaties* (Aldershot, 2004) 514–15.

operation of peremptory norms has to be kept low. The seventh argument, on action in Kosovo, again reveals a misunderstanding. A treaty is not void because some *material* acts are in violation of it. The voidness is limited to derogatory *legal* acts. Thus, if NATO States conclude a treaty to aggress a third State, this treaty will be void. Conversely, there is no clause contrary to peremptory norms in the NATO Charter, and thus no matter how many actions in violation of the non-use of force rule NATO States commit, this treaty will never thereby be void. Finally, there is no good reason to say that monstrous treaties are valid treaties, in the name of a wrongly understood realism. The legal order is not obliged to recognise any legal act whatsoever, no matter how little it strays from the main tenets of legal validity. Indeed, there is no legal order operating without the concept of nullity (this is also the case in international law, where nullity does not flow only from *jus cogens*). Why should international law be different? If law is only to recognise in all cases what actually is, as opposed to what ought to be, why do we have a prescriptive legal order at all? Reality of fact would then be enough.

* * *

Having reviewed a series of objections to the possibility or opportunity of *jus cogens*, we may conclude that none of these objections has so much merit as to render peremptoriness a concept which must remain alien to international law. The point rather is that some justified criticisms pose a caveat against too robust claims of what is peremptory in international law—an extensive tendency that is unfortunately gaining ground.[41] However, this is fundamentally a matter of degree and of construction. We are thus not hindered from proceeding with our inquiry into international *jus cogens*.

[41] Such as Orakhelashvili (n 20).

3

Theories of *Jus Cogens*

Having carefully considered the arguments of the deniers of international *jus cogens*, we may now analyse the positions of those who embrace the concept, be it on a bold or narrow basis.[1] We must at this point limit ourselves to the essential aspects of each theory.

I. *Jus Cogens* as an Expression of Natural Law

For some authors, *jus cogens* is a modern reflection of natural law.[2] According to them, a limitation on the freedom of sovereign States to choose the content of their agreements and on their general freedom of action—that is, a limitation of the reach of consent and will in international law—cannot be explained by instruments of positivistic legalism. This view is rooted in precisely that consent or will of States which *jus cogens* is there to limit or even to brush aside. It would therefore be circular to explain *jus cogens* on the basis of consent or will. Moreover, the concept of *jus cogens* is directly linked to moral absolutes, which in themselves necessarily lead back to natural law positions. Thus, *jus cogens* norms bind all States (or even all subjects of the law) by virtue of their intrinsic moral value, making them a legally necessary law. Unlike other positive norms of international law, they are not binding on States because States have accepted them by means of the ordinary legislative process, via different forms of consent. The fact that such norms are moral absolutes also entails the consequence that they cannot be modified.

[1] More detailed developments on some of these theories may be found in my monograph, R, Kolb, *Théorie du jus cogens international* (Paris, 2001).

[2] See D Dubois, 'The Authority of Peremptory Norms in International Law: State Consent or Natural Law?' (2009) 78 *Nordic Journal of International Law* 133ff (this author then admits in a short sentence on p 175 that these natural law values of *jus cogens* have to be somehow translated into the positive legal order—but on this essential point he says no more); MW Janis, 'The Nature of *Jus Cogens*' in L May and J Brown (eds), *Philosophy of Law: Classic and Contemporary Readings* (Chichester, 2010) 185; ME O'Connell, '*Jus Cogens*: International Law's Higher Ethical Norms' in DE Childress (ed), *The Role of Ethics in International Law* (Cambridge, 2012) 83, 86, 98. See FA von der Heydte, *Völkerrecht*, vol I (Cologne, 1958) 23; I Detter, *The International Legal Order* (Aldershot, 1994) 175; H Mosler, 'Ius Cogens im Völkerrecht' (1968) 25 *Annuaire suisse de droit international* 18.

This conception of *jus cogens* exhibits various weaknesses. *First*, there remains the problem of explaining how such norms become part and parcel of the existing and applicable legal order. If these natural law norms are not channelled through the ordinary process of law-creation, there must be some other means of recognising them. Their content alone is too weak a criterion: on such a question, opinions can and will largely differ, and great legal uncertainty will then ensue. The question becomes even more intricate if Western values are not self-evidently adopted as absolutes but different ideological conceptions in the world are taken into account. Moreover, each one of us can postulate norms of justice. The question whether these norms are part of the positive law, then, is still not settled. Article 53 of the Vienna Convention on the Law of Treaties (VCLT) requires that a norm be recognised as peremptory by the international community of States as a whole. This is not directed at content alone; it has mainly to do with form—that is, with a degree of recognition by States. This is understandable if one thinks about one of the main functions of a legal order: the limitation of otherwise boundless subjectivism. It would be strange if a concept whose aim is to achieve the progress of international law were to bring about considerable regression by allowing unlimited manipulations of the legal order as a function of constantly shifting subjective interests and perceptions.

Second, and more importantly, natural law theory suffers in our context from a technical insufficiency. Natural law (if one wants to admit its existence) addresses itself first of all to the legislator in order to impose some extreme limits on its creation and modification of the law. Its basis is therefore the question of creation and change of the law, that is, the plane of the creation and abrogation of norms. *Jus cogens*, conversely, concerns in the first place the nullity of derogations *inter se* from a legal regime which shall remain unique for all subjects. Thus, natural law is a meta-positive mechanism for orienting legislation, that is, for the making of law; *jus cogens* is conversely an intra-positive mechanism for issues of derogation, that is, for maintaining the unity of a general legal regime. To construe the latter as also being meta-positive is to move it into a realm which is not its own. The most that could be said is that the norms of natural law may form the most restricted core of *jus cogens* norms, since the rules that impose limits on the plenary legislator in the creation of objective law must *a fortiori* bind individual subjects in their more restricted dealings.

Third, natural law theory leads to a further misconception of the *jus cogens* mechanism from the point of view of substance. In the past, natural law theory rested on the idea that if any limits existed as to the freedom of sovereign States to contract, this could be admitted only in the context of the most reduced area of rationally, morally or socially necessary norms. However, this perspective paradoxically leads to excessively limited conceptions of *jus cogens*. If the latter is understood as legal technique of non-derogation, more practical and useful space is left for it to act; when it is limited to natural law propositions, its scope is either too narrow to be of great practical value, or else too ideologically inflated to be of wide practical acceptance in the international arena of States.

Fourth, on the modification issue, natural law theories may easily come into conflict with Article 53 VCLT. The latter explicitly acknowledges that *jus cogens* norms are subject to change. This quality brings such norms much closer to the realm of positive law than to the limbo of natural law. I do not intend to take a definitive position on natural law here. The point is rather that *jus cogens* is a positive law concept, a legal technique, which should not be confused with natural law.

II. *Jus Cogens* as the Public Order of the International Community, Giving Rise to Hierarchically Superior Norms (Rules of Vertical Collision)

This is the absolutely predominant theory today. In the narrowest sense, which was dominant in the past, public order concerns the lawful objects of agreements between States and is thus rooted in treaty law. In its robust versions, which completely dominate today, the public order of the international community gives rise to a series of constitutional norms of that community. These norms protect the fundamental values of the international community against impairment as a result of State derogation or action.[3] Commonly mentioned examples are the maintenance of international peace, the self-determination of peoples, the protection of fundamental human rights and humanitarian law, and the protection of the environment. The consequence of public order is to confer on those norms

[3] This conception is so common that it is impossible to give extensive references here. I have a list comprising 124 entries for this position. See, eg, A Orakhelashvili, *Peremptory Norms in International Law* (Oxford, 2006) 7ff; J Verhoeven, 'Sur les "bons" et les "mauvais" emplois du *jus cogens*' (2008) 5 *Anuario brasileiro de direito internacional* 133, 134; MM Magallona, 'The Concept of *Jus Cogens* in the Vienna Convention on the Law of Treaties' in J Scott Davidson (ed), *The Law of Treaties* (Aldershot, 2004) 495; R Puceiro Ripoll, 'Las normas de *jus cogens* en el campo del derecho internacional contemporaneo' in H Arbuet-Vignali and R Puceiro Ripoll (eds), *Derecho internacional publico, Breviarrio*, vol 1 (Montevideo, 2010) 117; Janis (n 2) 184; R Nieto-Navia, 'International Peremptory Norms (*Jus Cogens*) and International Humanitarian Law' in LC Vorah (ed), *Man's Inhumanity to Man: Essays in Honour of A Cassese* (The Hague/London/New York, 2003) 617; S Laghmani, 'Le jus cogens et la cohérence de l'ordre juridique international' in *Les droits de l'homme: une nouvelle coherence pour le droit international? Rencontre à la mémoire de D Jazi* (Paris, 2008) 65; S Schmahl, 'An Example of *Jus Cogens*: The Status of Prisoners of War' in C Tomuschat and JM Thouvenin (eds), *The Fundamental Rules of the International Legal Order, Jus Cogens and Obligations Erga Omnes* (Leiden/Boston, 2006) 45; U Linderfalk, 'Normative Conflict and the Fuzziness of International Ius Cogens' (2009) 69 *Zeitschrift für ausländisches öffentliches Recht und Völkerrecht* 977. See further references in Kolb (n 1) 68ff. Some are skeptical on this point, eg J Sztucki, *Jus Cogens and the Vienna Convention on the Law of Treaties: A Critical Appraisal* (Vienna/New York, 1974) 8–9; K Zemanek, 'The Metamorphosis of *Jus Cogens*: From an Institution of Treaty Law to the Bedrock of the International Legal Order?' in E Cannizzaro (ed), *The Law of Treaties Beyond the Vienna Convention* (Oxford, 2010) 355 (excessive analogy with the much more developed internal legal order). On the other hand, in favour of an analogy with the internal legal order, see M Kawano, 'The Role of Judicial Procedures in the Process of the Pacific Settlement of International Disputes' (2009) 346 *Recueil des cours de l'Académie de droit international de La Haye* 396. Against the merging of international *jus cogens* with public order, see Mosler (n 2) 22ff.

protecting such superior values a superior legal status. The norms cannot be derogated from; no exceptions to them are allowed (reservations, military necessity, etc); they have a superior hierarchical status[4] (which suggests that in case of a conflict with ordinary norms they should have precedence), etc. The public order here takes the place of (or complements) the natural law. Let us also note that there are some rare conceptions of the international public order which root that concept in State sovereignty and in an atomistic conception of international relations. Thus, it has been said that the public order must be reduced to the *raison d'Etat*. In the

[4] This proposition seems to have contaminated almost all legal writings on *jus cogens*: see for the older literature Kolb (n 1) 127. Add to these authors the following ones: D Shelton, 'Normative Hierarchy in International Law' (2006) 100 *American Journal of International Law* 291ff; C Tomuschat, 'International Law: Ensuring the Survival of Mankind on the Eve of a New Century. General Course of Public International Law' (1999) 281 *Recueil des cours de l'Académie de droit international de La Haye* 290, 330; T Meron, 'International Law in the Age of Human Rights: General Course of Public International Law' (2003) 301 *Recueil des cours de l'Académie de droit international de La Haye* 415; AA Cançado Trindade, 'International Law for Humankind: Towards a New Jus Gentium' (2005) 316 *Recueil des cours de l'Académie de droit international de La Haye* 336ff; Kawano (n 3) 397; WE Conklin, 'The Peremptory Norms of the International Community' (2012) 23 *European Journal of International Law* 838; C Espaliu Berdud, 'Reflexiones en torno a la presencia del *jus cogens* en el derecho internacional contemporaneo' in R Casado Raigon and I Gallego Dominguez (eds), *Personalidad y capacidad juridicas*, t I (Cordoba, 2005) 420, 435–36; S Knuchel, 'Words, Words, Words ... Where are the Values? Assessing the International Judge and *Jus Cogens*' in S Besson and A Ziegler (eds), *The Judge in European and International Law* (Paris/Geneva/Zurich/Basel, 2013) 87; A Cassese, 'An Enhanced Role of *Jus Cogens*' in A Cassese (ed), *Realizing Utopia: The Future of International Law* (Oxford, 2012) 159; L Haopei, '*Jus Cogens* and International Law' in S Yee and W Tieya (eds), *International Law in the Post-Cold War World: Essays in Memory of Li Haopei* (London, 2001) 521; Orakhelashvili (n 3) 7ff; S Knuchel, 'General Principles: The Surest Path for the Formation of *Jus Cogens*?' in S Besson and P Pichonnaz (eds), *Les principes en droit européen* (Paris/Geneva, 2011) 129; A Bianchi, 'Human Rights and the Magic of *Jus Cogens*' (2008) 19 *European Journal of International Law* 491, 494, 495, 501; Laghmani (n 3) 78; A Paulus, '*Jus Cogens* in a Time of Hegemony and Fragmentation' (2005) 74 *Nordic Journal of International Law* 297, 303, 319; Z Drnas de Clément, 'Las normas imperativas de derecho internacional general (*jus cogens*): dimension sustancial' in Z Drnas de Clément (ed), *Estudios de derecho internacional en homenja al professor EJ Rey Caro*, vol I (Cordoba, 2002) 667–68; O'Connell (n 2) 80, 81, 83. Even the ILC has indulged this position: *Report on the Fragmentation of International Law*, Doc A/CN.4/L.682 (2006), §§ 361ff. This position can also be found in judicial practice: eg *US v Matta-Ballesteros* (1995) 107 ILR 435 fn 5 (US Court of Appeals, 9th Circuit); International Criminal Tribunal for the Former Yugoslavia, *Furundzija* case (1998) 121 ILR 260–62; *Bouzari v Iran* (2002) 124 ILR 442 (Ontario Superior Court of Justice) (superior form of customary international law overriding ordinary rules of customary international law). Against this conception of hierarchy, see eg L Hannikainen, *Peremptory Norms (Jus Cogens) in International Law: Historical Development, Criteria, Present Status* (Helsinki, 1988) 11, noting that *jus cogens* must not be situated at the highest level of international law; H Mosler, 'Ius Cogens im Völkerrecht' (1968) 25 *Annuaire suisse de droit international* 9, 19; Schmahl (n 3) 45; M Virally, 'Réflexions sur le *jus cogens*' (1966) 12 *Annuaire français de droit international* 5, 18; L Alexidse, 'Legal Nature of *Jus Cogens* in Contemporary International Law' (1981-III) 172 *Recueil des cours de l'Académie de droit international de La Haye* 237, 259; J Vidmar, 'Rethinking *Jus Cogens* after Germany v Italy: Back to Article 53?' (2013) 60 *Netherlands International Law Review* 25. In favour of only a limited hierarchical effect, see Verhoeven (n 3) 153–54. The origin of this conception linking *jus cogens* with hierarchy can probably be traced back to Art 53 VCLT: there it is stated that a norm of general international law which is peremptory cannot be derogated from using a conventional norm. From there, it seems a logical step to infer that the customary peremptory norm must be superior, since it takes precedence in case of conflict, and it even takes precedence very radically, through the nullity of the contrary norm (thus, strictly speaking, there is no collision of norms here, since one of the norms is void). *Jus cogens* has here been taken as the starting point for a vertical reorganisation of the system of sources and norms of international law.

egoistic environment of international relations, a public order can only refer to the interests of States or groups of States—in other words, not lofty communitarian ideals but rather the reality of power relations.[5]

The precise reasons why I do not subscribe to this theoretical construction will become more apparent in chapters four and five. The general points will suffice here.

First, identification of the spheres of international public order and *jus cogens* leads to an excessive, unwarranted restriction of the latter concept. There is no reason why a legal technique of 'non-derogability' in view of a common interest to protect a legal regime against normative fragmentation should be limited to some fundamental norms and not be available in other contexts. However, the habit of seeing *jus cogens* as the exclusive realm of public policy norms is so entrenched in current legal thinking that many readers will not feel comfortable with the dissociation advocated here. The question remains: why should international *jus cogens* be limited only to public order, while municipal law *jus cogens* is precisely not so limited? The better view is therefore to admit that there exists some international public policy (to be defined)[6] and that *jus cogens* consequences (non-derogability) may be one of the effects of such public order norms. However, it would be right and proper to admit that there are *also* other phenomena of peremptoriness in international law, that is, situations where the technique of non-derogability may be used. That these latter expressions of peremptoriness may be beyond the lenitive grab of Article 53 VCLT is not a reason to ignore them. In short, there are different types of *jus cogens* which have a common core but also partly different functions within the legal order: one is public policy-related *jus cogens* and another is public utility-related *jus cogens* (see below). Thus, *jus cogens* should not be limited to public policy; it also exists outside and independently of public policy.

Second, as a legal technique, *jus cogens* is hierarchically neutral. It touches on the problem of derogation from a norm, that is, the attempt to replace to a general norm with a special norm which would enjoy priority of application *inter partes*. This legal phenomenon can take place at any level in the legal order, not only in the context of the relations between its highest norms and lower ones. The question is essentially relative: at all levels of the legal order there will be more general and more special norms *ratione personarum*. The essential point is that derogation comes from below, through the attempt of a special norm to earn priority (a special norm which is then voided through the imperative norm); hierarchy comes from

[5] GA Christenson, '*Jus Cogens*: Guarding Interests Fundamental to International Society' (1988) 28 *Virginia Journal of International Law* 585, 643ff.

[6] On international public policy, see eg H Rolin, 'Vers un ordre public réellement international' in *Essays in Honor of J Basdevant* (Paris, 1960) 441ff; G Schwarzenberger, 'The Problem of International Public Policy' (1965) 18 *Current Legal Problems* 191; G Jaenicke, 'Zur Frage des internationalen Ordre Public' in *Berichte der Deutschen Gesellschaft für Völkerrecht*, vol 7 (Karlsruhe, 1967) 77ff; W Levi, 'The International Ordre Public' (1994) 72 *Revue de droit international, de sciences diplomatiques et politiques* 55ff; M Gebauer, 'Ordre Public' in R Wolfrum (ed), *The Max Planck Encyclopedia of Public International Law*, vol VII (Oxford, 2012) 1008ff.

above, from a norm enjoying hierarchy in the realm of the objective sources of a legal system. In municipal law, it stands to reason that the constitution contains peremptory norms; but this cannot be taken as an argument to deny that there are also such norms in the context of ordinary legislation and even in petty administrative regulations of all types. Indeed, peremptory norms span the entire realm of public law. Put briefly, *jus cogens* is concerned with the relationship *lex generalis/lex specialis* and not with the relationship *lex superior/lex inferior*. The two are all but identical. It may also be noted that the *lex superior* rule, to the extent that it applies in a legal order, does not necessarily entail the nullity of the inferior rule; the superior rule may just enjoy precedence of application;[7] this is then a mechanism of collision of norms, which is to some degree separate from the voidness-logic of *jus cogens*. It may finally be noted that the hierarchy argument is not well suited to a relationship of two concrete and situated norms, the general and the special one, when one of both is voided. Hierarchy may be applicable to the general setting of objective norms of the legal system: one norm may here be said to be superior to another (but what consequences flow from that has still to be ascertained). But here, the peremptory norm can only and at best be said to be 'superior' to the derogatory norm whose formation it impeaches, nullifies or renders inapplicable. This 'superiority', if one really wants to employ the term, is thus purely relative: it is situated in the relationship between two concrete norms and does not move beyond them into the general setting of objective norms of the legal order. In other words, it is limited to the capacity or otherwise to derogate from one norm with respect to another.[8] If all priorities of application were rewritten as issues of hierarchy, one would also have to say that the special norm is hierarchically superior to the general norm (since it prevails over the general norm by virtue of the *lex specialis* rule when the general norm is not peremptory) or that the later norm is hierarchically superior to the earlier norm (since it prevails by virtue of the *lex posterior* rule). But this is hardly useful and is therefore rightly avoided.

Third, the hierarchy argument is profoundly misleading, and if only on that account it should be avoided. It tends to create the wrong impression that the superior norm will enjoy priority of application simply because of its superiority. But this is not true as a matter of positive law, and even less so as a matter of legal technique. In other words, the *lex superior* principle is not of general application in the various legal systems. The extent to which it applies and the consequences

[7] Even in international law such arguments can be found: thus, it has been claimed that the access of victims to justice is *jus cogens* and that therefore immunities must yield (see eg Orakhelashvili (n 3) 320ff)—but few would be prepared to argue that the general norm on jurisdictional immunities is now void under international law.

[8] This is rightly noted by Virally (n 4) 18. See also C Rozakis, *The Concept of Jus Cogens in the Law of Treaties* (Amsterdam/New York/Oxford, 1976) 22: 'The novel vertical scheme introduced in international law consists … of the hierarchically superior norms of *jus cogens* and the hierarchically inferior norms of particular law. All other categories of rules are not affected by the superiority of the *jus cogens* norms vis-a-vis particular treaties or rules; consequently the international legal system remains basically horizontal with all rules of law in a linear formation, side by side with the *jus cogens* norms.'

it produces depend on the legal order and thus on contingent legislative choices. Hence, an inferior law can perfectly well continue to exist alongside a contrary superior norm. It can even continue to enjoy priority of application—even if there will probably be some political pressure to remedy this situation under the umbrella of the *lex superior* argument. This is indeed a common occurrence in municipal law systems, like that in Switzerland, where there is no constitutional tribunal reviewing the constitutionality of federal laws. It happens with some frequency that legislation adopted at the federal level (especially when voted by the people) is contrary to the Swiss Constitution. There have been some famous recent cases, including that on the prohibition of minarets.[9] However, as long as the relevant federal law has not been abrogated by the legislator, it will be applied notwithstanding the fact that it is contrary to the Constitution. In legal terms, this means that the inferior law takes practical precedence over the superior one. A similar example exists in relation to certain Swiss communal autonomies: when the Swiss Constitution grants a municipality autonomy in a certain matter, the municipality can pretend that the cantonal laws do not interfere with these matters. In legal terms, the communal legislation would here enjoy priority over the contrary cantonal legislation—*lex inferior derogat legi superiori*! Put briefly, stating that a norm is superior does not say anything about its fate or function in a concrete setting (that is, in a specific legal order and context). Further arguments would have to be marshalled in order to justify an effective priority of application with regard to a so-called inferior norm. But these arguments are unfortunately never addressed in the legal literature. Authors limit themselves to stating that *jus cogens* is hierarchically superior and think that they have thus solved the problem. The reason why this cannot be true is easy to understand: no legal order could bear the amount of legal uncertainly that would ensue from a general application of the *lex superior* rule, particularly if the inferior rules are voided. It is not acceptable that each and every legal operator may decide for himself, in the most disparate legal contexts, which norms should apply and which not, which ones should be voided and which not, etc; this is little better than juridical chaos. Thus, there must be some formalised process in order to determine such issues of normative conflict; the best the judge can do is to give priority to a norm over another in case of conflict; but a power to void norms as he sees fit exceeds the bounds of his functions, unless he has been explicitly or impliedly entrusted with such a power.

The hierarchy point is also misleading from the point of view of practice. It generates the wrong impression that *jus cogens* norms will always prevail over other, contrary objective norms of international law. But that is simply not true as a matter of positive law. If certain human rights are *jus cogens*, it does not flow

[9] See the commentary in R Kolb, 'Völkerrecht und Völkerpolitik. Gedanken zur Minarettinitiative' (2009) 19 *Revue suisse de droit international et européen* 467ff.

therefrom that jurisdictional immunities of States do not apply any more, as the International Court of Justice (after the European Court of Human Rights in *Al-Adsani* (2001))[10] rightly ruled in the *Jurisdictional Immunities* case of 2012.[11]

A tool which tends to create false impressions and illusory expectations is analytically poor and should be revised. Certainly, it is still possible to use the term 'hierarchy' to describe the particular relationship between the norm of general law and the derogatory norm that is voided. However, because of the great potential for misunderstanding the true scope of this hierarchy, this petulant vocabulary is better avoided. The question should be addressed as one of 'voidness' rather than hierarchy. The stress is hereby rightly put on the concrete relationship between two norms and the main effect of the *jus cogens* norm. The foregoing is not to contest the claim that public order norms of international law (distinct from *jus cogens*!) can indeed have some hierarchical effects. But these effects have to be carefully worked out and tested with regard to both international practice and their contextual practicability. Overall, therefore, *jus cogens* is not a phenomenon of hierarchy but rather one of specific priority of certain norms, normally through nullity, and centred, at least in the context of sources, on the key concepts of derogability/non-derogability. The hierarchy argument masks this reality and confuses legal phenomena which are not of the same kind.

Fourth, under the theory discussed here, *jus cogens* is necessarily universal—that is, based on norms of general international law. This may indeed be true for Article 53 VCLT *jus cogens*, but it does not address all forms of peremptoriness in international law. When considered as a legal technique designed to protect the unity of a legal regime against normative fragmentation, it becomes apparent that *jus cogens* can exist at all levels and in all sources of international law, as well as in regional systems. There too are some legal regimes which are more general *ratione personarum* that others, and whose normative integrity falls to be protected against derogation. There is no valid reason—apart from dogmatic consequences drawn from the fundamental values of the international community—to deny a regional group, such as the Council of Europe, its own peremptory norms, applicable among the local States parties, and disallowing derogations from, for example, certain regional human rights, local understandings of the rule of law or democracy, etc. That this is only relative *jus cogens*, neither absolute nor universal, will disturb only those who have completely abandoned the legal technique aspect of *jus cogens* in favour of the current and somewhat lobotomising ideology under the flag of the fundamental values of the international community. Why should the general international community not be happy with regional experiences of *jus cogens*? Could these perhaps even be precursors of universal developments? We will return to these issues when dealing with the sources of *jus cogens*.

[10] (2001) 123 ILR 32, 41–43, 50–51.
[11] Judgment of 3 February 2012.

III. *Jus Cogens* as Rules of International Constitutional Law (Fundamental General Principles, Minimum Necessary for the Existence of an International Legal Order)

Here we find a plurality of theories, but they have certain common points. In the abovementioned theories centred on the fundamental interests of the international community, the substratum on which *jus cogens* is built is non-legal: various substantive interests compete for pride of place. In the present context, the foundational substratum is legal: the question turns on fundamental general principles of the legal order; these form the *jus cogens* of any legal order. The social fact that these principles reflect has already received formal legal clothing. The principles at stake are not only substantive ones, but also structural ones, such as rules on the distribution of jurisdiction, the law-creating agencies (sources), the definition of legal persons, precepts like *pacta sunt servanda* or *consuetudo est servanda*, etc. The essential functional norms of a legal system are protected against alteration and manipulation by the subjects of law. *Jus cogens* is limited to the most general and abstract juridical propositions, situated at the apex of the legal system. Indeed, certain authors prefer to reduce *jus cogens* to general principles of law, some of a structural nature (such as rules on the collision of norms) and others of a substantive nature (such as good faith);[12] others go much further towards a more concrete legal order, by considering notably the Charter of the UN, with its Article 103, as the depositary of an international constitution with *jus cogens* character.[13] A related theory views *jus cogens* as the legal device that maintains the minimum conditions of existence and proper functioning of the international legal order (a sort of existential minimum, *Existenzminimum*).[14]

The foundations of these theories are too narrow to adequately explain *jus cogens*. They are certainly adequate for what they include, but inadequate for what they exclude. *Jus cogens* cannot be narrowed down to the protection of the most necessary principles of the legal system, a protection which is in a certain sense

[12] See, eg, HB Reimann, *Jus Cogens im Völkerrecht* (Zurich, 1971) 57, 76; E Härle, 'Les principes généraux de droit et le droit des gens' (1935) 16 *Recueil des cours de l'Académie de droit international de La Haye* 663ff. See also P Ziccardi, 'Il contributo della Convenzione di Vienna sur diritto dei trattati alla determinazione del diritto applicabile dalla Corte internazionale di Giustizia' in *Comunicazioni e studi*, vol XIV (Milan, 1975) 1073.

[13] See notably B Conforti, 'Cours général de droit international public' (1988-V) 212 *Recueil des cours de l'Académie de droit international de La Haye* 129ff; and on all types of international organisations, Jaenicke (n 6) 94–96.

[14] See notably JA Carrillo Salcedo, 'Droit international et souveraineté des Etats' (1996) 257 *Recueil des cours de l'Académie de droit international de La Haye* 135–36: '[L]a cohésion du droit international, en tant qu'ensemble normatif, exige la reconnaissance par tous ses sujets *d'un minimum de règles impératives* … c'est-à-dire de règles auxquelles on ne peut déroger sans mettre en péril la survie même de l'ordre international' (emphasis in the original).

inherent in those very notions. As we have seen, *jus cogens* is also a legislative tool, which can be used on any normative plane to protect the integrity of a legal regime. In this sense, *jus cogens* is not limited to super-sources placed at the apex of the legal order. In other words, the supreme principles are certainly to a great degree *jus cogens*; but they are only one of the many different types of peremptory norms. Consequently they cannot offer a specific difference so as to furnish the ground for an autonomous theory of *jus cogens*.

IV. *Jus Cogens* as a Legal Technique Inherent in Law: Defining *Jus Cogens* by Its Effect (Non-Derogability)

Certain authors refuse to define *jus cogens* in terms of substantive content. They also refrain from indicating what might cause a legal regime to be peremptory. Instead, these authors concentrate on the effect(s) of *jus cogens*, that is, mainly the prohibition on fragmenting a normative regime into a sub-set of *leges speciales*.[15] The core of *jus cogens*, in the context of the validity of legal acts (which expresses the conceptual origin of peremptoriness), is the refusal of the legal order to ascribe the desired effects to an attempt at derogation: in short, non-derogability. To a significant extent, the International Law Commission (ILC) has engaged itself in this way. It has refrained from indicating which norms are *jus cogens* or according to what substantive criteria such norms may be defined; rather it has pinpointed the formal criteria for the definition of *jus cogens*, such as 'acceptance as general law from which no derogation is permitted'. This is a definition by effect. Contrary to what has often been claimed,[16] this is not a tautological definition:[17] it is a formal

[15] See, eg, A Pellet, 'The Normative Dilemma: Will and Consent in International Law-Making' (1992) 12 *Australian Yearbook of International Law* 38; JM Ruda in Lagonissi Conference, Carnegie Endowment for International Peace (ed), *The Concept of Jus Cogens in Public International Law: Papers and Proceedings* (Geneva, 1967) 101.

[16] See, inter alia, C de Visscher, 'Positivisme et *jus cogens*' (1971) 75 *Revue générale de droit international public* 7; K Wolfke, '*Jus Cogens* in International Law' (1974) 6 *Polish Yearbook of International Law* 146–47; J Crawford, 'The Criteria for Statehood in International Law' (1976/77) 48 *British Yearbook of International Law* 147; F Berber, *Lehrbuch des Völkerrechts*, 2nd edn, vol I (Munich, 1975) 473; B Simma, 'From Bilateralism to Community Interest in International Law' (1994-VI) 250 *Recueil des cours de l'Académie de droit international de La Haye* 286–87; G Morelli, 'A proposito di norme internazionali cogenti' (1968) 51 *Recueil des cours de l'Académie de droit international de La Haye* 111; Paulus (n 4) 302.

[17] See correctly N Ronzitti, 'La disciplina dello *jus cogens* nella conventione di Vienna sul diritto dei trattati' in *Comunicazioni e studi*, vol XV (Milan, 1978) 250; Ziccardi (n 12) 1073; ME Villiger, 'The 1969 Vienna Convention on the Law of Treaties: 40 Years After' (2009) 344 *Recueil des cours de l'Académie de droit international de La Haye* 141; Linderfalk (n 3) 370; S Kadelbach, '*Jus Cogens*, Obligations Erga Omnes and Other Rules: The Identification of Fundamental Norms' in C Tomuschat and JM Thouvenin (eds), *The Fundamental Rules of the International Legal Order, Jus Cogens and Obligations Erga Omnes* (Leiden/Boston, 2006) 29; Verhoeven (n 3) 135.

one, indicating the legal process of creation rather than the end product. It defines the criterion by which *jus cogens* norms must be determined at any given moment in time, that is, the recognition of a norm as having the specific effect of peremptoriness by the overwhelming majority of States. The fact of not listing these norms can hardly be considered a tautology. In municipal law there is no list of peremptory norms either. If one were to be created, such a list would cover almost the entirety of public law. Nobody claims there that there is any tautology in this municipal legal approach to peremptoriness. That it may be difficult to ascertain whether a given norm of general international law is also recognised as *jus cogens* is another matter. It goes to the concrete evidence in individual cases.

For the present author, this theory quite adequately reflects *jus cogens* as a legal technique. It allows the perspective to remain broad enough to encompass the whole phenomenon of peremptoriness, without limiting itself *a priori* to this or that category of *jus cogens* norms, such as public order *jus cogens* or any other category of *jus cogens*. Moreover, the stress is correctly put on the fact that *jus cogens* is first and foremost a legal technique and not a substantive rule. If one wants to give the substantive fundamental norms of international law a name, the correct expression is 'international public order' norms. These norms have some *jus cogens* effects, but also a series of other potential or already accepted effects in international law. The peremptory effect, however, is shared by some other norms of international law. Therefore, these latter norms should not be excluded from the radar in our attempt to provide a general theory of peremptoriness in the international legal order. In short, this theory reinstates in our minds the global approach which the excessive force of attraction of public order norms has completely obscured in the heads of mainstream authors. It will be appreciated that the present way of explaining *jus cogens* does not detract from the mainstream view: public order norms are not negated, nor is their *jus cogens* effect. Conversely, the effort to provide clearer concepts and terminology allows for a more adequate and holistic legal analysis.

V. *Jus Cogens* as a Specific Rule for Conflict of Successive Treaties (Rules of Horizontal Collision)

This theory is based firmly on traditional positivistic grounds and is therefore somewhat older. It starts from the 'coordinative' character of international law, where sovereign States confront each other without the intermediation of a superior power. Consequently the law is created essentially by agreement among States. Since the bulk of international law (if not all international law) is based on agreements, horizontal collisions between treaty norms become a frequent occurrence. *Jus cogens* becomes a technique for solving some of these horizontal conflicts. It rests on a voluntary limitation of the law-making power of States in certain matters: States may accept in a treaty provision a self-limitation on the creation of certain conventional norms in the future. Whether such a limitation has been assumed or not is a matter of interpretation. To the extent that such an intention exists, the previous norm is *jus cogens* and the posterior norm may be void.[18] We may add to this school of thought the authors[19] who in the past (before the adoption of the VCLT, which takes the opposite stance) considered that the conclusion of an incompatible later treaty leads to the voidness of that treaty if it is concluded by parties which are also bound by the previous treaty. *Jus cogens* is here the technical explanation for the nullity of the contrary later norm. Its role is to inverse the maxim *lex posterior derogat legi priori* (and not, as usual, the maxim *lex specialis derogat legi generali*): *lex prior derogat legi posteriori*. Finally, we may add the authors who discuss *jus cogens* in the context of 'integral treaties', that is, those agreements which cannot be split into a bundle of bilateral relationships but whose performance is always due to all the other parties to a treaty (such as a treaty on disarmament).[20]

These theories waned in popularity after the adoption of the VCLT. The latter fixed (if not petrified) *jus cogens* around Article 53 and did not mention it in the context of Article 41, which deals with incompatible *inter se* agreements in the context of previous multilateral conventional engagements. Moreover, the ILC has adopted an approach whereby a later incompatible treaty is not void.[21] The State bound by incompatible treaty commitments can elect which one it will honour. It will incur State responsibility for the provision it sacrifices and therefore violates. Since the question of treaty conflict has moved from the reach of validity of norms into the realm of subjective priority of application, garnished with ordinary consequences of responsibility, the *jus cogens* aspect has faded away. It is quite likely that many contemporary authors do not even remember that there ever was a purely conventional law theory of *jus cogens*. Such authors are convinced that *jus cogens* is inherently 'anti-positivistic'—how could it be heeded by hard and pure positivists? But reality is always richer than abstract speculation: *jus cogens* can be built into purely positivistic theories, as shown by D Anzilotti and G Morelli, two eminent protagonists of the Italian school of international law in the twentieth century.

In any event, even if we wanted to maintain peremptoriness in the context of collision of treaty clauses, we would have to be aware that the latter problem is considerably larger than that of *jus cogens* and also partly of another nature: there is (normally) nullity for *jus cogens* and (normally) priority of application for collision, automatic effect here, subjective choice of the obligation preferred for

[18] See D Anzilotti, *Corso di diritto internazionale* (Rome, 1928) 88–89; D Anzilotti, *Cours de droit international* (Paris, 1929) 96–101; G Morelli, 'Norme dispositive e diritto internazionale' (1932) 11 *Rivista di diritto internazionale* 388ff, 483ff; Morelli (n 16) 114–15. Compare the authors who consider that one treaty can never invalidate another (or one treaty norm invalidate another treaty norm): Verhoeven (n 3) 136, 138.

[19] See, eg, G Haraszti, *Some Fundamental Problems of the Law of Treaties* (Budapest, 1973) 304–05.

[20] G Jaenicke, 'Völkerrechtsquellen' in K Strupp and HJ Schlochauer (eds), *Wörterbuch des Völkerrechts*, vol III (Berlin, 1962) 773–74. On this category of treaties, see the regulations in the VCLT of 1969, Art 41, § 1, lit b and Art 60, § 2, lit c.

[21] See the references in Kolb (n 1) 150ff.

application there. This is not to say that some aspects of such collisions cannot be relevant for *jus cogens*. If the original parties provide for the sanction of nullity as regards derogatory *inter se* agreements between a restricted number of parties to the original agreement, and if that sanction is effectively applied, a special collision rule will have precedence over the general rule of international law which excludes nullity. The process then comes close to a *jus cogens* mechanism. This would be a purely conventional and thus relative *jus cogens*.

VI. The Theories of Cançado Trindade, Chaumont and Wengler

There are various highly personal views on *jus cogens*—that is, potent intellectual conceptions which have essentially remained limited to the authors proffering them. Three examples of such theories may be given here; no commentary on them is necessary.

A. Cançado Trindade

Brazil's AA Cançado Trindade[22] advocates a new *jus gentium* to replace traditional international law. The old-fashioned international law was centred on the inter-State level. It was based exclusively on the interests of States and had the aim of facilitating political dealings among them. The new *jus gentium* attempts to respond to the social needs and aspirations of the international community and of humankind as a whole. It places at its core not the State but the human being. Thus, this new international law is based on a universal humanist perspective. The common and superior interests of mankind are its gist: human rights, self-determination of peoples, protection of the environment, human development, disarmament, etc. In this context, it stands to reason that *jus cogens* has an eminent role to play.[23] It protects all these common human values and the legal norms giving expression to them against the revenge of States. The latter could be tempted to, and are often effectively attempting to, derogate, except, brush aside, diminish, weaken, or otherwise diminish the legal regime of the new *jus gentium*. *Jus cogens* is thus the cognate concept to the new *jus gentium*: it is its direct protector and follows it like a shadow or bodyguard. The extension of *jus cogens* here is remarkable. It is practically co-extensive with the whole realm of the new *jus gentium* protecting universal human values.[24] Thereby, *jus cogens* ensures a degree of verticalisation of the international legal order according to ethical standards.

[22] See Cançado Trindade (n 4) 331ff.
[23] ibid, 335ff.
[24] ibid, 345.

B. Chaumont

A theory of a quite different nature is that of C Chaumont. Its root is not harmony of universal values, but a struggle in the larger setting of Maoist ideology. For this eminent French author, *jus cogens* is centred on the revolutionary right of peoples to self-determination (as we can see, the period of anti-colonialist struggle had not yet passed). In his general course at the Hague Academy,[25] Chaumont had still cast *jus cogens* in an orthodox communist light. It was defined as a set of rules created by States in the context of peaceful coexistence between the Western and Eastern Blocs. In an article of 1985,[26] Chaumont recused his own former State-centred *jus cogens* of the 1970s and now put peremptory law at the exclusive service of peoples. Any *jus cogens* of States is dead, torn apart by the highly contradictory interpretations of governments in the real world. What remains is the spontaneous right of peoples to write their own history. *Jus cogens* is thus nothing more than the eternal right of peoples to revolution in order to safeguard their independence against foreign entities and against their own State apparatuses. In respect of this supreme finality, *jus cogens* is divested of any precise juridical form. Any such form would be inappropriate vis-a-vis its ability to safeguard the absolute political aim of formless revolution.

C. Wengler

The theory of W Wengler, from Germany, is different again. Having collaborated in the German resistance against the Nazi regime and witnessed the extreme weakness of legal norms, Wengler has been constantly obsessed in his legal theory with the sanction of law, that is, with the effectiveness of legal prescriptions. A legal norm is nothing but a multiplicity of relationships representing a power of action (active legitimation) and obligations to suffer an action (passive legitimation). There are regimes of general international law that States want to leave unaltered, not allowing any derogation. There is thus active legitimation on the part of all States to maintain this regime in its original form. This legitimation cannot be cast away by an agreement among only some parties. The *jus cogens* character of such norms with *erga omnes* interests lies in the fact that some States parties to the regime cannot alter it. That would be an attempt to expropriate the active legitimation of the other States parties in relation to these integral legal regimes.[27]

[25] C Chaumont, 'Cours général de droit international public' (1970-I) 129 *Recueil des cours de l'Académie de droit international de La Haye* 377ff.

[26] C Chaumont, 'Mort et transfiguration du *jus cogens*' in *Essays in Honor of PF Gonidec* (Paris, 1985) 469ff.

[27] W Wengler, *Völkerrecht*, vol I (Berlin, 1964) 409ff. Hence the following definition of *jus cogens*: 'Als zwingendes Völkerrecht sind … die durch kollektiven Rechtszwang seitens sämtlicher Staaten gesicherten Sätze des Völkergewohnheitsrechts zu verstehen' [*Jus cogens* is constituted by the norms of customary international law which are guaranteed by the collective coercion of all the States].

As can be seen, *jus cogens* here takes its place in the context of the multilateralisation of the sanction. It is not limited to the aspect of sources, that is, the possibility of derogation or not. It goes further into the realm of State responsibility (as a sort of counter-measure) and finally into sanction norms. It must be noted that the *erga omnes* interests of Wenger are only technical in nature. They are not centred on an international community, whose existence Wengler does not endorse.

* * *

This chapter has shown that there are many theories of *jus cogens*. The concept has attracted much attention and has spawned the greatest legal imaginings of a wide variety of lawyers. If we are still far from having a consensus—from the deniers of *jus cogens* to the most fervent panegyrists—it is fair to state that the bulk of legal writings identify *jus cogens* as a sort of substantive public order of the international community, enriched with some hierarchical superiority and producing a series of particular legal effects, such as the nullity of contrary legal acts. The moment has come to consider more closely what theory of *jus cogens* the present author can offer to the interested reader.

4

Legal Construction of International *Jus Cogens*

I. Relativity of *Jus Cogens*

The first and most important point to be made is that *jus cogens* as a legal technique does not have the absolute and monolithic nature and effects that a mainstream doctrine all too easily attaches to it. On the contrary, as has been correctly stated, *jus cogens* as a concept of positive law remains highly contextual, variable and multiple: this is true in time, since the number and quality of *jus cogens* norms evolves; it is true in space, since there is a regional *jus cogens*; and it is true in substance, as there is variability according to subject-matter, *jus cogens* in the law of treaties not operating in exactly the same way as in the law of State responsibility, or else in human rights law, etc.[1] Moreover, there are different types of *jus cogens* whose role and effects in international law are not the same.

True, our definition of *jus cogens* complicates the matter somewhat. For the mainstream opinion, the identification of *jus cogens* with substantive public order norms (up to the point of synonymy) leads to a simplified notion, with a unique set of legal consequences. However, the conceptual and consequential multiplicity that pops up in our approach is but the price to pay for a global analysis of all peremptory law phenomena of the international legal order. This price may be worth paying. There is also a unifying umbrella in our construction, and that is the concept of 'non-derogability'. The latter allows a broader inquiry than the current public order criterion. Might it be added that this broader view often also yields more satisfactory results? Thus, there are authors who adhere at the very outset of their study to the public order mainstream view, and end up disappointed that this fantastic public order they project according to their hopeful wishes is barely realised in positive international law ('*un ordre public international privé de ses moyens*').[2]

[1] P Tavernier, 'L'identification des règles fondamentales: un problème résolu?' in C Tomuschat and JM Thouvenin (eds), *The Fundamental Rules of the International Legal Order: Jus Cogens and Obligations Erga Omnes* (Leiden/Boston, 2006) 15–16.

[2] S Laghmani, 'Le jus cogens et la cohérence de l'ordre juridique international' in *Les droits de l'homme: une nouvelle coherence pour le droit international? Rencontre à la mémoire de D Jazi* (Paris, 2008) 63ff, 82ff.

It may be answered that the enquiry might perhaps be more promising if *jus cogens* were linked to positive law as a starting point, that is, considered as a legal technique rather than as a super-legality to which States do not yet adhere. It is a frequent problem that objects are not correctly grasped when dogmatic strictures excessively narrow down the perception at the beginning of an inquiry. The reader will appreciate that the present theory attempts to avoid all dogmatic parochialism in the starting hypotheses. It is certainly based on a distinctive criterion, as are all scientific inquiries; but it avoids any pre-conceived exclusion of phenomena which have some link to non-derogation from the arena of *jus cogens*. The extent to which such phenomena are indeed *jus cogens* falls to be analysed carefully and in context.

II. Types of *Jus Cogens*

There are fundamentally three types of international *jus cogens*. In clearer terms, there are three reasons which may lead a norm to be non-derogable or un-fragmentable under the guise of the *lex specialis* principle, that is, to be a norm imbued with the peremptory protective wall.

A. Public Order *Jus Cogens*

Fundamental norms of international law or, more precisely, *some aspects* of the non-use of force rule or self-determination,[3] some human rights guarantees and some international humanitarian law protections, as well as some group protections (like the prohibition of genocide) and perhaps some protections of the natural environment, are non-derogable. Their peremptory content (and only this content) cannot be contracted out or done away with by legal acts.[4] The extent to

[3] An additional interesting case is the one whereby a State renounces for a long time-span and in an excessive way its liberty to make fundamental political choices. This would be contrary to self-determination (and also to the principle of reciprocity, which however is not necessarily peremptory). In the context of private law, such contracts are regarded in German legal science as *Knebelungsverträge* (gagging treaties). See H Mosler, 'Ius Cogens im Völkerrecht' (1968) 25 *Annuaire suisse de droit international* 18, 32. The problem is to determine the point at which such agreements become 'excessive', since it stands to reason that a State can accept some far-reaching obligations even without perfect reciprocity. Historically, the issue has often been discussed in the context of the unequal treaties: cf L Caflisch, 'Unequal Treaties' (1992) 35 *German Yearbook of International Law* 52ff. See generally A Peters, 'Unequal Treaties' in R Wolfrum (ed), *The Max Planck Encyclopedia of Public International Law*, vol X (Oxford, 2012) 38ff.

[4] For a series of interesting examples where the concept of *jus cogens* has been or could have been invoked in international practice relating to various treaties, see W Czaplinski, '*Jus Cogens* and the Law of Treaties' in Tomuschat and Thouvenin (n 1) 93ff, mainly: (i) 1921 Treaty between Russia and Persia (unilateral right of Russia to intervene militarily in Persia); (ii) Cyprus Guarantee Treaty (1960) (question of the right of unilateral military intervention); (iii) Western Sahara Treaty (1975) (disrespect of the right to self-determination of the local population); (iv) Camp David Israel/Egypt Peace Treaty (1979) (infringement of self-determination?).

which this is true is however a complex matter, which is not sufficiently appreciated in legal doctrine. If it is certainly true that an agreement by which two States agree to aggress a third State and to divide its territory between them would be void, it is not possible to additionally hold that all agreements concluded in the context of an unlawful occupation of territory obtained by force are void.[5] This is clear from the law of occupation, under the law of armed conflicts, where it is conceded that the occupying power may conclude agreements necessary for the administration of that territory (separation of *jus ad bellum* and *jus in bello*).[6] By the same token, agreements concluded in order to seek a compromise solution for the status of a territory unlawfully occupied under *jus ad bellum* are not simply all void when they do not reinstate completely and integrally the *status quo ante* (for example, because of the peremptory principle of self-determination).[7] There is already instinctively a difference between the first example (conclusion of a treaty to aggress a third State) and the two latter ones. But the question of the exact legal criteria for the difference—or in other words the extension of the peremptory core of the public order norms—is a matter which has not been sufficiently examined in legal doctrine. Here we find ourselves in the context of lofty sentiments and sometimes fairy-tale adoration, instead of painstaking and precise legal analysis. It is not sufficient to sing the virtues of the 'fundamental rules of the international community'. A precise legal technique analysis must follow, in order to operationalise the concept as fully as possible. As long as this is not done, public order *jus cogens* will continue to frighten all those who are attached to a functioning international legal order, with its lot of legal certainty and respect for the pledged word.

It is not my purpose to present a refined analysis of this difficult legal issue in an introductory inquiry. But some reflections may be offered, since neither is it our purpose to step away from difficult matters. In the determination of the peremptory core of a principle, the following criteria are to be taken account of:

- State practice and judicial pronouncements have to be considered: for example for determining the precise scope of non-recognition peremptoriness in the context of territory obtained by the use of force (from there some analogies to other peremptory effects, such as the nullity of treaties, may be allowable).
- The legal regulations applicable in certain branches of the law have to be respected and may indicate useful distinctive criteria: thus, the cardinal distinction between *jus ad bellum* and *jus in bello* will show that certain legal acts are not void, at least if they respect the powers accorded by the law of armed conflict.

[5] On the principle of non-recognition of territorial situations obtained by force, see J Crawford, *The Creation of States in International Law*, 2nd edn (Oxford, 2006) 96ff, 157ff.

[6] See A Bouvier, M Sassoli and A Quintin, *How Does Law Protect in War?*, 3rd edn, vol I (Geneva, 2011) 114ff, with many references.

[7] This is a legitimate concern of authors such as Barnidge: se R Barnidge, 'Questioning the Legitimacy of *Jus Cogens* in the Global Legal Order' (2008) 38 *Israel Yearbook on Human Rights* 225.

- Recognised exceptions to certain norms may indicate that the scope of peremptoriness is reduced, for example in situations where some norms may be suspended[8] (which does not mean that they may be derogated from in any context, but probably only if the conditions for suspension are met, such as a state of emergency as defined under the norm) or where they may be set aside in certain circumstances (such as law of armed conflict norms under military necessity allowed by the norm,[9] and with the same limitation as the one mentioned above).
- For other cases, the question must be whether the legal act directly or only indirectly infringes the peremptory content (for example, a direct denial of any viable self-determination or merely less than full restitution for previous violations of public order norms, taking keenly into account the fact that the consequences of public order breaches under State responsibility are not themselves *jus cogens*; this makes possible compromise agreements on the status of contested territories). This latter also explains why certain agreements relating to Kosovo or even the recognition of Kosovo by a series of States at the moment of its declaration of independence is not necessarily contrary to the peremptory non-recognition rule for territorial situations created by force. Since almost 10 years had elapsed since NATO's unlawful use of force in 1999, many *intermediate facts* intervened. The final status of Kosovo was therefore no longer a direct and exclusive consequence of the use of force in 1999 (absence of direct causality). Recognition was thus perhaps not unlawful. But the matter is debatable, since the use of force of 1999 remains the main element that finally, after many intermediary changes, allowed for independence.

These examples show how difficult the administration of public order *jus cogens* can be in all but the simplest and mainly hypothetical cases, such as agreements to commit a genocide. It is to be considered a highly worrisome omission that legal writings have not given such aspects the attention they deserve, preferring the easy limelight of generous statements about the great values of the international community. If public order *jus cogens* is to be made operational, a degree of legal certainty will have to be secured in such concrete matters. Otherwise, public order *jus cogens* will remain too open-ended and a dangerous tool, and States will therefore hardly let it penetrate their effective legal dealings. It must be admitted that the task is all but easy; there is however no question that it must be tackled.

[8] As in human rights law under so-called derogation clauses (which are from a legal point of view suspension clauses), eg Art 4 International Covenant on Civil and Political Rights: see M Nowak, *UN Covenant on Civil and Political Rights: Commentary*, 2nd edn (Kehl/Arlington, 2005) 83ff.

[9] On military necessity, see R Kolb, 'La nécessité militaire dans le droit des conflits armés: essai de clarification conceptuelle' in *Colloque de Grenoble de la Société française de droit international* (Paris, 2007) 151ff.

B. Public Utility (or Public Law)[10] *Jus Cogens*

In municipal law, almost the entire area of public law is peremptory, not only the fundamental norms of the legal order; likewise, in international law there are peremptory regimes in the most varied contexts. They exist whenever the States parties to a legal regime want to protect it against fragmentation into more specific legal regimes. This public utility *jus cogens* is not linked to fundamental values or fundamental norms. It is linked to norms where the legislator spots a common interest in maintaining an unaltered, integrated and unique functioning. In international law, there are such public utility *jus cogens* norms mainly in two well-settled contexts. First, there are constitutive treaties, as well as derived sources, of international organisations or organs.[11] For example, the Statute of the International Court of Justice (ICJ) contains a series of norms which States cannot alter; they have to take or leave them as they stand (see below). Second, there are so-called 'integral treaties' (to some extent, constitutive instruments of international organisations are but an important example thereof), where the treaty regime supposes that all parties will apply the same rules and where any derogation into specific regimes applicable between some parties under *lex specialis* would defeat the object and purpose of the treaty.[12] Thus, derogatory treaties for a limited number of the original parties are not allowed. (Conversely, all the parties to the original treaty could depart from it, this not being derogation but modification of the original agreement.) The question whether these agreements *inter partes* are void, inapplicable, non-opposable to the original parties, or give rise only to consequences of State responsibility is of secondary interest here.[13]

[10] The term 'public law' is not preferred here, since it may suggest an excessive analogy with municipal legal orders.

[11] Many authors share this point of view: see eg J Jurt, *Zwingendes Völkerrecht: Ein Beitrag zur lehre vom objektiven Völkerrecht* (Wil (St Gallen), 1933) 103; A Miaja de la Muela, 'Ius cogens y ius dispositivum en derecho internacional publico' in *Essays in Honor of L Legaz y Lacambra*, vol II (Zaragoza, 1960) 1144–45; Mosler (n 3) 20–21; See also B Conforti, *Diritto internazionale*, 4th edn (Naples, 1992) 185–86; J L'Huillier, *Droit international public* (Paris, 1949) 72–73; J L'Huillier, *Eléments de droit international public* (Paris, 1950) 181; S Wittich, 'Permissible Derogation from Mandatory Rules? The Problem of Party Status in the Genocide Case' (2007) 18 *European Journal of International Law* 608ff. For the Statute of the ICJ as peremptory, see eg the developments in G Abi-Saab, *Les exceptions préliminaires dans la procedure de la Cour international de Justice* (Paris, 1967) 158ff; G Abi-Saab, 'Cours général de droit international public' (1987-VII) 207 *Recueil des cours de l'Académie de droit international de La Haye* 259. Contra: J Verhoeven, 'Sur les "bons" et les "mauvais" emplois du *jus cogens*' (2008) 5 *Anuario brasileiro de direito internacional* 133, 155.

[12] See the regime of Art 41, § 1, lit b VCLT. On this provision see F Rigaux and D Simon, 'Article 41' in O Corten and P Klein (eds), *The Vienna Convention on the Law of Treaties: A Commentary*, vol II (Oxford, 2011) 986ff, 1001ff; ME Villiger, *Commentary on the 1969 Vienna Convention on the Law of Treaties* (Leiden/Boston, 2009) 528ff, 534–35; K Odendahl, 'Article 41' in O Dörr and K Schmalenbach (eds), *Vienna Convention on the Law of Treaties: A Commentary* (Heidelberg/Dordrecht/London/New York, 2012) 719ff, 724–25.

[13] Legal writings deny the consequence of voidness, since the ILC rejected it after a heated discussion: Rigaux and Simon (n 12) 1008; Odendahl (n 12) 721. Art 30 VCLT is however applicable.

It is only if we determine that nullity is a necessary prerequisite of *jus cogens* that the mechanism could possibly fall outside the scope of peremptoriness. For the moment, it must be considered part and parcel of it, since it manifestly concerns the issue of derogability and non-derogability.

The example of the Statute of the ICJ, as a form of public utility *jus cogens*, may be briefly developed.[14] The parties to a specific case must take the rules governing the activities of the ICJ as they stand and cannot contract out of them; in other words, the Court's rules are beyond their control. They are not merely dispositive law, which must give way to contrary agreement between the parties. On the contrary, they are peremptory and even the Court cannot alter or dispense with them.[15] As the ICJ itself has stated: '[T]he international tribunal is no longer an arbitral tribunal constituted by virtue of a special agreement between the parties for the purpose of adjudicating on a particular dispute, but is an institution which has been pre-established by an international instrument defining its jurisdiction and regulating its operation, and is, in the present case, the principal judicial organ of the United Nations.'[16] As a logical consequence, as A Bustamante y Sirven wrote in 1925: '[T]he judge or tribunal, established in advance, [is] subject to rules … [that are] … prior and superior to the will of any party appearing before them. The judge and tribunal are not special creations of the parties, but have an existence prior to and superior to theirs, exercising their powers from above.'[17] Hence the fact that there can be no derogation from the Statute, as emphasised by G Schwarzenberger: '[I]ndividual parties to cases before the Court have but

[14] For a fully fledged development, see R Kolb, *Théorie du jus cogens international* (Paris, 2001).

[15] AS de Bustamante, *La Cour permanente de justice internationale* (Paris, 1925) 152: '[The] judge or tribunal, established in advance, [is] subject to rules which are prior and superior to the wills of the respective parties … The person charged with ruling on the dispute is not the special creature of the various parties, but on the contrary, exists, so to speak, "prior to" and "above" them, exercising his powers from above to below' (author's translation). This aspect can also be analysed, at a more theoretical level, as resulting from differing legal orders on the one hand applicable to isolated arbitrations, and on the other to permanent tribunals. For Morelli, 'isolated' arbitrations, especially bilateral ones, do not create a new legal order. All that happens is that the internal legal orders of the States in question govern the setting up of the arbitral tribunal. Relations between the arbitrators and the States are based exclusively on an arrangement for services. The creation of a permanent tribunal, by contrast, supposes the creation of a special legal system, the same in nature as internal law, but without any 'State' character. This is the system that regulates the activity of the judges and establishes their rights and obligations. After all, it is impossible to say that the obligations of the Court's judges are owed only to the parties to particular disputes: that conception would lead to a continual metamorphosis in judges' legal position—agents now of this State and now of that one; a conclusion which, at least for the Italian internationalist Morelli, is completely impossible. Here, the greater distance between the judicial body and the parties' wishes is explained as the effect (or the cause) of a *normative mediatisation*. This is a screen between international judges and individual States. See G Morelli, 'La théorie générale du procès international' (1937-III) 61 *Collected Courses of the Hague Academy of International Law* 282–83.

[16] *Nottebohm* case, *Preliminary Objection* [1953] ICJ Rep 119. See also the Pessôa Dissenting Opinion in the *Serbian Loans* case, PCIJ series A no 20/21, p 65; the Novacovitch Dissenting Opinion, ibid, 80; the Observation of Juge Pessôa annexed to the order in the *Free Zones* case, PCIJ series A no 22, pp 48–49; and the Observation of Judge Kellogg in the same case, PCIJ series A no 24, pp 32–33.

[17] de Bustamante (n 15) 152 (author's translation).

a limited choice: they may take the Statute as they find it or leave it.'[18] Certainly the Statute can be amended, but only by the procedures laid down in the text, not by derogation. It is therefore accepted that the parties to cases before the Court cannot, between themselves, make agreements which would require the Court to behave inconsistently with its Statute. On several occasions the Court has explicitly refused to follow the parties down that road, or has at least indicated that it might refuse if the request were to be made. In this sense, the Statute is, for litigating States, imperative law. Stipulations contrary to it will be of no avail. Possibly they are not null and void in themselves,[19] but they have no effect as regards the Court, and this, as a practical matter, certainly does make them sterile nullities.

In its practice, the Court has frequently reaffirmed the imperative nature of its Statute. The fundamental underlying reason was first explained with clarity in the *Nottebohm* case (Preliminary Objection, 1953): 'The seising of the Court is thus dominated by the declarations of the parties ... But the seising of the Court is one thing, the administration of justice is another. The latter is governed by the Statute, and by the Rules which the Court has drawn up by virtue of the powers conferred upon it by Article 30 of the Statute.'[20] This was reaffirmed in *Military and Paramilitary Activities in and against Nicaragua* (merits, 1986): 'The Court is bound by the relevant provisions of its Statute and its Rules ... provisions devised to guarantee the sound administration of justice, while respecting the equality of the parties.'[21] Respect for the Statute and the Rules is a matter of the international public interest in the proper administration of justice. This cannot be left to the desires and idiosyncrasies of parties. In this regard, the Court, and the Court alone, has to be the guardian. As the Court said in 1963 in the *Northern Cameroons* case: 'The Court itself, and not the parties, must be the guardian of the Court's judicial integrity.'[22]

This is not the place for a comprehensive list of the cases in which the Court has invoked the imperative character of the Statute when faced with a wide range of contrary wishes on the part of litigating parties. A few examples will suffice.

— A special agreement between the parties, agreeing to submit their dispute to the Court, cannot contravene an imperative provision of the Statute. In the

[18] G Schwarzenberger, *International Law—As Applied by International Courts and Tribunals*, vol IV (London, 1986) 723. In the same sense, see MO Hudson, *The Permanent Court of International Justice* (New York, 1943) 413; M Dubisson, *La Cour internationale de justice* (Paris, 1964) 205–06, 211: 'However the provisions agreed between the parties in the *compromis*, whether they relate to the procedure or the substance of the case, can never derogate from the Court's Statute, which, as is well known, is binding on all parties just as it is on the Court itself' (211, this author's translation).

[19] It has however been argued that stipulations contrary to the Statute are void, eg Dissenting Opinion of Guerrero in the *Norwegian Loans* case [1957] ICJ Rep 69; Individual Opinion of H Lauterpacht in the same case at 34ff; Dissenting Opinion of H Lauterpacht in the *Interhandel* case [1959] ICJ Rep 101ff. The argument is that automatic reservations to optional declarations under Art 36, § 2 of the Statute are void because they are contrary to Art 36, § 6 of the same Statute. The question as to whether the reservation can be severed from the rest of the declaration is a different one.

[20] [1953] ICJ Rep 122.

[21] [1986] ICJ Rep 39, § 59.

[22] [1963] ICJ Rep 29.

Free Zones case (Order, 1929) the special agreement contained a provision contrary to the Statute. The parties had jointly asked the Court to provide a non-official indication of the results of its deliberations prior to the giving of formal judgment. But under Article 54, § 3 of the Statute, the Court's deliberations were secret. The Court therefore refused this request: 'The spirit and letter of its Statute, in particular Articles 54, paragraph 2, and 58, do not allow the Court "unofficially" to communicate to the representatives of the Parties to a case "the result of the deliberation" on a question submitted to it for a decision; as, in contradistinction to that which is permitted by the Rules (Article 32 [now 101]), the Court cannot, on the proposal of the Parties, depart from the terms of the Statute.'[23] It would be difficult to find a clearer expression of the Statute's peremptory character.

— Even on the basis of an agreement between them, States do not have the right to request an advisory opinion. Articles 96 of the Charter and 65–68 of the Statute confine that right to certain organs of the UN and to certain affiliated organisations. This limitation is peremptory. Other entities, particularly States, cannot make such requests. At the time of the *travaux préparatoires* on the Statute, the idea was in fact proposed, but it was firmly rejected, for a number of reasons. One was that making advisory opinions available to States would profoundly disturb the functioning of the Court. States could obtain judicial pronouncements without being under a corresponding duty to carry them out. This would imperil the Court's prestige, and the Court would in effect turn into a legal advisory service for States. Its function in contentious disputes would suffer from the weight of the advisory work that could be anticipated. Also, it might have become possible to consult the Court on an advisory basis, with a view to finding out, in advance, the likely tenor of a decision in a future application for actual resolution of the dispute. States might then decide whether to agree to submit their cases to the Court, as a result of the advance knowledge thereby obtained. In addition, a kind of *de facto res judicata* would be established, with highly dubious effects. No tribunal likes to limit its future freedom of judgment by adopting advance positions on an abstract basis, where the case has not been sifted by the demanding processes of contentious proceedings in which claims have to be proved. The consensual nature of the Court's jurisdiction might also, in effect, be undermined if unilateral requests for opinions were allowed. The step would threaten the principle of equality between the parties, the more so since the requesting State would be the sole judge of the tenor and formulation of the question put to the Court. It would be necessary to anticipate intervention proceedings, and counter-requests for opinions, leading to procedural difficulties of various kinds. Finally, the consultative procedure would not have, for States, the importance it can sometimes have for international organisations. The latter can take action only on the basis of their

[23] PCIJ series A no 22, p 12.

constitutive texts, and so it is vital for them to know how to interpret those texts correctly. It is not the same for States—their *internal* laws apply to their internal affairs. Considering all these points, the Court has always considered this limitation on the right to seek advisory opinions a rule of imperative law. It has refused to respond to requests which appear to be simply seeking an opinion, whether the request is unilateral[24] or made jointly.[25]

— In some cases, the advance interpretation of a text can be incompatible with the Court's judicial function and consequently also with its Statute. In the *Free Zones* case (Order, 1929), the parties had asked the Court to declare whether the Versailles Treaty had abrogated, or was designed to abrogate, the free zones. The Court refused to allow itself to be boxed in by a predetermined interpretation, since the Treaty might have neither of those effects: 'The Court cannot as a general rule be compelled to choose between constructions determined beforehand none of which may correspond to the opinion at which it may arrive...'[26] The Court recognised that its rules contained an element of flexibility, it being accepted that the parties could limit its role, and thus have some influence on the law that would be applied. But the proposed restriction was considered excessive, the more so since the multilateral Treaty of Versailles had a far wider ambit than the relationship between the present parties. Such limitations will always be excessive if they would make it impossible for the Court to reach an adequate appreciation of the situation before it, thus placing the Court in a false position; or if the predetermined interpretation would be so partial as to prevent a reasonable application of the law—*part-interpretation* becoming partial interpretation. In all such cases, the limitations imposed by the law on parties' freedom are, plainly, derived from the need to maintain the Court's judicial integrity.

— Parties are not allowed to subordinate the binding or executory character of a judgment to conditions not recognised by the Statute. In the *Free Zones* case (1929–32), the special agreement provided that, if the judgment countenanced the importation of merchandise in bond or at reduced customs duties, that aspect of it would be subject to the assent of both parties. The Court considered that condition to be contrary to the Statute.[27] It went beyond merely providing for possible renegotiation. It amounted to giving binding force, in the Court Order itself, to the idea that there would have to be subsequent agreement for the ruling of the Court to become binding. In the circumstances, therefore, the Court refused to make the Order. The same question arose much later, in the *Continental Shelf* case (Tunisia/Libya, 1982).

[24] *Certain German Interests in Polish Upper Silesia* (1925), PCIJ series A no 6, p 21.

[25] *Interpretation of the Greco-Bulgarian Agreement of 9 December 1927* (Caphandaris-Molloff Agreement, 1932), PCIJ series A/B no 45, p 87.

[26] PCIJ series A no 22, p 15.

[27] PCIJ series A/B no 46, p 161: '[I]t would be incompatible with the Statute, and with its position as a Court of Justice, to give a judgment which would be dependent for its validity on the subsequent approval of the Parties.' See also PCIJ series A no 24, p 14.

> Libya interpreted the special agreement to mean that the Court's task would be confined to giving directions, on the basis of which the parties would then renegotiate while retaining almost complete freedom of manoeuvre. In the process of interpreting its decision, the Court reduced that view to proportions compatible with the Statute.[28] Judge Gros expressed much greater doubts still about the validity of the Libyan argument, because he took Libya's oral declarations literally.[29] Unlike in the *Free Zones* case, in this case the parties were not attempting to subordinate the Court's order to a subsequent agreement between them. One party was simply making an advance statement that the judgment would serve only as the basis for negotiation, and would not have immediate executory status. If the Court is warned in advance that the parties intend to nullify the executory character of a decision by negotiations on the very subject-matter of the rights and obligations ruled upon, it must refuse to decide the case. It is true that the parties are always free to decide, *ex post facto*, not to give effect to the obligations set out in a decision of the Court, in the same way that any ordinary judgment creditor can decide not to execute his judgment. That, however, is not the point. If that intention is known *in advance*, the Court must refuse to rule,[30] because to do so would put in issue its judicial integrity. In effect, its decision would simply amount to providing States with an advisory opinion, which would be contrary to the Statute. The parties can reserve to themselves a maximum degree of freedom of manoeuvre by asking the Court for a declaratory judgment. But even in that case, they cannot declare *in advance* that they do not necessarily intend to adhere to the Court's decision on the legal points on which it will rule. To sum up, then: (1) a peremptory rule of law prohibits the parties from subordinating the validity of the Court's decision to their consent, or from modifying *ex post facto* the findings of law in the judgment; (2) the Court cannot give judgment if the parties have declared in advance their intention not to give effect to the judgment in its entirety, or if that intention is established by other means; and (3) the parties do not lose the right to renegotiate the substantive issues—but not to renegotiate the judgment—by coming to an agreement on new terms, after judgment has been given.

The above examples show that these rules, which are necessary to protect the integrity of the Statute, were applied just as zealously by the Permanent Court of International Justice (PCIJ) as they have subsequently been applied by the ICJ. This attitude thus shows very clearly that no institutional international tribunal can allow itself to depart, in any way, from a cluster of functional rules centring upon the concepts of judicial integrity and the proper administration of justice—in other words, upon the public interest, of which the PCIJ was, and the ICJ now is, the sole and ultimate guardian.

[28] [1982] ICJ Rep 40.
[29] Dissenting opinion of Judge Gros, ibid, 143–46.
[30] ibid, 145.

This function of *jus cogens* is to be found across all questions relating to the constitutive instruments, resolutions and rules of international organisations, even in matters of a certain banality. Thus, for example, the legal advisor of the UN's Geneva Office had to consider the conclusion of certain agreements between the UN and private corporations, through which the Organisation would be funded and as a counterpart would allow the publication of its emblem/logo in commercial catalogues of the donors. However, by virtue of the fact that there are certain resolutions and regulations strictly protecting the UN logo, these agreements have been prohibited by the UN legal service in New York.[31] This prohibition stems from the fact that the regulations on the logo are peremptory. They protect a public interest of the Organisation in the use of its emblem and cannot be derogated from by means of special agreements. The fact that the agreement, once concluded, could not necessarily be considered void technically speaking, since it would have involved third parties (a corporation), does not change the gist of the matter. The prohibition on concluding such treaties took its place.

This larger conception of *jus cogens*, based on public interest rather than only on fundamental norms, reflects the most ancient continental legal tradition. Its roots go back to Roman Law.[32] In the Roman legal order there was a fundamental distinction between *jus publicum* and *jus privatum*. The former are the objective laws of the Roman State, while the latter concern State regulations on private dealings and legal relationships between individuals in the sphere of their private autonomy (that is, subjective legal acts). The distinction between the two levels of legislation is mainly casuistic. It is made according to the interests protected, here the interest of the collectivity (*utilitas publica*), there the interest of the individual (*utilitas singulorum*).[33] In view of these interests protected, the first is non-derogable and thus what we would now call *jus cogens*: *publicum ius privatorum pactis mutari non potest*.[34] This rule is considered important by the Roman lawyers; it is often

[31] Information given by the UN Legal Advisor in the Geneva Office, Markus Schmidt. The protection of the emblem and name is pursuant to GA Resolution 92(I) of 7 December 1946. See also the UN *Revised PPP Guidelines* (V) (November 2009), available on the internet.

[32] See notably M Kaser, 'Ius publicum und ius privatum' (1986) 103 *Zeitschrift der Savigny-Stiftung für Rechtsgeschichte, Romanistische Abteilung* 1ff, 75ff (one of the most eminent specialists of Roman Law). See also G Nocera, *Ius publicum (Dig. 2, 14, 38), Contributo alla ricostruzione storico-esegetica delle regulae iuris* (Rome, 1946); C Gioffredi, 'Ius, Lex, Praetor' in *Studia et documenta historiae et iuris (Rome)*, vols 13/14 (Rome, 1947/48) 90ff; A Guarino, *L'ordinamento giuridico romano*, 3rd edn (Naples, 1959) 242ff; O Robleda, 'En torno al binomio "ius publicum"—"ius privatum" en derecho romano' (1967) 47/48 *Miscellanea comillas* 541ff; M Lauria, *Ius: visioni romane e moderne*, 3rd edn (Naples, 1967) 243ff; B Schmidlin, *Die römischen Rechtsregeln* (Cologne/Vienna, 1970) 47ff; H Ankum, 'La nocion de "ius publicum" en derecho romano' (1983) 53 *Anuario de historia de derecho español* 523ff (cf (1980) 97 *Zeitschrift der Savigny-Stiftung für Rechtsgeschichte, Romanistische Abteilung* 302ff); G Aricò Anselmi, 'Ius publicum—ius privatum in Ulpiano, Gaio et Cicerone' (1983) 37 *Annali del seminario giuridico dell'Università di Palermo* 524ff; A Guarino, *Diritto privato romano*, 8th edn (Naples, 1988) 136ff (with further references). H Hausmaninger and W Selb, *Römisches Privatrecht*, 3rd edn (Vienna/Cologne, 1985) 65–66 use the terms *ius cogens/ius dispositivum*.

[33] Kaser (n 32) 4, 98.

[34] ibid, 75ff.

invoked in the sources.[35] The imperative effect of public law is such a distinctive feature of it that it tends to become a defining element; derogable *ius publicum* is considered a contradiction in terms.[36] In addition, subjective obligations under *ius civile* are also peremptory when the legislator does not allow the parties to contract out of them.[37] There is no evidence that the Roman lawyers limited public law and related *jus cogens* to a core of fundamental rules within *ius civile* (public order). On the contrary, the whole realm of public law and a series of private law rules and subjective positions were peremptory, according to the collective interest in prohibiting derogation.[38] It is also clear that *jus cogens* does not refer to the *inter partes* 'extinction' of objective norms, which is not in the power of the parties; *jus cogens* rather concerns the peremptoriness of the legal regime provided for in the norm, that is, the subjective legal positions flowing from the objective provision.[39]

In the Middle Ages, the notion of *jus cogens* was extended to the domain of the relations between sources of law. Thus, when the Italian municipalities gained power, from the fourteenth century onwards, they could impose the priority of their local statutes (*jus proprium*) over the common law (Roman and Canonic Law, *jus commune*) by virtue of the *lex specialis* principle, which was by then highly developed. However, it was accepted that these local laws could not derogate from certain 'common interest' rules of general law, such as a number of rules of canon law, the Aegidian Constitutions of 1357, and the common rules providing for criminal offences.[40] The interesting point is that nullity under *jus cogens* is here transferred to the production of local objective laws; it is not limited to derogatory subjective legal acts of private individuals. Here we see a significant analogy with international society. Power within it is decentralised, as it was in fourteenth-century Italy. In the Italian cities, there was a general common law and a particular local law; in international law there is a general international law and partial agreements, limited *ratione personarum*. In both situations the sphere of production of objective laws and of subjective legal acts is not entirely differentiated. The experience of the European Middle Ages shows that *jus cogens* can function perfectly well in such a setting. Its core elements remain the same: *utilitas publica*, non-derogability and nullity.

C. Logical *Jus Cogens*

This concerns the principles *pacta sunt servanda* and good faith. Neither principle can be derogated from as such, without falling into self-contradiction and thereby

[35] ibid, 75 fn 320.
[36] ibid, 76.
[37] ibid.
[38] ibid, 73.
[39] ibid, 78.
[40] See W Engelmann, *Die Wiedergeburt der Rechtskultur in Italien durch die wissenschaftliche Lehre* (Leipzig, 1938) 79–80, 105–06, 132. See also, on the relationship between *jus commune* and *jus proprium*, G Ermini, *Corso di diritto commune* (Milan, 1989) 33ff.

indirectly confirming them. If some States were to try to contract out from *pacta* ..., this would amount to them concluding an agreement to the effect that they would no longer respect the principle, at least in some circumstances. But in order to achieve the result thus stipulated for, these States would have to respect the derogatory agreement. Otherwise their derogation could have no effect. Consequently, in order to derogate from *pacta* ... there is the need for an agreement, and by this token the necessity to apply the *pacta* principle is upheld. The same reasoning applies to good faith. In order to stipulate out of good faith, the different-drummer States would have to respect their derogatory agreement ... in good faith, which brings back by the door the principle chased out of the window. For these reasons, several authors regard these principles as a form of *jus cogens*,[41] and this author agrees.

Conversely, there are some authors who refuse to factor these principles into the realm of *jus cogens*.[42] The arguments mustered are manifold. They boil down to essentially three aspects. First, this particular *jus cogens* is not envisaged by Article 53 of the Vienna Convention on the Law of Treaties (VCLT), which concerns substantive public order norms rather than structural principles which cannot logically be abandoned.[43] Second, it has been said that *jus cogens* is here legally superfluous. Since such principles are already peremptory on the logical plane, it is not necessary that the legal order confers a separate and additional peremptoriness

[41] See, eg, G Perrin, 'La nécessité et les dangers du *jus cogens*' in *Essays in Honor of J Pictet* (Geneva, 1984) 751; I Sinclair, *The Vienna Convention on the Law of Treaties*, 2nd edn (Manchester, 1984) 207, 215, 222; Miaja de la Muela (n 11) 1137–38; J Martensen, '*Ius Cogens* im Völkerrecht—Gibt es bindende Normen des Völkerrechts die durch völkerrechtliche Verträge nicht aufgehoben warden können?', PhD thesis (Hamburg, 1971) 176. See also the authors mentioned in L Hannikainen, *Peremptory Norms (Jus Cogens) in International Law: Historical Development, Criteria, Present Status* (Helsinki, 1988) 319–20 G Morelli, 'A proposito di norme internazionali cogenti' (1968) 51 *Recueil des cours de l'Académie de droit international de La Haye* 113 argues that only the derogability of the principle *pacta* allows the existence of concrete peremptory norms. This is so because only with a partial derogation from *pacta* can certain treaties be considered void, ie not covered by the duty of performance ('con ciò si limita l'efficacia di produzione giuridica conferita all'accordo da pacta sunt servanda'). The eminent Italian teacher here however confuses the limitation of the scope of application of *pacta* through a primary norm with the notion of derogation. It stands to reason that legally speaking *pacta* is not an absolute principle, but knows of exceptions: eg the invalidity of treaties obtained by coercion, concluded in violation of important formal requirements, etc. This limitation of the scope of application of the principle at the level of the primary norm has nothing to do with its 'derogation'.

[42] J Sztucki, *Jus Cogens and the Vienna Convention on the Law of Treaties: A Critical Appraisal* (Vienna/New York, 1974) 72, 80, 84; M Virally, 'Réflexions sur le *jus cogens*' (1966) 12 *Annuaire français de droit international* 10; AJ Leonetti, 'Interprétation des traités et règles impératives du droit international général (*jus cogens*)' (1973) 24 *Oesterreichische Zeitschrift für öffentliches Recht* (*Oesterreichische Zeitschrift für öffentliches Recht*) 96; JA Barberis, 'Le concept de "traité international" et ses limites' (1984) 30 *Annuaire français de droit international* 266–67; JA Barberis, *Formacion del derecho internacional* (Buenos Aires, 1994) 60–61; B Simma, 'From Bilateralism to Community Interest in International Law' (1994-VI) 250 *Recueil des cours de l'Académie de droit international de La Haye* 288.

[43] See, eg, J Crawford, 'The Criteria for Statehood in International Law' (1976/77) 48 *British Yearbook of International Law* 146; U Scheuner, 'Conflict of Treaty Provisions with a Peremptory Norm of General International Law and its Consequences' (1967) 27 *Zeitschrift für ausländisches öffentliches Recht und Völkerrecht* 525–26; Mosler (n 3) 30ff, because these norms usually have no direct normative content but must be used with other norms in order to give concrete effect to legal relationships.

on them; and what is redundant (*quid pluris*) is for that reason legally wrong.[44] Both arguments raise mainly definitional points. It *may* be true that Article 53 of the VCLT was not meant to open up to the peremptoriness of such structural principles. But that is not altogether certain; after all, such principles were mentioned by several members of the International Law Commission (ILC) as examples of *jus cogens*.[45] In any event, Article 53 VCLT is not exhaustive as to peremptoriness in international law. As to the second argument, it does not impeach a recognition that a certain principle is peremptory also in law. The order of logic is one thing, the order of law is another. The recognition that a certain quality in one also leads to a similar quality in the other is not redundant. Moreover, it is accepted that the two principles are non-derogable. The point about whether we want to call them *jus cogens* or simply non-derogable norms is after all secondary and purely definitional. In this study, which tries to provide a global analysis of legal peremptoriness in international law, it stands to reason that the more global approach is preferred.

There is a third argument which deserves to be mentioned. It has been argued that if *pacta* … were peremptory, any later derogatory agreement between some parties to an earlier multilateral treaty would be void. The reason for this lies in the fact that the adoption of the later conflicting treaty leads to direct jeopardy of the first treaty, contrary to the pledge of *pacta* … Such nullity, however, it is claimed, is not the position under the applicable conflict rules of Article 30 VCLT. Thus, *pacta* … can hardly be *jus cogens*.[46] This learned argument is based on a misunderstanding. The later agreement does not purport to derogate from *pacta* … itself (if it did, it could not itself stand as an agreement). It only derogates from the substantive content of an earlier treaty. This the principle *pacta* … does not disallow, nor does it then lead to a nullity by virtue of *jus cogens*. In other words, there are different planes which should not be confused: here the general bindingness of agreements; there the conflict between concrete incompatible aspects of formally valid treaties.

III. The Extension of *Jus Cogens*: What Legal Acts and Facts are Covered by the Notion?

The question to be analysed here is limited to the extension of *jus cogens* in its classical context of the validity or nullity of legal acts. Actual or potential further effects of peremptoriness will be considered in chapter six. The distinction between

[44] C Focarelli, 'Promotional *Jus Cogens*: A Critical Appraisal of *Jus Cogens*' Legal Effects' (2008) 77 *Nordic Journal of International Law* 451.

[45] See, eg, GI Tunkin in [1963-I] *Yearbook of the ILC* 197.

[46] See Czaplinski (n 4) 87–88. See also G Haraszti, *Some Fundamental Problems of the Law of Treaties* (Budapest, 1973) 304.

legal acts and legal facts has already been mentioned.[47] The former are acts of will producing normative effects (obligations and rights) according to the expressed will (which is normally congruent with the real intention): agreements, promises, resolutions, but also legislation, regulations, etc. The second are either material facts or intentions, producing legal effects (obligations and rights); in the case of an intention the effects are not congruent with the express or implicit intent (such as an unlawful act, producing the effect of responsibility). The effect of nullity is normally limited to the category of legal acts; it does not extend to legal facts. The reason for this is easily understood. A mere legal fact is not to be valid or void; it is legal or illegal—that is, it corresponds to the injunction of a norm or it is contrary to it. For example: if a norm provides that the State acquires territory by the natural fact of accretion, then the fact of accretion (the formation of new territory by natural events) has the consequence of triggering the legal consequence foreseen in the norm, namely the acquisition of that territory under the sovereignty of the State. Here, nullity is not at stake: the issue is only whether the fact is able to trigger the legal effect or not. As the fact is merely natural in the case of accretion, even the double category of legality and illegality disappears; the fact is rather simply existence or not (existence/non-existence), and if it is existent, it will trigger the effect provided for in the norm. In a second example, we can consider a fact flowing from human behaviour, let us say an unlawful act. A norm provides for the integrity of territorial sovereignty, and yet another State penetrates that territory with its armed forces, without the consent of the local sovereign. The fact of penetrating the territory is not to be judged under the categories of validity or nullity; it is to be judged under the umbrella of conformity or not with the norm at stake, that is, legality or illegality. It does not make sense to say that such a fact as the entry of armed forces into territory does not exist, when it is indeed foreseen in a legal norm. Conversely, in the particular category of legal acts (which are a special category of legal facts), the question of validity and nullity does arise, and it does so alongside the question of legality and illegality. If two subjects conclude an agreement and provide for legal rights and obligations, the legal order has the option to recognise these stipulations as being valid or to deny them the legal effect the parties wanted to create, that is, the rights and obligations they provided for. In addition, such stipulations can also be unlawful acts, albeit in the international legal order it is normally the case (that is to say, there are exceptions) that only the actual carrying out of the stipulations will lead to the admission of responsibility.[48] However, under particular international law this may be different: for example if the parties have agreed in another, prior agreement that any contrary stipulation will in itself amount to an unlawful act. The result of the foregoing is that with legal acts the quest for validity/nullity is central. Thus, the concept of *jus cogens* has its standing in this context. But which are concretely the legal acts covered by international *jus cogens*?

[47] For these categories, see the very precise developments in G Morelli, *Notions de droit international public* (Paris, 2014) 205ff.

[48] On this issue, see J Crawford, *The ILC's Articles on State Responsibility* (Cambridge, 2002) 130.

A. Agreements

The most typical legal acts in international law are the various agreements (called treaties when consigned in written form). For a long time, legal writings in international law concentrated on agreements (and sometimes even denied that unilateral acts could *per se* have normative legal effects).[49] That *jus cogens* applies to this category of legal act (that is, agreements) is today not contested.[50] This is the gist of Articles 53 and 64 of the VCLT, the former for treaties concluded when the peremptory norm they attempt to derogate from is already established, the latter for treaties contrary to a *jus cogens* norm which has developed after the conclusion of the treaty. Thus, Article 53 of the VCLT reads as follows: 'A treaty is void if, at the time of its conclusion, it conflicts with a peremptory norm of general international law…' The question of what constitutes an agreement must be referred to the legal literature on treaties.[51] Suffice it to say, at this point, that an agreement is based on four essential elements: (i) a meeting of minds on a certain subject-matter; (ii) subjects of international law as parties, to the exclusion of individuals (treaty-making power); (iii) having legal effects (and not only political effects, as do political agreements); and (iv) subject to public international law. If a treaty conflicts with *jus cogens*, it is void, either in totality (under Article 53) or possibly only in the conflicting provisions (under Article 64). This regime is today considered to reflect general international law.[52] There have not been many treaties openly conflicting with *jus cogens* norms. The acceptance of the notion may have had prophylactic value. However, two precedents may be mentioned. The first goes back to times before the Vienna Treaties Convention of 1969. The legal basis for the conclusion reached was therefore at least uncertain, if not rooted outright in justice and natural law considerations (or municipal law analogies). Thus, in the *Krupp* case[53] (US Military Tribunal at Nuremberg), defence counsel had made the argument that the transfer and exploitation of French prisoners of war contrary to the Geneva Convention of 1929 on Prisoners of War was justified by an Agreement between Germany and France (Vichy). The Tribunal did not have to rule directly on the point, since the evidence for the existence of such an agreement was insufficient. However, it affirmed, *obiter*, that such an agreement, if it existed, would have been void as *contra bonos mores*. It has to be added that the 1929 Convention contained no clause equivalent to Article 6 of the 1949 III Geneva Convention on

[49] See the discussion of the issue in JD Sicault, 'Du caractère obligatoire des engagements unilatéraux en droit international public' (1979) 83 *Revue générale de droit international public* 634ff.

[50] See, eg, A Orakhelashvili, *Peremptory Norms in International Law* (Oxford, 2006) 133ff; L Haopei, '*Jus Cogens* and International Law' in S Yee and W Tieya (eds), *International Law in the Post-Cold War World: Essays in Memory of Li Haopei* (London, 2001) 508ff; A Gomez Robledo, 'Le *jus cogens* international: sa genèse, sa nature, ses fonctions' (1981-III) 72 *Recueil des cours de l'Académie de droit international de La Haye* 88ff.

[51] See DB Hollis, 'Defining Treaties' in DB Hollis (ed), *The Oxford Guide to Treaties* (Oxford, 2012) 11ff.

[52] E Suy, 'Article 53' in Corten and Klein (n 12) 1226; Villiger (n 12) 677 (emerging rule).

[53] 15 ILR 626–27.

Prisoners of War, which expressly rules out special agreements between belligerents derogating from the guarantees due to prisoners. Another precedent, already mentioned, is the *Aloeboetoe* case (Inter-American Court of Human Rights). The problem arose in the context of a treaty of 1762 by which the Surinam authorities granted a local tribe the right to be governed by their own laws. However, this treaty also provided for cooperation between the tribes and the authorities in the lucrative slave trade. While there were once again other reasons for not applying this treaty to the question at the fore, the Court noted that in any event it could not have enforced such a treaty since it was inapplicable under *jus cogens*. This was a case of *jus cogens superveniens* under Article 64 of the VCLT: the slave trade was not prohibited at the time the treaty was concluded, nor did there exist *jus cogens* norms on the issue at that time. If the treaty had applied in the present case, the nullity would not necessarily have led to the lapse of the whole treaty: under Article 64 severability of the conflicting clauses by virtue of Article 44, § 3 of the VCLT is possible. As another example, we may mention reports in the press that some rulers proposed agreements which would have been squarely contrary to peremptory provisions. Thus, it has been said that S Milošević proposed to the Greek government a splitting up of Macedonia between the two States, which the Greek government seems to have refused. An agreement to that effect would have been contrary to the non-use of force and the peremptory self-determination rules.

B. Unilateral Legal Acts

Most writers accept that *jus cogens* also applies to unilateral (legal) acts. Most often, this result is reached on the basis of a reasoning *a fortiori*: if *jus cogens* voids bilateral legal acts, it must perforce also void unilateral engagements.[54] Such nullity

[54] See, eg, Hannikainen (n 41) 7; HB Reimann, *Jus Cogens im Völkerrecht* (Zurich, 1971) 41; Lagonissi Conference, Carnegie Endowment for International Peace (ed), *The Concept of Jus Cogens in Public International Law: Papers and Proceedings* (Geneva, 1967): Abi-Saab, 10; Fitzmaurice, 36; Suy, 75, 86; Ushakov, 93; Asamoah, 96; N Ronzitti, 'La disciplina dello *jus cogens* nella conventione di Vienna sul diritto dei trattati' in *Comunicazioni e studi*, vol XV (Milan, 1978) 245; EP Nicoloudis, *La nullité de jus cogens et le développement contemporain du droit international public* (Athens, 1974) 122ff; GA Christenson, '*Jus Cogens*: Guarding Interests Fundamental to International Society' (1988) 28 *Virginia Journal of International Law* 585, 611; K Zemanek, 'The Metamorphosis of *Jus Cogens*: From an Institution of Treaty Law to the Bedrock of the International Legal Order?' in E Cannizzaro (ed), *The Law of Treaties Beyond the Vienna Convention* (Oxford, 2010) 393–94; S Kadelbach, '*Jus Cogens*, Obligations Erga Omnes and other Rules: The Identification of Fundamental Norms' in Tomuschat and Thouvenin (n 1) 29; Laghmani (n 2) 76; FA Mann, 'The Doctrine of *Jus Cogens* in International Law' in *Essays in Honor of U Scheuner* (Berlin, 1973) 403–04; M Kreca, 'Some General Reflections on the Main Features of *Jus Cogens* as a Notion of International Public Law' in *Essays in Honor of W Abendroth* (Frankfurt/New York, 1982) 31; J Dugard, *Recognition and the United Nations* (Cambridge, 1987) 146; LA Sicilianos, *Les réactions décentralisées à l'illicite* (Paris, 1990) 34, 344; JA Barberis, *Formacion del derecho internacional* (Buenos Aires, 1994) 142–43; RSJ MacDonald, 'Fundamental Norms in Contemporary International Law' (1987) 25 *Canadian Yearbook of International Law* 135–36; T Meron, 'On a Hierarchy of International Human Rights' (1986) 80 *American Journal of International Law* 19; V Coussirat-Coustère, 'Israël et le Golan' (1982) 28 *Annuaire français de droit international* 200–10; J Verheoven, 'La reconnaissance internationale: déclin ou renouveau?' (1993)

will lie outside the realm of Article 53 of the VCLT, being rooted in general international law. This position has been contested by some authors,[55] but their arguments are generally based on a misunderstanding. Most of the authors refuting the application of *jus cogens* to unilateral acts do not make a clear distinction between material unilateral acts and legal unilateral acts. The former are simple facts, such as the invasion of a territory. It stands to reason that the issue of voidness is not at stake in such situations. In particular, the argument of the contesters is that the application of *jus cogens* to such (material) unilateral acts leads to a confusion of validity issues with violation issues:[56] unilateral (material) acts either conform or do not conform to the legal norm. Moreover, these authors recall that the law is always binding on the subjects taken *uti singuli*; they cannot derogate from the norms by their unilateral acts, so that *jus cogens* seems to be superfluous here.[57] But this is not truly the point of most of the authors admitting an extension of

39 *Annuaire français de droit international* 38; W Czaplinski and G Danilenko, 'Conflicts of Norms in International Law' (1990) 21 *Netherlands Yearbook of International Law* 9; R Provost, 'Reciprocity in Human Rights and Humanitarian Law' (1994) 65 *British Yearbook of International Law* 442; JA Carrillo Salcedo, 'Droit international et souveraineté des Etats' (1996) 257 *Recueil des cours de l'Académie de droit international de La Haye* 194–95; C Tomuschat, 'International Law: Ensuring the Survival of Mankind on the Eve of a New Century: General Course of Public International Law' (1999) 281 *Recueil des cours de l'Académie de droit international de La Haye* 82. See also Dissenting Opinion of Kreca in the *Genocide* case [1996-II] ICJ Rep 754. Expressing doubts: C Rozakis, *The Concept of Jus Cogens in the Law of Treaties* (Amsterdam/New York/Oxford, 1976) 16ff. For the extension of *jus cogens* to unilateral acts of international organisations (resolutions), see eg P Reuter, *Introduction au droit des traités*, 3rd edn (Paris, 1994) 126. L Grosse, 'Racines historiques et fondements contemporains des normes impératives (*jus cogens*) dans la théorie et la pratique du droit international' (1995) 73 *Revue de droit international, de sciences diplomatiques et politiques* 225ff, considers that legal unilateral acts have their main root in municipal law and that international *jus cogens* cannot void such acts for the purposes of municipal law—thus nullity under international law will in any case be insufficient. This argument does not seem entirely convincing. First, we may notice that there are authors who consider that international *jus cogens* may also void internal legal acts: see eg P Saladin, 'Völkerrechtliches ius cogens und schweizerisches Landesrecht' in G Jenny and W Kälin (eds), *Die schweizerische Rechtsordnung in ihren internationalen Bezügen* (Bern, 1988) 73–74; A Cassese, 'An Enhanced Role of *Jus Cogens*' in A Cassese (ed), *Realizing Utopia: The Future of International Law* (Oxford, 2012) 167–68. Other authors insist on the differences between the two legal orders, nullity under international law not necessarily entailing nullity under municipal law: T Meron, 'International Law in the Age of Human Rights: General Course of Public International Law' (2003) 301 *Recueil des cours de l'Académie de droit international de La Haye* 206–07. Second, the fact that international *jus cogens* cannot void the municipal law side of the act at stake does not mean that the international legal order should not void it for its own purposes. Why one 'gap' should perforce produce another is unclear.

55 K Marek, 'Contribution à l'étude du *jus cogens* en droit international' in *Essays in Honor of P Guggenheim* (Geneva, 1968) 441; P de Visscher, 'Cours général de droit international public' (1972-II) 136 *Recueil des cours de l'Académie de droit international de La Haye* 105; P Weil, 'Le droit international en quête de son identité' (1992) 237 *Recueil des cours de l'Académie de droit international de La Haye* 281–82. Some have contested the equation of *jus cogens* with public order to which the inclusion of (all) unilateral acts would lead: Mosler (n 3) 25. Sometimes, the absence of a basis in positive law is advanced as an argument: Perrin (n 41) 757.

56 Such a confusion would indeed be unwarranted: see eg Y Dinstein, 'The Interaction between Customary International Law and Treaties' (2006) 322 *Recueil des cours de l'Académie de droit international de La Haye* 400. However, see also Rozakis (n 54) 10ff, where *jus cogens* is also given a role in the prevention of violations of certain important norms; and Meron, 'International Law in the Age of Human Rights' (n 54) 208.

57 de Visscher (n 55) 105; Weil (n 55) 281–82.

peremptoriness to unilateral acts. The extension is limited to *legal* acts of unilateral nature—promises, recognition, reservations, etc. Such acts are also expressions of will, directed to the creation of legal effects concordant with the expressed will. In short, such legal unilateral acts have normative effects. Thus, they should be subject to the validity/nullity test. There is no reason why the legal order should consider void an agreement to commit a genocide but not a promise to commit one. Conversely, there is not much sense in extending *jus cogens* to material unilateral acts, as some authors continue to do.[58] That such acts may have a series of consequences flowing from the violation of a public order norm is undoubtedly true. But this is an issue of responsibility (rather than of validity), and furthermore an issue of public order more than of *jus cogens* (since, as we have seen, a distinction has to be drawn between the two concepts). Nullity is one thing, other effects are another. Let us take an example. The recognition of a territorial situation may be void if it is contrary to a *jus cogens* norm. Conversely, *jus cogens* does not found a duty of non-recognition of territorial situations obtained by force or through a denial of the right of self-determination.[59] The latter duty flows from customary international law (where it forms a separate norm); it is rooted in the international public order. Thus a distinction must be drawn between recognition (as a unilateral act, which can be void) and the duty of non-recognition (which is a free-standing norm of international law, rooted in public order, and which requires a specific abstention).

Considering what has been said above, legal doctrine and practice rightly extend *jus cogens* to the following *normative* unilateral acts:

— resolutions of international organisations, and in particular decisions of the UN Security Council;[60]
— acquiescence: impossibility to acquiesce in a derogation from *jus cogens*;[61]

[58] See, eg, Orakhelashvili (n 50) 205ff; D Dubois, 'The Authority of Peremptory Norms in International Law: State Consent or Natural Law?' (2009) 78 *Nordic Journal of International Law* 135, 144; R Puceiro Ripoll, 'Las normas de *jus cogens* en el campo del derecho internacional contemporaneo' in H Arbuet-Vignali and R Puceiro Ripoll (eds), *Derecho internacional publico, Breviarrio*, vol 1 (Montevideo, 2010) 123–24; VS Mani, 'Humanitarian Intervention Today' (2005) 313 *Recueil des cours de l'Académie de droit international de La Haye* 189. See also Saladin (n 54) 73–74.

[59] It has to be conceded, however, that the duty of non-recognition is often directly linked to *jus cogens*: Mann (n 54) 412ff; Ronzitti (n 54) 245; Orakhelashvili (n 50) 372ff; Dugard (n 54) 123ff. Or else, the breach of *jus cogens* is seen as grounds for withdrawal of recognition: E McWhinney, 'Self-Determination of Peoples and Plural-Ethnic States' (2002) 294 *Recueil des cours de l'Académie de droit international de La Haye* 261.

[60] See, inter alia, *Tadic* (1999) 124 ILR 181 § 296 (Judgment of the Appeals Chamber); *Yusuf and Barakaat* (2005) 149 ILR 237 § 281 (Court of First Instance of the European Communities); *Kadi* (2005) 149 ILR 296–97 (Court of First Instance of the European Communities); Orakhelashvili (n 50) 423ff; JA Frowein, 'Ius Cogens' in R Wolfrum (ed), *The Max Planck Encyclopedia of Public International Law*, vol VI (Oxford, 2012) 445. See also K Zemanek, 'The Legal Foundations of the International System: General Course of Public International Law' (1997) 266 *Recueil des cours de l'Académie de droit international de La Haye* 231. See further the famous Separate Opinion of E Lauterpacht in the *Genocide* case (Provisional Measures) [1993] ICJ Rep 440, § 100.

[61] Orakhelashvili (n 50) 398ff; Ronzitti (n 54) 245; Nicoloudis (n 54) 124–25; L Oppenheim, *International Law* (ed RY Jennings and A Watts), 9th edn, vol I (London, 1992) 8.

- nullity of an arbitral or judicial pronouncement contrary to *jus cogens*;[62]
- prescription: no acquisitive prescription contrary to a *jus cogens* position;[63]
- reservations: nullity of reservations contrary to *jus cogens*;[64] and
- waiver: no waiver possible for *jus cogens* positions.[65]

Conversely, some other often-mentioned effects linked to unilateral acts have to be considered separately in order to find out whether they are supported by a norm of general or particular international law, since they are not concerned with validity/nullity and are thus not inherent in the concept of *jus cogens* (but they are often treated in the context of *jus cogens*):

- consent to the jurisdiction of a tribunal;[66]
- consequences of State responsibility;[67]
- duties of non-recognition;[68]
- curtailment of certain privileges if a State is the aggressor;[69]
- availability of counter-measures or reprisals;[70] and
- role of reciprocity: no reciprocity arguments in the context of peremptory positions,[71] etc.

Thus, the non-availability of counter-measures, if their exercise is contrary to '*jus cogens* norms', is a consequence of public order rather than of *jus cogens*: not all types of *jus cogens* norms (such as public utility *jus cogens*) entail such limitations; and moreover the unavailability of these measures is not a question of validity or nullity. But it must be conceded that the terminological and conceptual distinctions made here have largely been lost in the line of mainstream thinking after the ILC, in its Articles on State Responsibility, largely intermingled these issues.

C. Customary International Law?

Does a *jus cogens* norm void or take precedence over a norm of general or regional customary international law? Or does the existence of a *jus cogens* norm render

[62] Ronzitti (n 54) 245.

[63] Orakhelashvili (n 50) 404ff; Sinclair (n 41) 223–24; J Crawford (n 43) 148.

[64] Orakhelashvili (n 50) 176ff; Zemanek (n 54) 391–92; Kadelbach (n 54) 29; Meron, 'International Law in the Age of Human Rights' (n 54) 238. Contra, but erroneously, see Verhoeven (n 11) 154.

[65] Orakhelashvili (n 50) 390ff; A Maresca, *Il diritto dei trattati* (Milan, 1971) 622; Kadelbach (n 54) 29.

[66] Tomuschat (n 54) 414; Focarelli (n 44) 431ff. See also Orakhelashvili (n 50) 489ff.

[67] Orakhelashvili (n 50) 241ff; Zemanek (n 54) 396–97; and see the various contributions in J Crawford, A Pellet and S Olesson (eds), *The Law of State Responsibility* (Oxford, 2010) 405ff.

[68] Often put in the orbit of *jus cogens*: Mann (n 54) 412ff; Ronzitti (n 54) 245; Orakhelashvili (n 50) 372ff; Dugard (n 54) 123ff; Meron, 'International Law in the Age of Human Rights' (n 54) 422.

[69] See, eg, I Brownlie, *Principles of Public International Law*, 4th edn (Oxford, 1990) 514.

[70] Kadelbach (n 54) 29; Zemanek (n 54) 396; Zemanek (n 60) 327; C Focarelli, *Le contromisure nel diritto internazionale* (Milan, 1994) 471ff; LA Sicilianos (n 54) 339ff; OY Elagab, *The Legality of Non-Forcible Counter-Measures* (Oxford, 1988) 96ff; de Visscher (n 55) 105; Oppenheim (n 61) 8; Provost (n 54) 442.

[71] Kadelbach (n 54) 29.

legally impossible the emergence of a contrary norm of customary law, at least so long as the *jus cogens* norm exists itself? This issue is considerably different from the one we considered previously. The point here is not that a norm of general international law (according to the requirement of Article 53 VCLT) voids a derogatory norm of a more restricted circle of participants, that is, a limited, *inter partes* derogatory legal act. The question is rather cast—for universal customary law[72]—as a conflict between two objective norms of general international law. The legal consequence of nullity would here have an entirely different scope than the one usually contemplated in the context of legal acts. It would not serve to maintain the integrity of a general regime against fragmentation into particular legal acts, but rather to ensure the superiority of one norm over another in case of conflict, either by simple precedence or perhaps even by radical nullity. Notwithstanding this, there are several international lawyers who accept the idea that *jus cogens* will nullify or take precedence over an ordinary norm of customary international law in case of collision;[73] and even the case law of tribunals hints in this direction.[74] It has thus been said that it would be doubtful to accept that public order norms cannot be derogated from by conventional acts but could be brushed away by customary norms; in other words, it would be odd to admit that they are not derogable by agreement but derogable by practice. Or else: why could an ordinary customary rule be derogable by agreement, but not 'derogable' by an imperative norm of customary law? The agreement would here be more potent than a *jus cogens* norm—is that sensible?

The question to be asked is whether we can accept this legal construction. The answer is in the negative, and this for a series of reasons. Let us consider first the situation for norms of general customary international law, before moving to issues linked with norms of particular customary international law (regional and bilateral custom).

[72] For the relationship between a universal peremptory customary rule and a regional derogatory customary rule the general/particular law link is upheld, but there remains the fact, to be discussed later in this text, that a customary norm is not a legal act.

[73] Zemanek (n 54) 394–95; Orakhelashvili (n 50) 340–41; Christenson (n 54) 611; Oppenheim (n 61) 8: '[N]or can a rule of customary international law which conflicts with a rule of ius cogens continue to exist or subsequently be created'; H Charlesworth and C Chinkin, 'The Gender of *Jus Cogens*' (1993) 15 *Human Rights Quarterly* 66; study of the ILC on *Fragmentation of International Law*, Doc.A/CN.4/L.682 (2006), § 367, the ILC seeming even to admit the invalidity of the contrary customary norm! On the whole question, see R Kolb, 'Nullité, inapplicabilité ou inexistence d'une norme coutumière contraire au *jus cogens* universel?' (2013) 117 *Revue générale de droit international public* 281ff. See also, even if we no longer agree with everything said at that time, Kolb (n 14) 93ff. Also rightly against such an extension to customary norms, see Verhoeven (n 11) 153–54; J Verhoeven, 'Considérations sur ce qui est commun—cours général de droit international public' (2008) 334 *Recueil des cours de l'Académie de droit international de La Haye* 235–36, 318.

[74] See, eg, International Criminal Tribunal for the Former Yugoslavia, *Furundzija* (1998) 121 ILR 261 (Trial Chamber); *Siderman de Blake* case (1992) 103 ILR 472 (US Court of Appeals); *Bouzari v Iran* (2002) 124 ILR 442 (Canada, Ontario Superior Court of Justice); *Ferrini* (2004) 128 ILR 668–69 (Italian Court of Cassation); *Prefecture of Voioitia* (2011) 150 ILR 720–21 (Italy, Court of Cassation); Separate Opinion of E Lauterpacht, *Genocide* case (Provisional Measures) [1993] ICJ Rep 440, § 100; Joint Dissenting Opinion of Rozakis, Caflisch, Wildhaber, Costa, Cabral Barreto and Vajic in *Al-Adsani* (see n 75), § 1. Contra: Separate Opinion of Dugard, *Armed Activities* case (*DRC v Uganda*) [2006] ICJ Rep 91, § 13.

First, State practice and the case law of the important international tribunals does not know of such an operation of *jus cogens*. On the contrary, when it came to such a collision, the international tribunals concerned refused to give precedence to the *jus cogens* norm (and even less to void the contrary norm) by the sole fact that it was peremptory. We may recall in this context the European Court of Human Rights in *Al-Adsani* (2001)[75] or the ICJ in *Armed Activities* (*DRC v Rwanda*, 2006)[76] as well as in *Jurisdictional Immunities* (2012).[77] In *Al-Adsani* and *Jurisdictional Immunities*, the issue was a conflict between on the one hand the possibly or actually peremptory right to access to justice for the victims of international crimes (human rights law), and on the other the jurisdictional immunities of States, which is certainly a non-peremptory norm of customary international law. The courts at stake upheld the immunity rule, from which State practice has not yet carved out an exception for access to justice in the context of international crimes. In *Armed Activities*, the ICJ refused to give precedence to the undoubtedly peremptory norm prohibiting the commission of genocide over the norm of its Statute (which is conventional in nature) that its jurisdiction is merely consensual. By the same token, State practice does not evidence in any way such an automatic precedence. In the context of immunities, the ICJ undertook a painstaking analysis in the *Jurisdictional Immunities* case and could find no diverging practice, apart from that of Italy and, in the meantime reversed, that of Greece. The capacity to override norms of ordinary customary international law is a possible expression of peremptoriness in international law; but, as long as it is not accepted in State practice—that is, not accepted by the international legislator—it cannot be taken as being part and parcel of positive international law. In particular, it cannot be deduced from the concept of *jus cogens* itself, if only since such a function would be deviant in relation to the accepted notion of peremptoriness. It would by far exceed the sphere of nullity of contrary *inter partes* legal acts and become a device of norm conflict resolution in the sense of an overall hierarchy (verticalisation) of international law. Such a novelty cannot just be deduced from a concept, lest any legal operator arrogates to himself the faculty of highest constitutional law-making in disguise. A practical argument may be added: the anarchy and disorder in a legal system that would ensue if each operator could choose to foster his or her own agenda by shuffling new normative combinations and priorities would be of such a magnitude as to alienate international law from its 'clients', namely States. If every subject can have its own law by some magic and powerful *jus cogens* manipulation, the question remains as to whether international law would still deserve the predicate of 'law'. What is certain is that the disservice rendered to international law would be huge. An additional and powerful reason not to take it seriously would be given to various States: they would stop seeing international law in their own law and practice and perceive it as a haphazard, growling and ideologised play

[75] (2001) 123 ILR 32, 41–43, 50–51.
[76] [2006] ICJ Rep 31–32, § 64.
[77] Judgment of 3 February 2012, § 92ff.

tool barely deserving of any respect. The paradox is that those who struggle for the greatest progress of international law could be those who will be responsible for an important regression.

Second, it is inadequate to say that *jus cogens* represents a hierarchically superior norm. But even accepting such a hierarchical construction, for the sake of argument as it were, the priority of the peremptory norm would not follow automatically. We have seen that even hierarchically superior norms do not necessarily impose themselves on hierarchically lower norms. In other words, the principle *lex superior imperat* (or *derogat*) *legi inferiori* is not of general application.[78] There are many cases where inferior norms continue to be applicable albeit they contradict hierarchically superior norms, such as norms of a Constitution. There are specific procedures for bringing the two norms into line. But a legal operator cannot always just give precedence to what he considers to be the correct interpretation of the superior norm, brushing aside the lower norm. Elementary considerations of legal certainty explain this position. Legal certainty is already particularly weak in international law, with its gaps, interpretive uncertainties, complexity of sources, etc. It should not be weakened even further. This brings us back to the point previously made. If the peremptory norm is to cast away the non-peremptory one, there must be some positive legal basis for that conclusion. The hierarchy argument in itself is *not* sufficient. The same is true for arguments that insist on the fact of *jus cogens* norms being based on a double *opinio juris*, one for the legality and generality of the norm, and one for its peremptory character.[79] However, the supplementary *opinio juris cogentis* (the opinion that a norm is not derogable) does not confer greater weight on that norm in relation to other ones; it just qualifies its mode of operation as not being subject to derogation.

Third, *jus cogens* is a mechanism centred on derogation (*vel* non-derogation), not on the collision of objective norms. In other words, the question of solving antinomies between objective norms (and not simple particular legal acts) of the system is one which must be solved by a contextual interpretation of the provisions at stake and not by nullity or wholesale non-application of one norm in favour of full application of another.[80] That one norm is peremptory does not change this state of affairs. In short: the better course is interpretation, not rigid derogation. Clearly, in the mutual adjustment of the spheres of application of two or more norms in conflict, the peremptory character of one of these norms may be taken into account in order to increase its weight and to tilt the balance. But—and

[78] It must be added once more that all forms of precedence in case of collision are not expressions of hierarchy: *lex specialis* and *lex posterior* give precedence to a norm over another in a concrete context, but it stands to reason that the more particular and the later law are not hierarchically superior to the more general or the older law.

[79] On the double legal opinion, see eg H Thirlway, 'Concepts, Principles, Rules and Analogies: International and Municipal Legal Reasoning' (2002) 294 *Recueil des cours de l'Académie de droit international de La Haye* 401.

[80] This is rightly admitted even by friends of a slightly bold *jus cogens*: see A Bianchi, 'Human Rights and the Magic of *Jus Cogens*' (2008) 19 *European Journal of International Law* 491, 505.

this is the cardinal point—the process is one of interpretive adjustment and not one where a lock, stock and barrel result flows from the peremptory character of one of these norms, by way of derogation and nullity, or by way of automatic precedence *en bloc*. The contrary approach leads to rigid and unsatisfactory results, which will often be unworkable or disproportionate. There can be no argument, for example, that jurisdictional immunities are void because of *jus cogens* rights to access to justice; or even that access to justice (if that is a *jus cogens* human right) always take automatic precedence over all immunities. If that were true, possibly even embassy buildings of a State could be seized and sold (if diplomatic law is not *jus cogens*) in order to realise a judgment rendered against a State and flowing from *jus cogens* access to justice. Who can believe that States would be prepared to go that way?

Fourth, if the concept of nullity (or even simply constant inapplicability, which is practically tantamount to nullity) is seen as being essential for describing the effect of peremptory norms, then this effect on a customary norm poses important problems of legal technique. In legal science, it is admitted that legal acts can be voided. These are declarations of will having normative legal effects (creating rights and obligations). A declaration of will can be considered void in that it will not have the normative legal effects it purports to have in the legal order where a *jus cogens* norm impeaches its validity.[81] What is essential, thus, is that a legal act is based on will. However, customary norms are considered as expressions of will and consent only by an old and now completely abandoned theory of international law, which construed such norms as tacit agreements.[82] Today it is accepted that customary law is not based on tacit agreement. Thus, not all States of the world must have agreed to a norm in order for the latter to be considered a norm of general international law. The relevant practice must be 'general', not unanimous.[83] Hence, customary norms are based on a social normative process constituted of practice and legal opinion. In legal technique, it is a 'legal fact in the narrow sense': a fact of social life, to which the legal order attaches certain legal consequences.[84] A legal fact in the narrow sense is a fact to which the legal order attaches some legal consequences of its own, independently of the will of the subjects involved (for example, responsibility for a wrongful act, creation of a customary norm, etc). Now, in current legal technique, a juridical fact cannot be void. It can produce certain legal consequences or not; it can be derogated from or

[81] Sometimes, the defect in the legal act is so grave that the legal order does not consider it as existent at all (hence there is no possibility of voiding it, since it already lacks legal existence). Thus, in some legal orders the expression of will obtained by coercion (*vis compulsiva*) is considered no expression of will at all; thus the legal act is inexistent, not void.

[82] Se eg K Strupp, 'Les règles générales du droit de la paix' (1934-I) 47 *Recueil des cours de l'Académie de droit international de La Haye* 301ff, 303–04, 319; D Anzilotti, *Corso di diritto internazionale* (Rome, 1928) 64, 68–69. See generally H Günther, *Zur Entstehung von Völkergewohnheitsrecht* (Berlin, 1970) 22ff.

[83] On these issues, see eg M Akehurst, 'Custom as a Source of International Law' (1974/75) 47 *British Yearbook of International Law* 1ff.

[84] See the very precise developments in Morelli (n 47) 24ff.

not; it can be lawful or unlawful (wrongful act); it can exist or not; it can be compatible with the law or not; but it cannot be void.[85] This is true for facts in general: they are or they are not, they produce certain consequences or they do not. But what could be the reach and impact of a statement that such a fact is void? If it is not a legal fact at all (since it is not provided for in a legal norm), it does not exist for the legal order, and there is consequently no nullity: you cannot void a non-existent fact. If it is a legal fact, that is, recognised by a legal norm as producing a legal effect, then only the nullity of the norm referring to that fact would have the effect of also voiding, consequently, the fact itself. Conversely, as long as the norm applies, the fact cannot be said to be void. It is not severable from the operation of the norm that bears it.

In our context, it could perhaps be said that the *norm* of customary law arising out of the law-creating agency of custom could be voided. However, as a norm of objective international law, and not a subjective legal act, this process of voidance would have to occur through a special legal process geared to that effect. The nullity of that norm cannot simply be deduced from the peremptory character of another norm, since that precisely goes beyond the age-old accepted concept of peremptoriness. As already claimed, there must be some basis in positive law for such new effects of *jus cogens*; they cannot be smuggled into the system disguised as the accepted *jus cogens* notion. Technically speaking, 'inapplicability' of the customary norm contrary to *jus cogens* would not incur the same criticisms under legal technique. But there remains what was said above: wholesale inapplicability is an all too harsh and disproportionate consequence in case of collision of norms. The issue must rather be perceived as one of harmonising interpretation.

Fifth, there remains the question of the extent to which a customary *jus cogens* norm can *de lege lata* coexist with an incompatible norm of ordinary customary law.[86] We must consider two hypotheses. First: if the non-imperative customary norm is still *in statu nascendi*, the peremptory customary rule should normally impeach its birth or provide for an exception in the respective scopes of application so as to avoid a normative conflict. Conversely, if the ordinary later customary rule establishes itself, this occurrence can only mean that the older peremptory rule has lost its positive law status. A customary rule can uphold itself only if it continues to be supported by practice and legal opinion. But if that practice and opinion now go in another and incompatible direction, then the previous norm is totally or partially modified.[87] In such a situation, no room for true conflict is left.

[85] Grosse (n 54) 244.

[86] Legal writings consider the point, albeit only in a cursory manner. See Dinstein (n 56) 399–400: if ordinary customary international law is older, it falls into desuetude due to the newer peremptory norm; and if the ordinary customary rule is newer, this may lead to a modification of the older peremptory rule.

[87] In this sense, Art 53 VCLT is imprecise when it affirms that a peremptory norm can be modified only by a norm having the same status. This may be at best true for the direct replacement of one peremptory norm with another, especially in a process of treaty making. But it is not true for modification arising out of abandonment, desuetude or obsolescence of the older norm, which is not supported by practice or opinion. Clearly, there remains a presumption that practice contrary to a public order *jus*

Second: here the peremptory norm (or the recognition of the peremptory quality of a norm)[88] is posterior to the non-peremptory norm. But if the former is not terminated as discussed above (whence the conflict disappears), the only question that remains is whether the newer norm has or has not carved out a new exception to the old one. This flows from the fact that the material fact at the basis of the two customary rules is identical: it is State practice and legal opinion. If the latter contradicts the former, the former norm is terminated in whole or in part and the conflict disappears; or alternatively the newer norm provides for an exception to the reach of the former one, solving the conflict through harmonisation of the scopes of application of the two norms, the conflict disappearing once again. Let us take as an example a conflict between the right to access to justice for the victims of international crimes and jurisdictional immunities of States. If both are customary rules, the question is not so much whether one takes precedence over the other because it is peremptory; rather it is a distinct question as to whether State practice and opinion wanted to limit the rule of immunity in this context so that it would no longer apply. The point turns on the carving out of a new exception, analogously to the *jure gestionis* exception to immunity. If an exception is admitted, the immunity rule will not apply in such cases: there is no normative collision for which *jus cogens* as '*lex superior*' is needed. If an exception is not admitted, the rule of immunity will continue to apply and there will again be no conflict between the two rules. *Jus cogens* then could not change this deliberately assumed legal position. In short, the 'legislator' has to determine which norms in the customary process shall apply and how. The interpreter must try to ascertain this 'intention' through careful analysis of international practice (thus, for example, States have not, to date, agreed to make the right to access to justice an exception to jurisdictional immunities).

Sixth, a short reply to two arguments presented above may be ventured. These were: 'It has … been said that it would be doubtful to accept that public order norms cannot be derogated from by conventional acts but could be brushed away by customary norms; in other words, it would be odd to admit that they are not derogable by agreement but derogable by practice. Or else: why could an ordinary customary rule be derogable by agreement, but not "derogable" by an imperative norm of customary law? The agreement would here be more potent than a *jus cogens* norm—is that sensible?' The first argument confuses derogation with law-making (abrogation and modification). Peremptory norms may be changed by the

cogens norm does not intend to depart from it, and is therefore to be analysed as a simple violation of the rule. The *jus cogens* character of the rule thus heightens the threshold a contrary practice must pass before being able to establish itself as a lawful modification of a *jus cogens* norm. See Abi-Saab, 'Cours général de droit international public' (n 11) 378; M Kohen, 'The Use of Force by the US after the End of the Cold War, and its Impact on International Law' in M Byers and G Nolte (eds), *United States Hegemony and the Foundations of International Law* (Cambridge, 2003) 228.

[88] A new interpretation is given to an existing norm, which leads to a new apparent conflict: eg the norm on access of the victims to justice is given a peremptory status, so that it *now* apparently collides with the jurisdictional immunities.

legislator, that is, the community of States; this is even provided for in Article 53 VCLT. The second argument confuses two different processes of law. An agreement derogates as *lex specialis* from an ordinary rule of customary law. A peremptory customary rule does not have the function of derogating from a former custom, since it is not a legal act with a restricted scope *ratione personarum*. It rather terminates (abrogates) the older customary rule, carves out a new exception to it, or is placed separate and parallel to the older rule, with which it is held not to be in conflict.

We may now move to the second limb of the question asked at the beginning of this sub-section: what about the relationship between universal norms of peremptory law and ordinary norms of *regional customary law*? Does *jus cogens* void regional customary law norms? In this context, we are confronted with a peremptory norm of general international law and a 'derogatory' norm of particular international law, that is, a norm binding only a restricted number of subjects. If the general norm is not *jus cogens*, the particular customary norm will prevail by virtue of the *lex specialis* principle. The scheme seems almost ideally one of *jus cogens*. It is therefore no accident that many authors[89] admit that derogation from a universal *jus cogens* norm by regional or bilateral custom is not legally possible, which is tantamount to applying *jus cogens* in this context. Some authors[90] explicitly mention the fact that local customary law is essentially based on adherence to a practice by the States concerned, that is, it is much closer to a tacit agreement than universal customary law (only the States parties to that special practice and opinion will be bound by the special custom).

This view is to some extent sound: local customary rules cannot depart from peremptory universal rules. There is here a *lex specialis* and there is also non-derogation; this triggers a form of *jus cogens*, even if the process remains outside Article 53 of the VCLT. But there is the technical point that the local customary rule is probably still a legal fact in the narrow sense and not a legal act. Can it thus be void in the proper sense of the word, or must we look for another legal category? If the universal peremptory norm already exists, in most cases the contrary regional norm will not be able to establish itself. A regional legal opinion contradicting peremptory legal opinion at the general level cannot see the light of day or is not recognised by the legal order as triggering the ordinary consequences of norm-creation. The regional norm is in such cases merely non-existent, not void. If, conversely, the regional norm already exists and the peremptory universal norm develops later, or its peremptory character is accepted later, the regional

[89] See, eg, Virally (n 42) 19; Rozakis (n 54) 22; M Shaw, *International Law*, 6th edn (Cambridge, 2008) 125; GI Tunkin, 'International Law in the International System' (1975-IV) 147 *Recueil des cours de l'Académie de droit international de La Haye* 93; FA von der Heydte, 'Die Erscheinungsformen des zwischenstaatlichen Rechts; *jus cogens* und *jus dispositivum* im Völkerrecht' (1932) 16 *Zeitschrift für Völkerrecht* 469; A Verdross and B Simma, *Universelles Völkerrecht*, 3rd edn (Berlin, 1984) 359.

[90] Rozakis (n 54) 22. See also, generally, P Haggenmacher, 'La doctrine des deux éléments du droit coutumier dans la pratique de la Cour internationale' (1986) 90 *Revue générale de droit international public* 35.

norm terminates as soon as the universal one is established. There is here an analogy with Article 64 VCLT. Again, this is a process of extinction of the norm, not of formal nullity. The reason for the extinction lies in the fact that the later law abrogates the former; and the later universal customary law binds all States. In the rare case of a bilateral or local custom with States having constantly objected to the new customary law, the answer lies in the fact that legal doctrine generally denies the availability of persistent objections to peremptory norms.[91] While there are certain problems here (for example, if the peremptory status of the merging norm is not yet clear), we concur. Thus, once more, the subjection of customary rules to *jus cogens* leads to categories of non-existence or abrogation rather than of nullity.

D. General Principles of Law?

A question never asked—and situated outside the scope of Article 53 VCLT—is whether a universal *jus cogens* norm can derogate from a general principle of law. Admittedly, the question does not seem very practical, and it therefore does not need to be canvassed at length. It is hardly imaginable that a *jus cogens* norm would be contrary to a general principle of law.

There are fundamentally two types of general principles of law.[92] The first category is made up of a series of principles of international law (some of them being inherent in every legal order, such as good faith/reasonableness). The position here is the same as for universal customary law. The principles at stake form—together with the general customary norm—the substratum of what is called 'general international law'. *Jus cogens* is not thought to void the objective norms and principles of a legal order. The second category is based on municipal law analogies in order to fill gaps in international law. In this second case, a conflict with a *jus cogens* norm of international law is impossible. The analogous application of principles from municipal legal orders is conceded in order to fill gaps (or eventually to contribute to the interpretation of a norm of international law). If there is a *jus cogens* norm on a certain subject-matter, there will be no gap in the international legal order and thus no possibility of an analogy in the sense presented here.

For other actual or potential effects of *jus cogens*, outside the realm of validity or nullity, the reader is referred to chapter six.

[91] See, eg, Ronzitti (n 54) 256; Christenson (n 54) 622; J Vidmar, 'Rethinking *Jus Cogens* after Germany v Italy: Back to Article 53?' (2013) 60 *Netherlands International Law Review* 23; M Akehurst, 'The Hierarchy of the Sources of International Law' (1974/75) 47 *British Yearbook of International Law* 285; MacDonald (n 54) 136; Simma (n 42) 292; Meron, 'International Law in the Age of Human Rights' (n 54) 395–96. Contra: U Linderfalk, 'The Source of *Jus Cogens* Obligations: How Legal Positivism Copes with Peremptory Norms' (2013) 82 *Nordic Journal of International Law* 385ff; and on a strictly third-world positivistic view, M Magallona, 'The Concept of *Jus Cogens* in the Vienna Convention on the Law of Treaties' in J Scott Davidson (ed), *The Law of Treaties* (Aldershot, 2004) 503, where it is added that there will hardly be any dissenting State in the context of *jus cogens* norms.

[92] For a much more detailed account, see B Vitanyi, 'Les positions doctrinales concernant le sens et la notion de "principes généraux de droit reconnus par les nations civilisées"' (1982) 86 *Revue générale de droit international public* 48ff.

IV. Some Special Issues

We may at this point explore some specific problems in the context of peremptoriness in international law. The aim here is not to be exhaustive, but rather to present various points which are rarely spotted or developed in the literature on *jus cogens*. The latter was characterised for a long time by rather theoretical debates about the nature of the international legal order as well as natural law versus positivistic approaches. Later, attention has focused exclusively on a sort of adoration of the international public order, without a concomitant analysis of all the technical legal issues entailed by the existence of *jus cogens* norms. Some problems of this type have already been mentioned, and we therefore do not need to revisit them—such as the question of the extension of the chain of causality for construing certain acts and facts as contrary to a *jus cogens* prescription (for example the potential voidness of the recognition of Kosovo if the territorial situation was created contrary to a universal peremptory norm concerning the use of force). We will return to some of the issues linked with such extended chains of arguments in chapter seven, which is devoted to conflicts of *jus cogens* norms. Here, the following points seem of interest.

A. Extent of Peremptoriness

The first point to be addressed concerns a sort of subject-matter ontology of *jus cogens*. Many statements limit themselves to indicating that a certain norm is peremptory. But they do not indicate to *what extent* this norm is peremptory. It stands to reason that a norm often has many layers and that not all must be peremptory, or peremptory to the same degree. This gradualism in the analysis has been obfuscated by the current ideology whereby *jus cogens* is a matter of absolutes;[93] thus conceptions which unveil relativity, grades and shades, and also uncertainties, are not welcome. We may take as examples two sets of norms: first the rule on the non-use of force; and second the rules on the law of armed conflict containing a 'military necessity' clause.

(i) The Non-Use of Force Rule (Hereinafter NUFR)

This rule is considered to be one of the classic examples of *jus cogens*.[94] It was mentioned already by the ILC when drafting the VCLT.[95] A discussion has arisen

[93] See, eg, Maresca (n 65) 618, 622–23; Z Drnas de Clément, 'Las normas imperativas de derecho internacional general (*jus cogens*): dimension sustancial' in Z Drnas de Clément (ed), *Estudios de derecho internacional en homenja al professor EJ Rey Caro*, vol I (Cordoba, 2002) 668, listing an impressive number of purported 'absolute' qualities of *jus cogens*. See also Separate Opinion of Cançado Trindade in the *Kosovo Opinion* [2010-II] ICJ Rep 608–09.

[94] See O Corten, *Le droit contre la guerre* (Paris, 2008) 293ff, with many references.

[95] Hannikainen (n 41) 163, with references.

as to the scope of the prohibition and thus the extent of its *jus cogens* character. Indeed, as we know, the prohibition is not absolute but knows of three accepted exceptions:[96] (i) self-defence according to Article 51 of the UN Charter (UNC) and related customary international law; (ii) authorisation by the UN Security Council under Chapter VII of the UNC; (iii) invitation by the government of a State to undertake military action on its territory. In international law, there are thus lawful and unlawful uses of force. The scope of *jus cogens* must be modelled on the scope of the prohibition: it concerns only unlawful uses of force. Thus, it is possible to conclude a treaty organising collective self-defence, since the UNC and related customary law allow collective self-defence. The same is true for legal acts falling under the other two exceptions, such as Article 43 UNC agreements, status of forces agreements, agreements as to coordination of armed action in execution of a mandate by the Security Council, and so on. It will be noted that consent of a government is a valid exception regarding armed action on its territory: the principle *volenti non fit injuria* applies.[97] This may seem strange in the context of a fundamental norm of international law said to be *jus cogens*. The current expectation would be that consent cannot possibly validate a position contrary to a *jus cogens* rule. This is even the gist of peremptoriness—consent cannot free something from peremptory norms. However, the point here is not one of derogatory consent, which would be void. It is rather a matter of the primary rule defining its material scope of application and allowing for consent. The scope of *jus cogens* adapts to the scope of the primary rule. The foregoing shows the extent to which the legal analyst must guard against hasty conclusions in the field of positive law, especially through inflexible thinking nourished by purported 'absolutes'.

The exact scope of the peremptoriness of the NUFR has still been controversial. Some authors limit the peremptory scope of the rule to the prohibition of aggression.[98] But there is a difference between the scope of unlawful uses of force and aggression. The former is a broader category, since it includes uses of force which are contrary to international law but do not reach the threshold of gravity to qualify as aggression. The correct view is probably that the *jus cogens* scope covers all unlawful uses of force. In this sphere of 'unlawfulness', no legal acts can derogate from the norm. For example, an agreement to intervene militarily in a third State without the consent of the local government or any other permissive

[96] C Gray, *International Law and the Use of Force* (Oxford, 2004) 59ff, 95ff, 195ff. As for the lack of other exceptions, see O Spermann, 'Humanitarian Intervention as a Necessity and the Threat or Use of *Jus Cogens*' (2002) 71 *Nordic Journal of International Law* 523ff.

[97] Under the law of State responsibility, consent does not cure *jus cogens* breaches (Art 26 Articles on State Responsibility; Crawford (n 48) 164, 187–88), but in our context the special primary rules on the use of force (with their exceptions) prevail.

[98] T Christakis, 'Unilatéralisme et multilatéralisme dans la lutte contre la terreur: l'exemple du terrorisme biologique et chimique' in K Bannelier et al (eds), *Le droit international face au terrorisme* (Paris, 2002) 173; G Cahin, 'L'Etat défaillant en droit international: quel régime pour quelle notion?' in *Essays in Honor of J Salmon* (Brussels, 2007) 207.

title would be void.[99] If an intervention takes place in that State as a matter of fact, we are not situated in the realm of traditional *jus cogens*; the question here turns on a simple breach of the rule and not on a derogation from it.

It has to be noted, furthermore, that the argument whereby the recognised exceptions 'derogate' from the NUFR is technically incorrect (if that were true, these derogations would be void, and the NUFR would be turned into an absolute prohibition). The recognised exceptions are not derogations from the rule (priority of *inter se* agreements or titles) but true exceptions placed on the same normative level as the main rule. They concern the definition of the proper material scope of the NUFR under international law, and are consequently highly relevant for determining the scope of *jus cogens* itself.[100]

In short, it is often true that a rule or principle said to be *jus cogens* is so only to some extent. Only a core of a provision may be peremptory, and this core has to be carefully defined. With the NUFR, the position is not particularly complicated. For the rule on self-determination of peoples, the question is much more difficult, if only because the layers of that right are much more loosely and gradually defined as for the NUFR. We will return to the various problems raised in this context in chapter seven, on conflicts between *jus cogens* norms.

(ii) *Provisions of International Humanitarian Law (Law of Armed Conflict) Containing a 'Military Necessity' Clause*[101]

The rules of international humanitarian law (IHL) are often considered a prominent example of *jus cogens* norms in that they contain minimum guarantees for

[99] In real life this is already a matter of concern: were all the agreements linked with the unlawful interventions in Kosovo (1999) and Iraq (2002/03) considered void? Or would one again have to distinguish between agreements going directly to the unlawful use of force (eg organising the military interventions) and consequential agreements for *jus post bellum* issues? The latter seems more in line with observable international practice.

[100] See, rightly, Corten (n 94) 295–96. See, by contrast, JA Green, 'Questioning the Peremptory Status of the Prohibition of the Use of Force' (2011) 32 *Michigan Journal of International Law* 215ff. On the question, see also Hannikainen (n 41) 323ff.

[101] On this principle, see Y Dinstein, 'Military Necessity' in R Wolfrum (ed), *The Max Planck Encyclopedia of Public International Law*, vol VII (Oxford, 2012) 201ff; Y Dinstein, *The Conduct of Hostilities under the Law of International Armed Conflict* (Cambridge, 2001) 16ff; J Gardam, *Necessity, Proportionality and the Use of Force by States* (Cambridge, 2004) 59ff; C Greenwood, 'Historical Development and Legal Basis' in D Fleck (ed), *The Handbook of Humanitarian Law in Armed Conflicts*, 2nd edn (Oxford, 1995) 35–38; Kolb (n 9) 151ff; H McCoubrey, 'The Nature of the Modern Doctrine of Military Necessity' (1991) 30 *Revue de droit pénal militaire et de droit de la guerre* 215ff; PA Pillitu, *Lo stato di necessità nel diritto internazionale* (Perugia, 1981) 347ff; E Rauch, 'Le concept de nécessité militaire dans le droit de la guerre' (1980) 19 *Revue de droit pénal militaire et de droit de la guerre* 205ff; L Sbolci, 'Sulla necessità militare nel diritto internazionale applicabile nei conflitti armati' in *Essays in Honor of G Barile* (Padova, 1995) 653ff; G Venturini, *Necessità e proporzionalità nell'uso della forza militare in diritto internazionale* (Milan, 1988) 123ff. Older contributions are: NCH Dunbar, 'Military Necessity in War Crimes Trials' (1952) 29 *British Yearbook of International Law* 442ff; WG Downey, 'The Law of War and Military Necessity' (1953) 47 *American Journal of International Law* 251ff; GIAD Draper, 'Military Necessity and Humanitarian Imperatives' (1973) 12 *Revue de droit pénal militaire et*

the protection of persons during warfare.[102] What is the position of provisions which concede exceptions? Consider for example Article 23, letter g, of the Hague Regulations of 1907: '[It is forbidden] to destroy or seize the enemy's property, unless such destruction or seizure be imperatively demanded by the necessities of war.' Could a provision containing such a clause qualify today as peremptory, or does the potentially significant exception of military necessity preclude such a possibility? For those holding *jus cogens* to be an 'absolute', the exceptions may seem an obstacle to peremptoriness. The same cannot be said for those who analyse the matter under the guidance of legal technique. Exactly as for the use of force, the present rule contains an exception which limits its scope at the level of the primary norm (that is, not by a derogatory act). The difference with the non-use of force rule is that the exception is here quite subjective in nature, referring to the fluctuating military circumstances on the ground and their appreciation by the Commander. However, it stands to reason that a rule such as the one under discussion can be peremptory at its core, meaning it is not affected by the exception. For example, an agreement which attempted a derogation from the rule *outside* the context of military necessity would not be valid. Thus, if belligerents agreed to destroy private property even in circumstances not covered by military necessity, such an agreement would be void to the extent that the IHL norm is *jus cogens*. Conversely, if the belligerents conclude an agreement for the destruction of private property by clarifying what circumstances they will consider as amounting to military necessity in the current armed conflict, such an agreement will be valid. It falls within the realm of the accepted exception to the rule.

Consequently, the general point to be made is that the precise scope of peremptoriness depends on the material scope of application of the *jus cogens* rule. This scope depends on the reach of primary norms. Normative exceptions have to be factored in by reducing the scope of peremptoriness.

de droit de la guerre 129ff; WV O'Brien, *The Development of the Concept of Military Necessity and its Interpretation in the Modern Law of War*, PhD thesis (Georgetown, 1953); WV O'Brien, 'The Meaning of Military Necessity in International Law' (1957) 1 *World Polity* 109ff; G Schwarzenberger, 'Military Necessity: A Misnomer' in *Essays in Honor of S Séfériadès* (Athens, 1961) 13ff. See also MG Cowling, 'The Relationship between Military Necessity and the Principle of Superfluous Injury and Useless Suffering in the Law of Armed Conflict' (2000) 25 *South African Yearbook of International Law* 131ff; J De Breucker, 'La réserve des nécessités militaires dans la Convention de La Haye de 1954 sur la protection des biens culturels' (1975) 14 *Revue de droit pénal militaire et de droit de la guerre* 255ff; C Eustathiadès, 'La réserve des nécessités militaires et la Convention de La Haye pour la protection des biens culturels en cas de conflit armé' in *Essays in Honor of J Basdevant* (Paris, 1960) 183ff; M Messerschmidt, 'Völkerrecht und Kriegsnotwendigkeit in der deutschen militärischen Tradition seit den Einigungskriegen' (1983) 22 *Revue de droit pénal militaire et de droit de la guerre* 211ff; PA Ragone, 'The Applicability of Military Necessity in the Nuclear Age' (1984) 16 *New York University Journal of International Law and Politics* 701ff; M Schmitt, 'Military Necessity and Humanity in International Humanitarian Law: Preserving the Delicate Balance' (2010) 50 *Virginia Journal of International Law* 795ff. Documents on the notion can be found in M Whiteman, *Digest of International Law*, vol 10 (Washington, 1968) 298ff. In the context of the protection of the natural environment, see K Mollard-Bannelier, *La protection de l'environnement en temps de conflit armé* (Paris, 2001) 117ff.

[102] See, eg, E David, *Principes de droit des conflits armés*, 5th edn (Brussels, 2012) 107ff; Hannikainen (n 41) 596ff.

B. Human Rights Law and So-Called 'Derogation' Clauses

The point of the present sub-section is not to determine which human rights are peremptory in international law, or the extent to which they are so.[103] It is rather to consider what type of legal relationship exists between *jus cogens* and so-called 'derogation' clauses contained in many human rights treaties. The word 'derogation' seems to bring these clauses close to the technique of peremptoriness. Article 4 of the International Covenant on Civil and Political Rights (1966) reads as follows:[104]

1. In time of public emergency which threatens the life of the nation and the existence of which is officially proclaimed, the States Parties to the present Covenant may take measures derogating from their obligations under the present Covenant to the extent strictly required by the exigencies of the situation, provided such measures are not inconsistent with their other obligations under international law and do not involve discrimination solely on the ground of race, colour, sex, language, religion or social origin.
2. No derogation from articles 6, 7, 8 (paragraphs 1 and 2), 11, 15, 16 and 18 may be made under this provision…[105]

Technically speaking, the wording is imprecisely drafted. The matter does not involve derogation in the proper sense, that is, a particular legal regime applicable among some parties by virtue of the *lex specialis* principle. Nor could a derogation take place by self-exemption. Municipal law by which some human rights guarantees are suspended does not derogate from the International Covenant on Children's and Peoples Rights (ICCPR), since one State alone cannot exempt itself from

[103] On this issue, see eg Hannikainen (n 41) 425ff; Orakhelashvili (n 50) 53ff; T Meron, 'On a Hierarchy of International Human Rights Law' (n 54) 1ff; T Koji, 'Emerging Hierarchy in International Human Rights and Beyond: From the Perspective of Non-Derogable Rights' (2011) 12 *European Journal of International Law* 921ff; G Cohen-Jonathan, 'Le *jus cogens* et les droits de l'homme' in *Essays in Honor of J Charpentier* (Paris, 2008) 61ff; M Iovane, 'Peremptory Norms in the Field of Human Rights and General Principles of Law recognized by Civilized Nations' in Centro Internazionale di Studi Gentiliani (ed), *Alberico Gentili: l'ordine internazionale in un mondo a più civiltà* (Milan, 2004) 155ff. There are also a series of sectorial studies on human rights-related *jus cogens*, eg AA Cançado Trindade, 'Enforced Disappearances of Persons as a Violation of "*Jus Cogens*": The Contribution of the Jurisprudence of the Inter-American Court of Human Rights' (2012) 81 *Nordic Journal of International Law* 507ff; J Sarkin, 'Why the Prohibition of Enforced Disappearance has Attained *Jus Cogens* Status in International Law' (2012) 81 *Nordic Journal of International Law* 537ff; D Adams, 'The Prohibition of Widespread Rape as a *Jus Cogens*' (2005) 6 *San Diego International Law Journal* 357ff. See also C Maia, 'Le jus cogens dans la jurisprudence de la Cour interaméricaine des droits de l'homme' in L Hennebel and H Tigroudja (eds), *Le particularisme interaméricain des droits de l'homme* (Paris, 2009) 273ff.

[104] See also Art 15 European Convention on Human Rights (1950); Art 30 European Social Charter (1961); Art 27 Inter-American Convention on Human Rights (1969); Art 4 Arab Charter on Human Rights (2004). The African Charter on Human and Peoples' Rights (1981) lacks such a clause: see on the legal significance of this absence see F Ouguergouz, *The African Charter on Human and Peoples' Rights* (The Hague/London/New York, 2003) 423ff.

[105] See Nowak (n 8) 83ff, with references. See generally W Kälin and J Künzli, *The Law of International Human Rights Protection* (Oxford, 2009) 143ff.

the reach of a conventional rule. Nor, finally, could a derogation take place across different legal orders. Only norms of the same legal order can enter into a relationship of derogation, not norms pertaining to different legal orders. This is true even for monistic States: the difference between international and municipal law does not disappear in such systems, nor is the difference between state and federal law erased therein. In a technically correct use of the words, the point at issue is one of temporary 'suspension' of certain human rights guarantees by legal acts of municipal law. This suspension is linked to a series of conditions, such as the existence of a state of emergency as described in the conventions, an official proclamation of the state of emergency and of the intent to derogate, strict proportionality in suspension of rights, non-discrimination, etc. In order not to disturb the entrenched terminology, we shall use the word 'derogation' in what follows in order to designate suspension. It should moreover be noted that most human rights guarantees can be limited outside the emergency context in view of concurring rights and/or of public interest. The necessary and proportionate limitations must be contained in a piece of legislation (formal or sometimes material).[106] Thus, only few human rights—such as the prohibition of torture—constitute, from this vantage point, 'absolute' obligations. Conversely, the concept of an intangible core of the various human rights protections has been developed—a core which cannot be limited by legislation even if there is a preponderant public interest.[107]

Considering these elements, it may seem that there exist some relationships between *jus cogens* and 'derogation' clauses, and also between *jus cogens* and the 'intangible' core. The argument is not that there is identity between the notions, in the sense that, for example, derogation clauses constitute the domain of peremptory human rights. There are various reasons for this non-identity.

First, the rights specially protected by derogation clauses vary from one treaty to another, notwithstanding that some rights are invariably non-derogable (like the prohibition of torture). If there was an identity of peremptoriness and derogation clauses, we would therefore be limited to a variable conventional *jus cogens*. Conversely, only non-derogable rights under general international law (or under UN Conventions largely ratified, such as the ICCPR) would give rise to *jus cogens* according to the requirements of Article 53 VCLT.[108] There is an argument that such universally non-derogable rights are those which all human rights instruments treat as non-derogable.[109]

Second, and more substantively, it would be wrong to limit *jus cogens* solely to the domain of non-derogable rights. It is not possible to conclude from the fact

[106] This is typically the content of the many of the second paragraphs to the substantive provisions of the European Convention on Human Rights, See also, for example, Art 18, § 3 ICCPR.

[107] For an excellent treatment of this notion see JP Müller, *Eléments pour une théorie suisse des droits fondamentaux* (Bern, 1983) 147ff. See further M Schefer, *Die Kerngehalte von Grundrechten* (Bern, 2001); for the UN system see J von Bernstorff, 'Kerngehaltsschutz durch den UN-Menschenrechtsausschuss und den EGMR' (2011) 50 *Der Staat* 165ff.

[108] See T Meron, *Human Rights in Internal Strife* (Cambridge, 1987) 59, 137–39.

[109] ibid, 59.

that certain rights may be suspended in certain circumstances of emergency that other rights can be contracted out freely[110]—and this latter issue is the one of *jus cogens*. The point is to some extent the same as for IHL clauses containing various exceptions, such as the one regarding military necessity. Such a conclusion would moreover stand somewhat at odds with the fundamental nature of many human rights guarantees. Similarly, it would be wrong to conclude from the list of rights and guarantees applying in occupied territory under IHL even one year after the general close of hostilities (Article 6, § 3 Geneva Convention IV of 1949) that only those provisions are *jus cogens* for occupied territories. This conclusion would be incompatible with Article 7 of the same Convention, which denies legal effect to special agreements which lower the protections of the persons covered by the Convention.

There are thus many different techniques for 'hardening' certain legal positions. Some arguments may be made from one or other of these techniques towards *jus cogens*, but the translation must always remain limited and critical. The non-identity of the two sets of situations—that is, 'non-derogability clauses' and *jus cogens*—is buttressed by the fact that the relevant circumstances are not the same in the two cases. Thus, some rights are not listed in non-derogability clauses simply because it is never practically necessary to 'derogate' from them in times of emergency. This is the case, for example, with Article 11 ICCPR, the right not to be imprisoned for contractual debts. In other words, it is not the lack of (fundamental) importance of this right which has given rise to its exclusion from the list of non-derogable rights; it is rather the fact that it is not relevant to the situation of public emergency. This shows once more that the legal logic of the two circles ('derogation clauses' and *jus cogens*) and not identical. As an example of 'derogable' rights which are often seen as peremptory, it is possible to mention the right to a fair trial.[111]

Third, 'derogation clauses' are coloured by conceptions at the time of adoption of the convention, for example 1966 for the ICCPR. However, conceptions change over time. What is considered a fundamental right is also a question of epoch. Thus, some rights may gain greatly in importance, or some new specific rights may be developed according to new needs (such as: enforced disappearances since the 1980s and the events in Central and Latin America). The *jus cogens* character of rights has to keep pace with these developments and cannot be limited to historical derogation clauses.

However, conversely, 'derogation clauses' (as well as the intangible core) may provide some useful, albeit only fragmentary, indications for determining the

[110] This is also the position of the UN Human Rights Committee in its General Comment no 29, § 11: '[T]he category of peremptory norms extends beyond the list of non-derogable provisions as given in article 4, paragraph 2.'

[111] As for Art 14, § 5 ICCPR, see eg the *Sam Hinga Norman* case, 2003, Special Court for Sierra Leone, case no 2003-08-PT, § 19. See also Inter-American Court of Human Rights, *Judicial Guarantees in Times of Emergency*, Advisory Opinion, 1987, series A, no 9, §§ 23–25 (92 ILR 405ff).

domain of *jus cogens* in the realm of international human rights law.[112] There is an argument that these clauses indicate *some* rights which are to be considered peremptory. If States agree that rights shall not be liable to temporary suspension (in municipal law) even in time of emergency threatening the life of the nation, there is much to be said for the corollary argument that these rights may not be subject to contracting out by *leges speciales* (under international law). This argument holds good even a fortiori, since contracting out would in fact amount to a suspension *sine die*, if not bluntly to a permanent suspension. But if a temporary suspension is prohibited by the clauses, a permanent or unlimited one must be prohibited all the more. Such a suspension by *lex specialis* would moreover circumvent the conditions for suspension under derogation clauses. Derogation clauses could therefore be seen as a common minimum core for *jus cogens* in the domain of human rights, as would the intangible core. There would here be two series of peremptory norms, some on the basis of the respective treaties, and some under general customary law. Any contrary stipulation or legal act in these core domains would suffer from invalidity under international law. The difficulty is to determine with sufficient clarity the respective extension of these notions. If the 'intangible core' remains too vague a notion, the legal uncertainty ensuing from the voiding of contrary legal acts may seem too great. How, for example, could one ensure a *jus post bellum* administration of territory by international forces, if all sorts of legal acts could be attacked as contrary to peremptory human rights stipulations? Conversely, if the core notions are sufficiently defined and restricted, such arguments do not have much weight. Similarly, in municipal law the notion that contracts *contra bonos mores* are void leaves great leeway for appreciation in the particular circumstances—with the significant difference that there are regular tribunals to hear the disputes.

From another perspective, 'derogable' peremptory rights are not necessarily *jus cogens in all their parts*. As we have seen, 'derogation' is subject to a series of formal and substantive requirements. If two States conclude an agreement regarding the manner in which they will apply these conditions for suspending the peremptory rights at stake, and if the agreement does not derogate from these conditions but only elaborates on them, it is not void. In other words, even peremptory human rights may give rise to limitations, either under public interest municipal legislation, or under suspension/derogation clauses. Legal acts under international law relating to these allowable restrictions are valid; legal acts under international law situated beyond the scope of these allowable restrictions will be void, if the right at stake is *jus cogens*. This shows once more how misleading it may be to take peremptoriness as a sort of absolute of moral or other nature, and to neglect the indications of legal technique.

[112] See, eg, International Criminal Tribunal for the Former Yugoslavia, *Furundzija* case (1998), § 144 (see 121 ILR 257–58).

C. International Humanitarian Law, in Particular Articles 6/6/6/7 of Geneva Conventions (GC) I–IV

The basic provisions of IHL for the protection of human persons during warfare are commonly considered to be a significant domain of *jus cogens* norms.[113] This is a sort of minimum protection law directed against the dangers of barbarity and unleashing of passions during armed conflict. The legal literature identifies a series of elements militating in the direction of *jus cogens*:[114] the formulation of certain norms as applicable 'at all times' (for example Articles 3 common, 15 GC I, 13 GCIII, 18 GC IV, 48 Additional Protocol (AP) I, 11, § 1, AP II); the fact that the breach of certain provisions does not give rise to reprisals (see for example Article 51, § 6 AP I, protecting the civilian population); and the fact that breaches of important IHL rules constitute international crimes. The most interesting peculiar peremptoriness element of modern IHL is that contained in Articles 6/6/6/7 of the four Geneva Conventions of 1949.[115] The main feature of these provisions reads as follows: 'No special agreement shall adversely affect the situation of protected persons, as defined in the present Convention, nor restrict the rights which it confers upon them.'[116] IHL features many provisions which allow or even invite belligerents to conclude special agreements, either in order to implement IHL duties (for example Article 109, § 2 GC III for the repatriation of seriously wounded or seriously sick prisoners of war) or in order to assume new obligations not automatically applicable *ex lege* (for example Article 3, § 3 GC I–IV, as the extension of various prisoners of war guarantees to persons captured in the context of a non-international armed conflict). Such special agreements are frequently concluded during armed conflict.[117] The quoted provision is directed at allowing such special agreements, but at the same time at guaranteeing that they shall not be used to contract out or to diminish the rights and protections of the persons covered by the Geneva system. During World War II, some disquieting examples took place. Collaborating governments concluded agreements with Germany for cooperation

[113] David (n 102) 107ff; Hannikainen (n 41) 596ff; Orakhelashvili (n 50) 61ff. Too limited a view can be found in R Nieto-Navia, 'International Peremptory Norms (*Jus Cogens*) and International Humanitarian Law' in LC Vorah (ed), *Man's Inhumanity to Man: Essays in Honour of A Cassese* (The Hague/London/New York, 2003) 627ff, who restricts *jus cogens* in IHL essentially to common Art 3 GC of 1949.

[114] David (n 102) 111–12.

[115] Orakhelashvili (n 50) 62.

[116] On these provisions see J Pictet's Commentaries on the Geneva Conventions: *Commentary I, Geneva Convention for the Amelioration of the Condition of the Wounded and Sick in Armed Forces in the Field* (Geneva, 1952); *Commentary II, Geneva Convention for the Amelioration of the Condition of Wounded, Sick and Shipwrecked Members of Armed Forces at Sea* (Geneva, 1960); *Commentary III, Geneva Convention relative to the Treatment of Prisoners of War* (Geneva, 1960); *Commentary IV, Geneva Convention relative to the Protection of Civilian Persons in Time of War* (Geneva, 1958).

[117] See the list in F Bugnion, *Le Comité international de la Croix-Rouge et la protection des victimes de la guerre* (Geneva, 1994) 1205ff. For later agreements, the annual reports of the ICRC would have to be consulted.

in the deportation of protected persons.[118] The abovementioned provisions in the GC are thus a remarkable example of a (i) conventional and (ii) unidirectional *jus cogens*.[119] Let us explore these points.

First, the peremptoriness is *conventional*: it is organised under the GC and not put under the umbrella of general international law. It thus reinforces the legal mechanism as was later inserted in Article 41, § 1, letter b, ii of the VCLT. The legal consequence of the contrary agreement is not nullity, as under Article 53 VCLT. For a treaty to be void, this consequence would have to be indicated in the said provisions, Articles 6/6/6/7 GC or 41 VCLT; silence on this point must be taken as an indication that nullity cannot apply. But the special agreement cannot have the effect of rendering inapplicable or diminishing the rights of the protected persons. The latter is therefore inapplicable to the extent that it attempts to diminish these rights. This is largely tantamount to partial nullity.

Second, the peremptoriness is *unidirectional*. A special agreement may provide for further rights to be granted to the protected persons, that is, rights to be added to those already guaranteed in the Conventions (in this sense, 'positive derogation'[120] is allowed). Conversely, it may not detract from the rights and protections granted in the provisions of the GC (in other words, 'negative derogations' are prohibited).[121] The exact extent of *jus cogens* thus depends on the sum of rights and guarantees of the protected persons under the Geneva Conventions—and later the two Additional Protocols of 1977, which are part and parcel of this system. The question as to what exactly amounts to diminishing or contracting out of rights may not always be crystal clear. But it will in almost all cases be of great practical importance. Municipal civil law knows of similar (but not identical) problems in the context of minors, who may in their own right acquire favourable positions but may not be burdened with charges without the consent of their legal guardian. The interesting cases are those where advantages are acquired but where these advantages are linked with some concomitant duties or charges. In our context, the question would turn on the question whether some advantage given to the protected person neatly prevails over a concomitant charge, and the latter does not interfere with basic rights under IHL. Let us look at three examples:

> **Example 1**: Prisoners of war may be granted a favourable regime of semi-liberty during daylight hours, limited by some duties, such as presenting oneself at a checkpoint every three hours. This is allowed, and could be the object of a special agreement between belligerents. The duty to present oneself, even if onerous, is not contrary to any IHL right of prisoners of war.

[118] One trace is to be found in the *Krupp* case (1948) 15 ILR 626–27.

[119] The link with *jus cogens* is made by a series of authors: see eg Orakhelashvili (n 50) 61–62; P Weckel, 'Un exemple remarquable d'application du *jus cogens*, le statut de prisonnier de guerre' in Tomuschat and Thouvenin (n 1) 69ff.

[120] The term is not very precise, since the provision is not 'derogated from' at all, there are just some adjunctions to it. It would be better to speak of 'ad-rogation', but that is not a legal term of art.

[121] On these issues see R Kolb, '*Jus cogens*, intangibilité, intransgressibilité, dérogation "positive" et "negative"' (2005) 109 *Revue générale de droit international public* 305ff.

Example 2: The same situation, but this time the semi-liberty is purchased by a renunciation of the right to receive correspondence (contrary to Article 71 GC III). Such a special agreement could be concluded between belligerents or possibly with prisoners themselves (in the latter case, see Articles 7/7/7/8 GC I–IV). This aspect of special agreement would not be able to prevail over Article 71 GC III. The advantage can be considered to have been granted, but the disadvantage cannot be upheld. The rule of Articles 6/6/6/7 thus operate as a limitation on the maxim 'he who bears the advantages must also bear the burdens', *qui habet commoda, ferre debet onera*. The core criterion is what is granted as a right in the Conventions. These rights cannot be diminished, even if some other compensatory advantages are granted. However, even with this criterion there remain doubtful cases. (1): What if only certain classes of prisoners of war receive more favourable treatment? This entails a relative disadvantage for other classes, which might be contrary to the non-discrimination rule (or right) under Article 12 GC III. Would that agreement consequently be inapplicable? Would it have to be automatically extended to the other classes of prisoners? Could that not be a reason for the detaining power not to conclude it at all, if for example it lacks sufficient resources to grant the advantage to all prisoners? Would such a solution not be detrimental, at the end of the day, since then nobody at all would obtain the advantage? (2): a prisoner of war obtains a seeming advantage, such as an agreement providing that prisoners of war shall not work. But is that really an advantage? From one point of view, it could be seen as such: the prisoner is liberated from a burden. But from another perspective, the opposite may be true. For many prisoners, idleness in prisoner-of-war camps, without any activities to pass the time, is difficult to sustain.

Still further problems are raised by **Example 3**: prisoners of war receive the promise not to be criminally prosecuted for grave breaches of the Conventions. Viewed from their perspective, this is certainly an advantage; but it is an unlawful advantage. Indeed, the GC provide for the *duty* of the States parties to prosecute 'grave breaches' of the Conventions (Articles 50/51/130/147 GC I–IV). This is another provision with *jus cogens* character. Thus, such an agreement cannot stand, even if it contains only advantages for the protected persons. In other words, Article 6/6/6/7 is only one modality of humanitarian *jus cogens*; it is not the only one. If it conflicts with other peremptory norms in the Conventions, it may yield.

Three further refinements to the foregoing deserve to be mentioned here. *First*, it stands to reason that a protected person must not *exercise* a right which is granted to him or her.[122] This issue stands on another plane to the one as to whether the right is peremptory for belligerents. *Second*, the primary law of the Convention sometimes provides that a protected person can renounce, voluntarily, a certain

[122] See S Schmahl, 'An Example of *Jus Cogens*: The Status of Prisoners of War' in C Tomuschat and JM Thouvenin (eds), *The Fundamental Rules of the International Legal Order, Jus Cogens and Obligations Erga Omnes* (Leiden/Boston, 2006) 64–65, who gives the example of refusing repatriation according to Art 118, § 1 GC III. By the same token, in another area of the law, a State may renounce the peremptory non-use of force rule by inviting a foreign State to send military forces onto its territory.

protection. Thus, Article 52, § 1 GC III reads as follows: 'Unless he be a volunteer, no prisoner of war may be employed on labour which is of an unhealthy or dangerous nature.' This is a *lex specialis* with regard to Article 6 GC III. It is situated not on the plane of derogation by legal acts of some parties to the Convention (which would not be allowed) but at the level of the primary law itself. In other words, there is no vertical relation between all the parties to the Convention and some of them attempting a derogation by special agreement. There is rather a horizontal relation of harmonising two provisions situated on the same normative level. The point is—as with the use of force and its exceptions—the proper determination of the respective scope of application of the different provisions. In this regard, Article 52, § 1 limits the scope of Article 6. This means for our purposes that an agreement between belligerents for organising voluntary 'unhealthy' or 'dangerous' work for their respective prisoners is valid. Conversely, an agreement organising involuntary work of that nature, or work which is absolutely prohibited (such as military service for the enemy force), would not prevail over the prohibition under Article 6 and would therefore be inapplicable. *Third*, there may be situations where the loss of some formal rights or guarantees of protected persons, in the circumstances of a particular case, effectively improves their protection rather than diminishing it. A teleological interpretation of the Geneva Conventions should then exceptionally allow such action, but be placed under the control of the International Committee of the Red Cross in order to prevent abuse. Consider, for example, the following situation. During the Falklands (Malvinas) War in 1982, UK armed forces proposed to transfer Argentinian prisoners of war onto ships. The reason was that there were no adequate camps on the islands and also that the temperatures were quickly dropping in these barren southern lands. This transfer was, however, contrary to Article 22 of GC III, which stipulates that prisoners of war must be detained 'on premises located on land'. The purpose of this long-time provision is to ensure a place of safe internment for prisoners and to avoid disappearances, as occurred during the Napoleonic Wars. In the particular circumstances of the case, internment on the ships was the safest and most adequate option. Therefore, the ICRC accepted the transfer in this case and even visited the prisoners on-board the ships. It thereby placed the spirit of the provision above its letter.[123] Such an approach had already been endorsed in the abovementioned *Pictet Commentaries*. They envisage a profound change of circumstances which turns a protection into a non-protection. In such a case the *Commentaries* give preference to the pragmatic idea of non-aggravation of the fate of protected persons.[124] Overall, then, the definition of the advantage or disadvantage may depend, in special circumstances, on a teleological interpretation of the provisions at stake. At the same time, too open-ended an interpretation may

[123] Bugnion (n 117) 754.
[124] Pictet, *Commentary I* (n 116) 75.

leave too much room for manoeuvre and abuse. Unfortunately, these are not rare events, especially during armed conflicts.

Taken together, all the previous developments reveal a significant amount of legal complexity in the issues to be tackled.

D. Differentiation of *Jus Cogens* According to Legal Subjects?

It is almost unchallenged mainstream thought that *jus cogens* is applicable to all subjects of international law in the same way and to the same extent, as a sort of absolute and invariable obligation. But is that necessarily true? Can there not be a *jus cogens* for the inter-State level (universal and regional) and another for international organisations, say the UN?[125] It stands to reason that the difference would only be a relative one. Many *jus cogens* provisions would apply to both levels in the same way, such as the prohibition of genocide. But take the important non-use of force rule. It does not apply in the same way to both subjects: for States, recourse to force is prohibited, unless in self-defence, authorised by the UN Security Council or by invitation from the local government. For the UN Security Council, the use of force is an option which it can use with a great amount of political discretion (Article 42 of the UNC and subsequent practice). In other words, the domain of lawful and unlawful uses of force is different in the two cases. The consequence would be that an agreement between States providing for the use of force outside the recognised exceptions would be void, but an agreement concluded by the UN, through the Security Council, in the context of the exercise of its Chapter VII power and relating to a use of force in the broader context of those special powers, would be valid. In short: An Agreement X concluded among States is void; but concluded with the UN, the same Agreement is valid.

In other contexts, reflections are more intricate and muddled. Would the UN be able to limit to a greater extent than States the right of self-determination of peoples, in its *jus post bellum* administrations, notably because it represents the interests of the international community as a whole? One may think here of such powers as those of the high international representative in Bosnia-Herzegovina, and in particular his faculty to veto local legislation.[126] Might such a power be acceptable if considered necessary by the UN Security Council, but not if imposed by one State on another (since then it would be contrary to the self-determination of the local people)? This example is already much more controversial politically

[125] That the UN Security Council, for example, is bound by *jus cogens* is generally accepted; even international and national jurisprudence has recognised this. See, eg, E de Wet, *The Chapter VII Powers of the United Nations Security Council* (Oxford/Portland, 2004) 187ff. As to the case law, see eg the *Yusuf* and *Kadi* decisions of the European Court of First Instance (2005) 149 ILR 237, 296–97, 230.

[126] See Orakhelashvili (n 50) 453–54.

and legally than the one relating to the use of force. Another example comes from the law of occupation. That a series of rules of this branch of the law are *jus cogens* for States—so that derogation is not allowed—is generally accepted. But the question as to whether territorial administrations under the mandate or directly placed under the aegis of international organisations, in particular the UN, are subject to the law of occupation at all is at the very least uncertain.[127] In practice, the law of occupation has generally yielded to the mandate in UN Security Council resolutions, probably also taking into account Article 103 of the UNC—and to the extent that occupation law has been recognised as being applicable at all. This matter can be seen as referring to the proper subjective and material scope of application of occupation law rather than to its derogability. But it has to be admitted that the concrete picture of the applicability of *jus cogens* norms in the two sets of situations is not necessarily identical. This was the point to be made here.

Perhaps it is necessary to consider more closely this potential subjective multiplicity of *jus cogens*, rather than remaining under the hypnotic influence of its purported 'absoluteness'. The latter course unfortunately erases any sensitivity to such issues. A cartography of which norms apply to different subjects and which ones are *jus cogens* for each of them would certainly be of great scientific and practical interest.

E. Definition of the Proper Normative Conflict

There is always some form of normative conflict behind the operation of *jus cogens*. This is particularly apparent in hierarchical theories of the concept. These are based on the idea that conflicts between different norms of international law can be solved by a hierarchisation of these normative expressions under the guise of *jus cogens*. But even for classical theories based on non-derogability and nullity, the issue remains one of a conflict between a general norm and a particular derogatory norm, the latter being voided by the peremptory character of the former. The conflict may in this latter case be an apparent one, in the sense that the effect of nullity makes it disappear. But in order to apply the effect of nullity, it must first be determined that the two provisions conflict—that is, that one attempts to derogate from the other. If that relationship cannot be established, we are not in the legal context of peremptoriness and the effects of *jus cogens* cannot apply. Thus, the normative conflict in the form of an attempt at derogation must always be ascertained. Derogation means, as we may recall, that a special legal regime between various parties is substituted for a more general one. The conflict in this context lies in the fact that legal regime A and legal regime B cannot be applied at the same time: the obligations under one are incompatible with the obligations under the other. But when is this the case? The answer may be simple in some

[127] R Kolb and S Vité, *Le droit de l'occupation militaire: perspectives historiques et enjeux juridiques actuels* (Brussels, 2009) 99ff, 234ff.

classical situations, such as the prohibition of genocide and the conclusion of an agreement organising the contribution of three States to the commission of genocide against a national minority of all three States. But in other contexts, the point may give rise to complex discussions.

An example is the recent debate about the relationship between *jus cogens* (right to access to justice) and jurisdictional immunities.[128] For some authors,[129] there is no relationship of conflict here, since no derogation is at stake. The rule of immunity has a procedural nature, barring access to certain judicial fora, but not to other judicial fora (for example, access to the ICJ is always open). The rule is then one channelling the claims to the most convenient forum. Thus, this procedural rule may at most be said to hinder the *full enforcement* of a *jus cogens* rule such as access to justice. But it does not technically derogate from it. Therefore, there is no room for the application of *jus cogens* in this context. The ICJ largely followed this view in its 2012 judgment on *Jurisdictional Immunities*, at § 92ff. The question is surely also linked with the definition of the concrete extent of *jus cogens*. The war crimes committed by Germany during the Second World War may have been violations of *jus cogens* (if the concept applied at that time, which is doubtful). However, the consequences of these violations must not all have a *jus cogens* character. For example, there is not necessarily a *duty* under international law to give access to a specific type of remedy when *jus cogens* breaches are involved. But it is also possible to hold that access to justice is itself a rule of *jus cogens*, or at least a rule of *jus cogens* when international crimes have been committed. Other authors[130] have stressed the fact that a true conflict exists. If *jus cogens* entails the positive obligation to provide a remedy for this type of breach, then there is a conflict with the rule on immunity. True, this is a conflict between objective norms of the same level (customary international law) and not technically speaking a derogation. But if *jus cogens* is applied as a general technique of hierarchical conflict solving, the issue becomes one of *jus cogens*.

This brief discussion has shown that there is not sufficient agreement as to the types of conflict that trigger *jus cogens*. Are they only derogation in the strict sense or are they also conflicts of objective norms? Is it useful to distinguish procedural from substantive norms? What is the role of positive obligations flowing from *jus cogens* breaches in the definition of the possible conflict? The present writer must confess that if peremptory norms in international law trigger such complexities with them, the risk is that they will not be taken seriously by State practice. Their

[128] There has been much literature on this. For contrasting views, see Orakhelashvili (n 50) 320ff (immunity yields); Vidmar (n 91) 1ff; and Focarelli (n 44) 444ff (immunity does not yield).

[129] S Talmon, '*Jus Cogens* after Germany v Italy: Substantive and Procedural Rules Distinguished' (2012) 25 *Leiden Journal of International Law* 989.

[130] C Esposito, '*Jus Cogens* and Jurisdictional Immunities of States at the International Court of Justice: "A Conflict Does Exist"' (2011) 21 *Italian Yearbook of International Law* 161ff. See also P Tarre Moser, 'Non-Recognition of State Immunity as a Judicial Countermeasure to *Jus Cogens* Violations: The Human Rights Answer to the ICJ Decision on the Ferrini case' (2012) 4 *Göttingen Journal of International Law* 809ff.

adequate digestion and proper handling by the international legal system can no longer be guaranteed. The argument here is thus that the type of relevant conflict for peremptoriness should be narrowed down to its classical content, that is, 'derogation' in its proper sense. *Jus cogens* is not yet, and should not become, a device for the solving of any type of conflict between objective norms, into which all sorts of positive and consequential *jus cogens* obligations are poured. By engaging in such avenues, the panegyrics of *jus cogens* follow the surest path to first discredit and then to kill their baby. And that would be prejudicial for the international legal order.

5

Sources of *Jus Cogens*

I. The General Issue

The question of what sources of international law may bear *jus cogens* norms is confused, to say the least. There is a doctrinal position for almost every conceivable source or combination of sources. This reflects the extremely diverse legal constructions of *jus cogens*, as reviewed in chapter three. The issue is further complicated by the fact that Article 53 of the Vienna Convention on the Law of Treaties (VCLT) can hardly be considered an exclusive expression of all international *jus cogens*. In other words, there are *jus cogens* phenomena beyond the VCLT, rooted directly in general or particular international law, and also in legal technique. Thus, the source of *jus cogens* indicated in Article 53 with the words 'norm of general international law' does not provide the whole answer. It answers the question only for the purposes of the VCLT.

As we know, the main sources of international law are considered to be customary law, agreements, and general principles of law.[1] All other sources of law and often of obligations can be attached to these. Thus, for example, resolutions of international organisations are secondary norms derived from treaty (for example, resolutions of the Security Council derive their force from the Charter). Unilateral normative acts of States, such as promises, are a source of subjective obligation more than a source of objective norms. They can however attach to the norms of customary international law providing for their operation. Regional and bilateral custom can attach to the concept of customary law, even if letter b of Article 38 speaks only of 'general' practice.

In order to illustrate the confusion that reigns regarding the issue of the sources of *jus cogens* norms, we may start by taking stock of the different positions that

[1] See Art 38 ICJ Statute, which is considered by most (but not all) authors to reflect the sources of international law.

exist in this regard. For different clusters of authors, *jus cogens* appears in the following law-creating agencies:

— Only general customary international law: Asamoah,[2] Cahier,[3] Czaplinski,[4] Focarelli,[5] Linderfalk,[6] Ronzitti,[7] Thierry,[8] Thirlway.[9] At the Vienna Conference on the Law of Treaties, this stance received support from Italy.[10] Later, this seemed also to be the position of the Ontario High Court of Justice (Canada).[11]
— Only multilateral, quasi-universal treaties and general customary international law: Akehurst,[12] Dinstein,[13] Magallona,[14] Puceiro Ripoll,[15] Rozakis,[16] Shaw,[17] Virally.[18] At the Vienna Conference, Trinidad & Tobago[19] voiced an opinion specifically excluding general principles from consideration.

[2] Lagonissi Conference, Carnegie Endowment for International Peace (ed), *The Concept of Jus Cogens in Public International Law: Papers and Proceedings* (Geneva, 1967) 96.

[3] P Cahier, 'Cours général de droit international public' (1985-VI) 195 *Recueil des cours de l'Académie de droit international de La Haye* 198.

[4] W Czaplinski, '*Jus Cogens* and the Law of Treaties' in C Tomuschat and JM Thouvenin (eds), *The Fundamental Rules of the International Legal Order: Jus Cogens and Obligations Erga Omnes* (Leiden/Boston, 2006) 92.

[5] C Focarelli, 'Promotional *Jus Cogens*: A Critical Appraisal of *Jus Cogens*' Legal Effects' (2008) 77 *Nordic Journal of International Law* 444ff.

[6] U Linderfalk, 'The Source of *Jus Cogens* Obligations: How Legal Positivism Copes with Peremptory Norms' (2013) 82 *Nordic Journal of International Law* 379; U Linderfalk, 'The Creation of *Jus Cogens*—Making Sense of Article 53 of the Vienna Convention' (2011) 71 *Zeitschrift für ausländisches öffentliches Recht und Völkerrecht* 359, 363.

[7] N Ronzitti, 'La disciplina dello *jus cogens* nella conventione di Vienna sul diritto dei trattati' in *Comunicazioni e studi*, vol XV (Milan, 1978) 241ff.

[8] H Thierry, 'Cours général de droit international public' (1990-III) 222 *Recueil des cours de l'Académie de droit international de La Haye* 59.

[9] H Thirlway, *International Customary Law and Codification* (Leiden, 1972) 97; H Thirlway, 'Concepts, Principles, Rules and Analogies: International and Municipal Legal Reasoning' (2002) 294 *Recueil des cours de l'Académie de droit international de La Haye* 400–01.

[10] United Nations Conference on the Law of Treaties, Official Documents, First Session, New York, 1969, No F.70.V.7, 311.

[11] *Bouzari v Iran* (2002) 124 ILR 442.

[12] M Akehurst, 'The Hierarchy of the Sources of International Law' (1974/75) 47 *British Yearbook of International Law* 283.

[13] Y Dinstein, 'The Interaction between Customary International Law and Treaties' (2006) 322 *Recueil des cours de l'Académie de droit international de La Haye* 397.

[14] M Magallona, 'The Concept of *Jus Cogens* in the Vienna Convention on the Law of Treaties' in J Scott Davidson (ed), *The Law of Treaties* (Aldershot, 2004) 502.

[15] R Puceiro Ripoll, 'Las normas de *jus cogens* en el campo del derecho internacional contemporaneo' in H Arbuet-Vignali and R Puceiro Ripoll (eds), *Derecho internacional publico, Breviarrio*, vol 1 (Montevideo, 2010) 121–22.

[16] C Rozakis, *The Concept of Jus Cogens in the Law of Treaties* (Amsterdam/New York/Oxford, 1976) 22, 58.

[17] M Shaw, *International Law*, 6th edn (Cambridge, 2008) 127.

[18] M Virally, 'Réflexions sur le *jus cogens*' (1966) 12 *AFDI* 15, 25–28.

[19] United Nations Conference on the Law of Treaties (n 10) 355.

— Only general international law, that is, general customary law and general principles of law: Barberis,[20] Dahm,[21] Drnas de Clément,[22] Mann,[23] Mosler,[24] Orakhelashvili,[25] Paulus,[26] Verhoeven.[27] That was also the view taken by the Federal Republic of Germany[28] at the Vienna Conference.
— Only general principles of law: during the Inter-War Period, Härle[29] and von der Heydte,[30] later Jaenicke,[31] Miaja de la Muela,[32] Quardi,[33] Reimann.[34] In recent times, some authors, mainly Alston/Simma,[35] have considered that general principles of law are the most suitable source for (universal) *jus cogens*.
— Only agreements/treaties, that is, particular international law: Schwarzenberger.[36]
— All three main sources of international law (agreements, customary law and general principles of law): Alston/Simma,[37] de Visscher,[38] Gomez Robledo,[39]

[20] JA Barberis, 'La liberté de traiter des Etats et le *jus cogens*' (1970) 30 *Zeitschrift für ausländisches öffentliches Recht und Völkerrecht* 44.
[21] G Dahm, *Völkerrecht*, vol I (Stuttgart, 1958) 17.
[22] Z Drnas de Clément, 'Las normas imperativas de derecho internacional general (*jus cogens*): dimension sustancial' in Z Drnas de Clément (ed), *Estudios de derecho internacional en homenja al professor EJ Rey Caro*, vol I (Cordoba, 2002) 664.
[23] FA Mann, 'The Doctrine of *Jus Cogens* in International Law' in *Essays in Honor of U Scheuner* (Berlin, 1973) 401.
[24] H Mosler, 'Ius Cogens im Völkerrecht' (1968) 25 *Annuaire suisse de droit international* 30, 38.
[25] A Orakhelashvili, *Peremptory Norms in International Law* (Oxford, 2006) 104ff.
[26] A Paulus, '*Jus Cogens* in a Time of Hegemony and Fragmentation' (2005) 74 *Nordic Journal of International Law* 302 (but the statement is expressly limited to the purposes of the VCLT).
[27] J Verhoeven, 'Sur les "bons" et les "mauvais" emplois du *jus cogens*' (2008) 5 *Anuario brasileiro de direito internacional* 136.
[28] United Nations Conference on the Law of Treaties (n 10) 319, § 33.
[29] E Härle, 'Les principes généraux de droit et le droit des gens' (1935) 16 *Recueil des cours de l'Académie de droit international de La Haye* 680.
[30] FA von der Heydte, 'Glossen zu einer Theorie der allgemeinen Rechtsgrundsätze' (1933) 33 *Die Friedenswarte* 297.
[31] G Jaenicke, 'Zur Frage des internationalen Ordre Public' in *Berichte der Deutschen Gesellschaft für Völkerrecht*, vol 7 (Karlsruhe, 1967) 91.
[32] A Miaja de la Muela, 'Ius cogens y ius dispositivum en derecho internacional publico' in *Essays in Honor of L Legaz y Lacambra*, vol II (Zaragoza, 1960) 1141.
[33] R Quadri, *Diritto internazionale pubblico*, 5th edn (Naples, 1968) 109.
[34] HB Reimann, *Jus Cogens im Völkerrecht* (Zurich, 1971) 57.
[35] P Alston and B Simma, 'The Sources of Human Rights Law: Custom, *Jus Cogens*, General Principles' (1988) 12 *Australian Yearbook of International Law* 102ff.
[36] G Schwarzenberger, *International Law—as Applied by International Courts and Tribunals*, 3rd edn, vol I (London, 1957) 427; also Lagonissi (n 2) 88, 100, 103, where Schwarzenberger admits the possibility of a customary *ius cogens*, but claims to have found no trace of it in an unstructured international society (p 103). The same argument is used against general principles (p 100). See also G Schwarzenberger, 'International Ius Cogens?' (1964/65) 43 *Texas Law Review* 455ff.
[37] Alston and Simma (n 35) 103.
[38] P de Visscher, 'Cours général de droit international public' (1972-II) 136 *Recueil des cours de l'Académie de droit international de La Haye* 107.
[39] A Gomez Robledo, 'Le *jus cogens* international: sa genèse, sa nature, ses fonctions' (1981-III) 172 *Recueil des cours de l'Académie de droit international de La Haye* 103.

Guggenheim/Marek,[40] Hannikainen[41] (if in a very restrictive way for general principles), Kadelbach,[42] Nahlik,[43] Nieto-Navia,[44] Saladin,[45] Suy,[46] Ténékidès,[47] Wolfke,[48] Verdross/Simma,[49] and also the present author.[50]

— A special, *sui generis* source:[51] either a hierarchically superior source, which thus expresses this particular superior quality of *jus cogens* (Monaco,[52] O'Connell[53]); or an expression of original consensus between the States of the international community at international conferences (Onuf /Birney[54]); or natural law (Janis,[55] Dubois[56]).
— The only possible remaining combination, that of treaties and general principles of law to the exclusion of other sources, seems to have found no support in doctrine. But even with that category, the variation in legal opinion remains remarkable, to say the least.

It is not necessary here to go into the detail of all the arguments advanced for and against every source.[57] Let us merely note the following aspects.

First, for Articles 53 and 64 VCLT *jus cogens* there is a conventional (and thus particular law) requirement, contained in the wording of these provisions, that

[40] P Guggenheim and K Marek, 'Verträge, Völkerrechtliche' in K Strupp and HJ Schlochauer (eds), *Wörterbuch des Völkerrechts*, 2nd edn, vol III (Berlin, 1962) 532.
[41] L Hannikainen, *Peremptory Norms (Jus Cogens) in International Law: Historical Development, Criteria, Present Status* (Helsinki, 1988) 216ff.
[42] S Kadelbach, *Zwingendes Völkerrecht* (Berlin, 1992) 182ff, esp 189.
[43] Nahlik in Lagonissi (n 2) 97.
[44] R Nieto-Navia, 'International Peremptory Norms (*Jus Cogens*) and International Humanitarian Law' in LC Vorah (ed), *Man's Inhumanity to Man: Essays in Honour of A Cassese* (The Hague/London/New York, 2003) 613–14.
[45] P Saladin, 'Völkerrechtliches ius cogens und schweizerisches Landesrecht' in G Jenny and W Kälin (eds), *Die schweizerische Rechtsordnung in ihren internationalen Bezügen* (Bern, 1988) 72.
[46] Suy in Lagonissi (n 2) 74–75.
[47] Tenekides, ibid, 112.
[48] K Wolfke, '*Jus Cogens* in International Law' (1974) 6 *Polish Yearbook of International Law* 154.
[49] A Verdross and B Simma, *Universelles Völkerrecht*, 3rd edn (Berlin, 1984) 331, 414.
[50] R Kolb, 'The Formal Source of Ius Cogens in Public International Law' (1998) 53 *Zeitschrift für öffentliches Recht* 69ff.
[51] Against the idea of a special source, see eg GM Danilenko, *Law-Making in the International Community* (Dordrecht/Boston/London, 1993) 223ff; K Zemanek, 'The Legal Foundations of the International System: General Course of Public International Law' (1997) 266 *Recueil des cours de l'Académie de droit international de La Haye* 136; S Knuchel, 'General Principles: The Surest Path for the Formation of *Jus Cogens*?' in S Besson and P Pichonnaz (eds), *Les principes en droit européen* (Paris/Geneva, 2011) 129.
[52] R Monaco, 'Observations sur la hiérarchie des normes du droit international' in *Essays in Honor of H Mosler* (Berlin, 1983) 106ff.
[53] ME O'Connell, '*Jus Cogens*: International Law's Higher Ethical Norms' in DE Childress (ed), *The Role of Ethics in International Law* (Cambridge, 2012) 83.
[54] N Onuf and R Birney, 'Peremptory Norms of International Law: their Source, their Function and Future' (1974) 4 *Denver Journal of International Law and Policy* 193ff.
[55] MW Janis, 'The Nature of *Jus Cogens*' in L May and J Brown (eds), *Philosophy of Law: Classic and Contemporary Readings* (Chichester, 2010) 184–85.
[56] D Dubois, 'The Authority of Peremptory Norms in International Law: State Consent or Natural Law?' (2009) 78 *Nordic Journal of International Law* 134, 137.
[57] For a detailed account, see Kolb (n 50) 69ff.

the norm be of the nature of 'general international law'. This normally designates norms of universal application, namely universal customary law and universal general principles of law. It is therefore not surprising that legal doctrine centred on analysis of the VCLT concludes that *jus cogens* must be embodied in such a norm of general reach.[58] However, since the International Law Commission (ILC) admitted that a norm of *jus cogens* could be found in a multilateral convention,[59] many authors have concluded that all three sources can satisfy the criterion of Article 53[60] (the conventional norm in a quasi-universally ratified convention will then in most cases be regarded as reflecting a norm of universal customary law). This position is based on the broader of the two possible understandings of the term 'general international law'.

Outside the narrow compass of Articles 53 and 64 VCLT, there is no need to reduce *jus cogens* norms to any particular source of law. As in municipal law, peremptory norms (norms which inhibit the operation of the *lex specialis* principle) can be found in all the layers of the law, that is, in all the sources. There are at almost all levels norms of law which are more general than other ones *ratione personarum* and which the legislator seeks to protect against fragmentation in special regimes applicable on a priority basis between parties. If that is the gist of *jus cogens*, the conclusion must be that it exists in all the sources.

For general customary law, this is most obvious, since that law is *par excellence* the general law *ratione personarum*. Hence, a great number of norms to be protected against legal fragmentation will be situated there. Moreover, this source accords particularly well with the public order view of *jus cogens* so commonly held and so intensely cherished.

For multilateral conventions, in particular those tending to universality, a similar argument may be made, particularly since these conventions are often the starting point for customary rules (such as the Genocide Convention of 1948 or the Geneva Conventions on international humanitarian law (IHL) of 1949). Moreover, if public utility *jus cogens* is admitted, the conventional source becomes an important bearer of *jus cogens*. Legal regimes of these types, for example statutes of international organisations and organs, are always contained in agreements. Thus, if the Statute of the International Court of Justice (ICJ) constitutes a form of *jus cogens*, in the sense that the Court cannot ignore the rules of its Statute by upholding special agreements between the litigants in a particular case (on the basis of *lex specialis* and *lex posterior*), the treaty is certainly a source containing *jus cogens* norms. Note that this is true even for public order norms. In 1949, the time of their adoption, it could hardly be said that the Geneva Conventions on

[58] C Maia, *Le concept de jus cogens en droit international public*, thesis (University of Bourgogne, 2006) 275ff.

[59] [1966-II] *Yearbook of the ILC* 248 § 4. See Kolb (n 50) 84.

[60] See, eg, ME Villiger, *Commentary on the 1969 Vienna Convention on the Law of Treaties* (Leiden/Boston, 2009) 670.

IHL were already customary; nor were these Conventions immediately ratified by a great number of States. Yet, the previously described mechanism contained in Articles 6/6/6/7 was from that time a *jus cogens* mechanism, applicable between the parties to the Conventions and denying effect to special agreements diminishing the rights of protected persons.

The position with regard to general principles of law is more complex, notably because these principles are subject to extremely diverse views in legal doctrine. Suffice it to say here that some great principles of international law (such as the non-use of force) and some great general principles of all legal orders (such as *pacta sunt servanda*) are peremptory. Conversely, general principles as gap-filling municipal law analogies can hardly be peremptory, if only on account of their subsidiary status. They may however become peremptory if their normative proposition is transformed into one of customary international law and if they are granted peremptory status through a fresh *opinio juris cogentis*. This is the case, according to some writers, with the principle of access to justice for individuals.[61]

In sum, *jus cogens* can be based on sources of general and particular international law. Its reach thus varies. Public order *jus cogens* will more often be embodied in sources of general international law; public utility *jus cogens* will more often be embodied in sources of particular international law.

Second, the main reason why some authors tend to narrow down the available sources has to do with their restrictive conception of *jus cogens* as *necessarily* embodying universal public order norms. But this view is unfounded, for at least two reasons. The first is that even public order norms can exist at all normative levels. There is no reason to claim that since there exists some universal public policy, there cannot exist a series of regional public policies. If the prohibition on genocide is a universal public policy norm, there is no reason to deny that the legal regimes governing democracy and the rule of law within the Council of Europe are European public policy, even if such positions are not yet accepted to the same degree at a universal level. Thus, there might be a valid reason for not allowing derogation from such regional public policy norms as among the States of the regional system. The separate question as to whether the existence of such divergent public policies does not lead to potential conflicts (and the way of solving them) must be considered later, in the context of the question as to the existence of a regional *jus cogens* (below, II). The second reason is that the identification of *jus cogens* with public policy is unwarranted. There is a public policy *jus cogens* (*jus cogens* being merely one quality of public policy norms), but there is also public utility *jus cogens*, or logically non-derogable norms. To the extent that *jus cogens* is perceived as a legal technique, it seems evident that it can reinforce the unity of all types of legal regimes

[61] See, eg, A Bucher, 'L'immunité de l'Etat confronté à ses crimes' (2014) 24 *Revue suisse de droit international et européen* 553ff.

in all types of sources. Conversely, if *jus cogens* is conflated with universal public policy, the sources will be narrowed down to those of 'general international law'. This leads us back to the reasons for narrowing down the concept in this way, so different from municipal law experiences. One powerful reason is the unwarranted influence of images such as the 'absolute moral nature' of *jus cogens*. How could the path then be kept clear for the legal technique dimension of the notion, when compared with its so eminent superior status? The position defended here is based on the conception that a norm can be technically *jus cogens* and yet not bind all States. *Jus cogens* can be relative in the domain of legal technique.

Third, some of the most commonly presented objections to each of the main sources of international law may be briefly presented and refuted.

Against *general customary international law*, the main objection is that *jus cogens* must perforce be contained in a separate and new source, since it is hierarchically superior to all the other sources or norms of international law. This hierarchical status could not be obtained if *jus cogens* norms were created similarly to the other, ordinary norms of international law, which precisely are not granted such a superior law status.[62] This objection is technically incorrect on many counts. In the first place, as we have already seen, it is wrong to equate *jus cogens* with hierarchy. If that conception were correct, a series of consequences would ensue which we cannot observe in positive law. For example, *jus cogens* norms would have to trump non-*jus cogens* norms every time. It would then not be clear why State practice and tribunals do not automatically brush away jurisdictional immunities as against the right of access to justice, or other claimed *jus cogens* positions; or why sovereignty does not automatically yield to human rights concerns. In the second place, even if *jus cogens* were inseparably linked with hierarchy, it would be wrong to consider that a new source of international law is necessary to confer that status. Law-making in the international community of States always takes place in the mould of recognised law-creating agencies. Thus, it is possible to create norms of customary international law which are given a superior status by virtue of a special *opinio juris*. These norms would be based on a double or enriched *opinio juris*: one for the legal character of the proposition and one for its superior rank. Even with treaty law, it is possible to create mechanisms going some way towards hierarchy, as is shown by mainstream interpretations of Article 103 of the UN Charter.[63] There is thus a non sequitur in this argument according to which traditional sources cannot create hierarchies.

Against *quasi-universal multilateral conventions* the main argument is that they will not bind all the States of the world (relativity of treaties).[64] But again this

[62] See, eg, Monaco (n 52) 106ff; O'Connell (n 53) 83.

[63] This is at least the view of the great majority of writers; see eg Verhoeven (n 27) 154. The views of the present writer are different: R Kolb, 'L'article 103 de la Charte des Nations Unies' (2013) 367 *Recueil des cours de l'Académie de droit international de La Haye* 235ff.

[64] See, eg, E Sciso, *Gli accordi internazionali confliggenti* (Bari, 1986) 335ff, 394ff.

argument proves too much. In the first place, and most decisively, the conception that only universally binding norms of law can be *jus cogens* is erroneous. As a legal technique, *jus cogens* can apply to partial legal communities. In the second place, it is possible to think of an exception to the principle of relativity in the context of *jus cogens*. Such exceptions to the *pacta tertiis* rule have indeed been discussed in the legal literature,[65] such as that of objective regimes. In the third place, even customary norms of general reach are based on State practice, which need not be absolutely universal. In other words, even in the context of a customary norm a State may be bound without having contributed to its formation, and in some cases even if it persistently objected to it (since according to overwhelming opinion persistent objection is not available for emerging *jus cogens* norms).[66] In the fourth place, it would remain possible to have recourse to the somewhat fictional device of considering that if a quasi-universal treaty embodies a norm the legislator wants to be of universal *jus cogens* reach, this fact transforms it automatically into a customary rule. This is a slightly extended view of the legislative function in international affairs. As already noted, the ILC acknowledged that *jus cogens* would often be created voluntarily by some treaty device rather than growing amorphously in State practice.

Against *general principles of law as municipal law analogies* (thus not the general principles of international law or the general principles inherent in each legal order), the main argument is their subsidiary status, called to fill in the gaps left by the main sources of international law.[67] This argument is certainly weighty. It shows that such principles will hardly be recognised as peremptory. There obviously remains the possibility that general principles taken from municipal law and considered to be peremptory might as a consequence simply no longer be subsidiary.[68] But such principles would then also have to be more than mere occasional gap-fillers.

Overall, the result is that *jus cogens* can be embodied in any of those sources, be they customary norms, treaties or some general principles.

[65] PF Smets, *Les effets des traités internationaux à l'égard des tiers* (University of Paris, Institut des hautes éltudes internationales, 1965–66).

[66] See, eg, Ronzitti (n 7) 256; GA Christenson, '*Jus Cogens*: Guarding Interests Fundamental to International Society' (1988) 28 *Virginia Journal of International Law* 622; J Vidmar, 'Rethinking *Jus Cogens* after Germany v Italy: Back to Article 53?' (2013) 60 *Netherlands International Law Review* 23; Akehurst (n 12) 285; RSJ MacDonald, 'Fundamental Norms in Contemporary International Law' (1987) 25 *Canadian Yearbook of International Law* 136; B Simma, 'From Bilateralism to Community Interest in International Law' (1994-VI) 250 *Recueil des cours de l'Académie de droit international de La Haye* 292; T Meron, 'International Law in the Age of Human Rights: General Course of Public International Law' (2003) 301 *Recueil des cours de l'Académie de droit international de La Haye* 395–96.

[67] See, eg, Ronzitti (n 7) 260; Akehurst (n 12) 283; G Balladore Pallieri, *Diritto internazionale pubblico* (Milan, 1937) 143.

[68] A Verdross, 'Forbidden Treaties in International Law' (1937) 31 *American Journal of International Law* 573: 'The principle of merely subsidiary validity of the general principles of law cannot be true without exception. It is only reasonable as far as it applies to non-compulsory norms.'

II. Regional *Jus Cogens*? Bilateral *Jus Cogens*?

One of the areas where dogmatism has overshadowed most aggressively dispassionate legal analysis is the question whether regional *jus cogens* can exist or indeed does exist. A series of authors have emphatically denied the legal possibility of any regional *jus cogens*;[69] it clearly does not fit with the triumphant 'absolutes' with which they have invested and perhaps infested the notion. On the other hand, a series of authors accept regional *jus cogens*, but sometimes hesitantly. Thus, for example, it has been said: 'No convincing reason has ever been given for ruling out the possibility of the existence of non-universal, or "regional" peremptory norms.'[70] More robustly, it has been added that regional *jus cogens* has been recognised in practice, for example in the Inter-American Commission on Human Rights in *Roach and Pinkerton* (1987), relating to the death penalty for minors.[71] An example often given is that of the European public order, which goes further than the universal one on issues of democracy, pre-eminence of the law and separation of powers.[72] Still another example encompasses regional human rights treaties.[73]

If one follows the legal technique view of *jus cogens*, as advocated in this monograph, there is no reason to deny the existence of regional peremptory norms. These norms may have some distinctive qualities with respect to universal public order *jus cogens*. But they remain peremptory in that they protect the integrity

[69] See, inter alia, Cahier (n 3) 198 ('l'idée d'une norme impérative régionale est contraire à sa notion même'); I Diaconu, *Contribution à une étude sur les norms imperatives en droit international (jus cogens)* (Geneva/Bucharest, 1971) 80ff; O Kimminich, *Einführung in das Völkerrecht*, 3rd edn (Munich, 1987) 228–29; M Kreca, 'Some General Reflections on Main Features of *Jus Cogens* as Notions of Public International Law' in *Essays in Honor of W Abendroth* (Frankfurt/New York, 1982) 33; Dinstein (n 13) 397–98; J Martensen, '*Ius Cogens* im Völkerrecht—Gibt es bindende Normen des Völkerrechts die durch völkerrechtliche Verträge nicht aufgehoben warden können?', PhD thesis (Hamburg, 1971) 80a, 90; Orakhelashvili (n 25) 38–39.

[70] See, inter alia, G Gaja, '*Jus Cogens* beyond the Vienna Convention' (1981-III) 172 *Recueil des cours de l'Académie de droit international de La Haye* 284. The following authors are favourable towards regional *jus cogens*: P de Visscher (n 38) 105 fn 85; F Domb, '*Jus Cogens* and Human Rights' (1976) 6 *Israel Yearbook on Human Rights* 110; Gomez Robledo (n 39) 23; Kadelbach (n 42) 203–04; Miaja de la Muela (n 32) 1127; Rozakis (n 16) 56; J Sztucki, *Jus Cogens and the Vienna Convention on the Law of Treaties: A Critical Appraisal* (Vienna/New York, 1974) 106–07; Puceiro Ripoll (n 15) 120 (it can exist, but does not exist today in fact); L Haopei, '*Jus Cogens* and International Law' in S Yee and W Tieya (eds), *International Law in the Post-Cold War World: Essays in Memory of Li Haopei* (London, 2001) 514–15; P Tavernier, 'L'identification des règles fondamentales: un problème résolu?' in C Tomuschat and JM Thouvenin (eds), *The Fundamental Rules of the International Legal Order: Jus Cogens and Obligations Erga Omnes* (Leiden/Boston, 2006) 16; Czaplinski (n 4) 93; K Schmalenbach, 'Article 53' in O Dörr and K Schmalenbach (eds), *Vienna Convention on the Law of Treaties: A Commentary* (Heidelberg/Dordrecht/London/New York, 2012) 940.

[71] Tavernier (n 70) 16.

[72] See, eg, Czaplinski (n 4) 93. See also Verdross and Simma (n 49) 334.

[73] Schmalenbach (n 70) 940.

of a regional legal regime against derogation by some of the States parties to the regional system. Even in the regional setting there is some 'general law' *ratione personarum* and some more 'particular law' *ratione personarum*; even there, the principle *lex specialis derogat legi generali* consequently operates; and even there, the contrary legal technique, *lex specialis non derogat legi generali*, may be of utility if the legislator wants to protect the integrity of the legal regime at stake. It would indeed be strange to argue that in Europe some legal acts contrary to the local conception of democracy *cannot* be treated as being void as between those very European States because the same conception of democracy has not yet been accepted on the universal plane. Such an argument confuses an ideological postulate with a point of legal technique.

As already suggested, the contrary conception is fundamentally based on the contestable mainstream conception of 'absolutes'. Thus, in the words of the Mali delegate at the Vienna Conference: 'The moral and spiritual values inherent in *jus cogens* could only assert themselves with the desired peremptory force if no geographical limits were placed on their applicability. Hence there could be no question of a regional *jus cogens*.'[74] *Jus cogens* is perforce a moral absolute—the most fundamental and high-standing rules of human existence on earth. The main practical argument against regional *jus cogens* is then that such a norm could apply only to States parties to the regional system and not to third States. Consequently, it would have to yield in relations between a State party to the regional system and a State not party to the system. This fact is seen as being incompatible with its peremptory nature. Indeed, if it were truly *jus cogens*, how could this regional 'peremptory' norm just be displaced by the universally applicable norm? A non-peremptory universal norm would here cast away a purportedly peremptory one—which in this perspective shows only one thing: that the latter one is not really peremptory.[75]

From the point of view of legal technique, this argument is plainly wrong. *Jus cogens* operates against *derogation*; conversely, its peremptory character does not entail as a consequence that the *scope of application* of the norm itself must be such that it applies in a given set of circumstances or towards a given set of persons (thus, a norm of *jus cogens* may be modified; or the non-use of force rule contains

[74] United Nations Conference on the Law of Treaties, Official Documents, First Session, New York, 1969, No F.70.V.7, p 327, § 73.

[75] See, eg, Diaconu (n 69) 81. See in particular also Orakhelashvili (n 25) 38–39. The latter's argument that regional *jus cogens* norms would introduce chaos into the system through conflicts between differing regional peremptory norms can hardly be taken seriously. Must it be recalled that a conflict of norms exists only for subjects bound by the same norms? In relations between States from different regions, such regional *jus cogens* norms would thus not apply at all; instead, general international law and the applicable treaties would apply. Where is the chaos here? Further, the argument that no regional *jus cogens* has ever been identified is wrong on the facts. Examples have been given in the text. Finally, the argument that the ILC has 'excluded' regional *jus cogens* is at best partial. The exclusion was directed to the proper scope of activities of the ILC, which purported to reflect only on universal *jus cogens* norms.

exceptions going to its scope of application; or the Geneva Conventions may have recourse to peremptory techniques even if they do not apply to all States, etc). True, universal public order *jus cogens* norms will apply to all.[76] But to equate the whole peremptory spectrum with this sole type of *jus cogens* is abusive. A norm is not *jus cogens* if and because it applies to *all* subjects of a given legal order. This is not a defining element of peremptoriness in legal technique. A norm is *jus cogens* if it does not allow a limited number of subjects from *within* a given legal regime to stipulate or adopt among themselves derogatory legal regimes, applicable by priority among themselves by virtue of the *lex specialis* principle. The gist of the matter is that the peremptory mechanism looks towards the *inside* of the system (and the ability or otherwise to split the unity of a legal regime), not towards the *outside* at subjects not party to that system. It is therefore entirely compatible with regional or particular *jus cogens* status to inhibit particular legal acts within the system, but at the same time to yield to other norms in external relations. This is the essence of the matter: the latter point concerns the spatial and subjective scope of application of the *jus cogens* norm and not its non-derogable character *inter se*. It remains true, however, that this form of regional *jus cogens* is distinct from Articles 53 and 64 VCLT. But regional customary international law is not mentioned in Article 38, § 1, letter b of the ICJ Statute either, yet it is not contested that it exists.[77] In short, fewer 'absolutes' and some more precise legal analysis would be of great value.

In a previous contribution, the present author argued that there could be *jus cogens* norms even in a bilateral agreement.[78] I admitted that such a *jus cogens* was of little practical relevance, if only because of the ease of the contrary act,[79] that is, a new bilateral agreement considered to be *jus cogens* by the parties. The main arguments in favour of the position taken were as follows: (i) the peremptory character could rule out any possibility of simple desuetude of the treaty; and (ii) the peremptory character would inhibit the mechanical application of the *lex posterior* rule by requiring some evidence that the parties want to depart from the previous peremptory rule. These arguments have some weight, but it must be admitted that the whole proposition remains somewhat artificial. In a bilateral agreement, there is no 'general law' to be opposed to a 'particular law': there are only two parties and hence there is no room for restricted *inter se* derogation (one party alone cannot derogate in any event).[80] Furthermore, the issues indicated under (i) and (ii) are

[76] Universal public order *jus cogens* will evidently apply to all subjects, but this is simply because by its very nature it is based on *general* international law, which binds all States. In other words, it is not its peremptory character that explains its universal binding reach, but rather the fact that this *jus cogens* is based on norms of general international law.

[77] See, eg, the classical *Right of Passage (Merits)* [1960] ICJ Rep 39.

[78] Kolb (n 50) 102–03.

[79] See also Kadelbach (n 42) 204.

[80] A reservation to a bilateral treaty, to the extent that it is allowed at all, would have to be tested against general international *jus cogens*, or the object and purpose, or some express provision in the treaty. The latter take the place of any *jus cogens* created by the bilateral agreement itself.

matters of interpretation rather than strictly of *jus cogens*. Finally, there does not seem to be relevant international practice for bilateral *jus cogens*. Therefore it does not seem excessive to lay this category to rest. Technically speaking, there must be at least a trilateral treaty in order for *jus cogens* to obtain some standing: in other words, the protection of the integrity of the general regime against restricted *inter se* derogations.

III. Modification of *Jus Cogens* Norms

Some words should be said on the modification of *jus cogens* norms. Article 53 VCLT allows such modification: '[A peremptory norm] can be modified only by a subsequent norm of general international law having the same [peremptory] character.' This formula calls for some immediate comments. *First*, Article 53 VCLT *jus cogens* may be changed. It is thus formatted as a notion of positive law, not of natural law. That it also covers some moral 'absolutes' has not led to all *jus cogens* norms being conferred the status of unalterable norms.[81] *Second*, the question of modification concerns the 'abrogation' of the norm and its potential or actual replacement by another norm. We remain situated at the level of the objective norm. This norm is terminated in its effects as against all States which it previously bound. Contrariwise, the point is not 'derogation'. In this latter category, the objective norm remains in force and applicable, but its application is suspended between some States that have adopted a special legal regime under the *lex specialis* rule (normally through an agreement). In this latter situation, the objective general norm applies among all States not parties to the special regime, and the special regime-norm applies only among the States parties to that special regime. There are thus two norms in parallel application: the general norm (for some subjects) and the special one (for other subjects). The mechanism of derogation is ruled out for peremptory norms, but the former one of modification applies to them. There are, however, certain difficulties when dealing with the modification of *jus cogens* norms, which are often discussed in the legal literature. It is therefore useful to consider those points below. *Third*, modification is said to require the same form as the creation of a new peremptory norm (parallelism of form: 'can be modified only by a subsequent norm of general international law

[81] Some authors have insisted, however, that some civilisational norms could not be considered modifiable (but whether this is posited on the basis of positive law or of natural law remains unclear): see S Schmahl, 'An Example of *Jus Cogens*: The Status of Prisoners of War' in C Tomuschat and JM Thouvenin (eds), *The Fundamental Rules of the International Legal Order, Jus Cogens and Obligations Erga Omnes* (Leiden/Boston, 2006) 50; M Lachs, 'General Course on Public International Law' (1980-IV) 169 *Recueil des cours de l'Académie de droit international de La Haye* 204–05; P Reuter, *Introduction au droit des traités*, 2nd edn (Paris, 1985) 128. At the Vienna Conference, only one delegate, namely that of Tanzania, voiced the idea that *jus cogens* cannot be modified: *United Nations Conference on the Law of Treaties*, Official Documents, First Session, New York, 1969, No F.70.V.7, vol I, p 321, § 2.

having the same [peremptory] character'). A new rule of *jus cogens* must be based, for the purposes of the VCLT, on general international law. Thus, any modification of that rule supposes a new rule of general international law, and that rule must be peremptory. Even more precisely, there must be, for the new rule, a triple *opinio juris*: that it is legal; that it is peremptory; and that it shall replace the old peremptory rule (the third can however be implicit in the first).

Two series of problems deserve to be discussed at this juncture. First, there is a conundrum as to the concrete way in which a *jus cogens* norm may be practically modified. Second, there remains the question of whether the parallelism of form is truly indispensable.

A. Modification

The argument has been made that the modification of a *jus cogens* norm by customary international is difficult, if not impossible, so that it would be sensible to admit a modification by way of multilateral treaty. In the latter situation, a consensus of the assembled universal community of States can be obtained and ascertained at once. The noted difficulty lies—for some authors[82]—in the fact that the material acts constituting the new practice would constitute a 'breach' of the old *jus cogens* norm and thus be considered void. Thus, such acts could not legally effectuate a change to the old norm. Conversely, it has been said that a treaty cannot modify a *jus cogens* norm. The new treaty norm, a legal act incompatible with the old *jus cogens* norm, would simply be void.[83] Taking these two arguments in conjunction, some authors have drawn the overall conclusion that *jus cogens* norms cannot truly be changed; it remains possible to develop new *jus cogens* norms, but not to abrogate old ones.[84] This result is remarkable, since it tends to sterilise the words contained in Article 53 VCLT. The drafters of the Convention would seem to have wanted something which is impossible to realise under the tools of international legal technique.

These conclusions are not solid. In the first place, modification of an old *jus cogens* norm by contrary material acts might occur if these material acts are accompanied by legal opinion whereby the challenge to and change to the old rule is intended, and this challenge and change is shared by a great number of subjects of law. Contrariwise, simple material acts contrary to a *jus cogens* norm will be considered mere violations of the norm and not acts able to change its normative content. These material acts may be unlawful for a transitory time from the point of view of responsibility of States, but they are certainly not void. Material acts are

[82] See, eg, Dinstein (n 13) 402–03; Haopei (n 70) 516–17; Magallona (n 14) 514–15 (the material practice will not be yet peremptory so the *jus cogens* norm remains even if its practice-basis will be weakened). The difficulties are also stressed in Schmalenbach (n 70) 917. Some authors do not share such concerns: see eg Villiger (n 60) 673. In general, see also Hannikainen (n 41) 265ff.

[83] O'Connell (n 53) 93.

[84] Orakhelashvili (n 25) 129–30.

facts and deeds. As already discussed, such acts are not subject to the roster of nullities. Only legal acts are valid or void; material acts are lawful or unlawful. In the second place—and this is certainly a sensible course—it remains possible to issue statements whereby a subject no longer considers the old rule peremptory, binding or even existent. Such statements make it possible to avoid being pushed to violate the norm in order to change it. The declaring subject thereby refuses to uphold the legal opinion necessary for the maintenance of the old peremptory rule. If it is followed by a sufficiently significant number of other subjects, the old customary rule is deprived of one of its constituent elements, namely its *opinio juris*. Thus, it will disappear. If it is a *jus cogens* rule, the threshold of required evidence for its vanishing will be particularly high and strict.[85] The number of States and the quality of the statements will have to be very significant.[86] The same is true, in the third place, for a new treaty purporting to change an old peremptory norm. The point is not the nullity of the new provision, by virtue of the continued operation of the old one. It lies rather in the fact that the States assembled in a conference may take the opportunity to issue statements as to how they see the status of the old norm. If many States declare that they consider the old norm to be no longer applicable, the legal opinion necessary for its continued existence is immediately lacking. The old norm then disappears—it is abrogated; there is then room for the creation of a new peremptory norm by the conventional process. Again, the number of States required and the quality of the statements must be particularly demanding when the old norm at stake is peremptory.

As far as the more extreme 'non-modifiability' opinion is concerned, it rests on ideological rather than positive law grounds. It is certainly desirable that the main public order norms be maintained in the future. However, unfortunately, from the standpoint of positive law, even these may be changed. A fight for their preservation would then have to take place—after having been temporarily lost on the ground of positive law—in the context of political mobilisation and natural law arguments. In short, modification of peremptory norms is possible since the secondary legal rules on changing peremptory norms are not themselves peremptory: that is, the acts necessary for the change are not themselves voided under *jus cogens*.[87]

[85] See, eg, G Abi-Saab, 'Cours général de droit international public' (1987-VII) 207 *Recueil des cours de l'Académie de droit international de La Haye* 378; M Kohen, 'The Use of Force by the US after the End of the Cold War, and its Impact on International Law' in M Byers and G Nolte (eds), *United States Hegemony and the Foundations of International Law* (Cambridge, 2003) 228; G Abi-Saab, 'The Concept of International Crime and its Place in Contemporary International Law' in J Weiler, A Cassese and M Spinedi (eds), *International Crimes of States: A Critical Analysis of Article 19 of the ILC's Draft Articles on State Responsibility* (Berlin, 1989) 146, considering that simple desuetude is not enough.

[86] Legal writings rightly stress that the approval must emanate from the international community as a whole, ie from the overwhelming number of States: Schmalenbach (n 70) 917. See also Haopei (n 70) 510.

[87] Linderfalk, 'The Creation of *Jus Cogens*' (n 6) 377.

B. Parallelism of Form

Article 53 VCLT requires that the modification of an old *jus cogens* norm be brought about by a norm of the same formal status—that is, a norm of general international law versus a norm of general international law. However, this perspective covers only one of the possible scenarios of modification: that of *replacing* a *jus cogens* norm with another norm of the same type. But there may also be cases of simple *abrogation* of a *jus cogens* norm, without the creation of a new one;[88] or the simple *return* of a *jus cogens* norm to *jus dispositivum*.[89] It would perhaps be possible to say that the new norm is the one which provides for the abrogation of, or the return to, the old one. This new norm would then have to be of general international law. However, such conceptualisations may seem all too theoretical. In most practical situations, there will be the erosion of the old rule by challenges, contrary opinions and statements before a new norm will establish itself, if at all.[90] When the legal opinion sustaining the old rule disappears, the latter rule cannot maintain itself. Thus, a simple (but clear and shared) contrary *opinio juris* could bring the old rule to its knees.

Parallelism of form, then, is not perfect in all cases. It is not always a new rule of general customary law that casts away the old rule. A new and contrary legal opinion may suffice to abrogate the old rule. The parallelism is however there if and when a new rule is to take the place of the old one. In order to be established it must, like the old rule, be based on peremptory general international law, at least for the purposes of the VCLT.

[88] Villiger (n 60) 673, using the imprecise word 'desuetude'.

[89] On this latter case, see Verhoeven (n 27) 138.

[90] A relevant process was seen—and fortunately it remained a long way off fulfilling the conditions for a change to the applicable *jus cogens* norms—when in the aftermath of 9/11 the US and some of its allies called into question the reach of the non-use of force rule and challenged the absoluteness of the prohibition on torture (see eg TH Cheng, *When International Law Works: Realistic Idealism after 9/11 and the Global Recession* (Oxford, 2012) 227ff, 290ff). If these views had been shared widely in the international arena, the positive lawyer would have had to accept the disappearance of certain norms in certain contexts (and with them their peremptoriness). The same could occur if States limited the reach or the peremptoriness of the non-refoulement principle in view of massive migrant streams. All these developments may seem extremely unwelcome and worrisome—and they are to some degree—but the fight against the turning back of the clock would have to take place on the level of politics. It could not be made by ignoring or negating the law as it stands. The modification of public utility *jus cogens* does not pose similar 'moral' problems; thus, a change to the Statute of the ICJ is a purely technical question.

6

Effects of *Jus Cogens*

The question of the effects of *jus cogens* norms did not give rise to particularly heated problems in the past. However, recently it has become one of the most intricate and grave problems of *jus cogens*. The issue is linked with the proper scope of action and the dangers of an over-extensive, potentially subversive reach of *jus cogens*.[1] The question is thus at once delicate, intricate and important.

I. An Extension of Possible Effects: From Nullity of Legal Acts to Consequences of Breach, to Potentially Unlimited Effects

A. Nullity

In legal history, the sole generally accepted effect of *jus cogens* was the nullity of the derogatory act. *Jus cogens* was therefore concerned only with the validity of legal acts and voided derogation. In international law, it was discussed whether a larger conception of this effect was admissible. The discussion turned on the fact that in a decentralised system, the role of nullity was somewhat more uncertain than in centralised municipal legal systems, which are blessed with regular judges. Legal opinion quickly split into those authors who maintained that validity and nullity were necessary ingredients of international *jus cogens*,[2] and those

[1] On the effects, see in the newer literature: C Focarelli, 'Promotional *Jus Cogens*: A Critical Appraisal of *Jus Cogens*' Legal Effects' (2008) 77 *Nordic Journal of International Law* 429ff; A Orakhelashvili, *Peremptory Norms in International Law* (Oxford, 2006) 131ff; J Verhoeven, 'Sur les "bons" et les "mauvais" emplois du *jus cogens*' (2008) 5 *Anuario brasileiro de direito internacional* 140ff; S Laghmani, 'Le jus cogens et la cohérence de l'ordre juridique international' in *Les droits de l'homme: une nouvelle coherence pour le droit international? Rencontre à la mémoire de D Jazi* (Paris, 2008) 76ff; U Linderfalk, 'The Effect of Jus Cogens Norms: Whoever Opened Pandora's Box, Did You Ever Think About the Consequences?' (2007) 18 *European Journal of International Law* 853ff. In the older literature, see in particular L Hannikainen, *Peremptory Norms (Jus Cogens) in International Law: Historical Development, Criteria, Present Status* (Helsinki, 1988) 293ff.

[2] See, eg, A Bernardini, 'Qualche riflessione su norme internazionali di *jus cogens* e giurisdizione della Corte nella Convenzione di Vienna sul diritto dei trattati' (1975) XIV *Comunicazioni e studi* 87–88, 93; A Pellet, 'The Normative Dilemma: Will and Consent in International Law-Making' (1992)

who were prepared to take a broader view,[3] allowing some functionally similar effects, such as inapplicability, non-prevalence, absence of the effect stipulated for, impeachment of a contrary norm in its formative stage, prohibition on concluding agreements (limitation of treaty-making power), non-opposability, or even some inhibiting role vis-a-vis attempts to derogate or vis-a-vis breaches.[4] In any event, it is often added that nullity under Article 53 of the Vienna Convention on the Law of Treaties (VCLT) is not automatic, but that the procedure of Article 65 VCLT has to be followed. As a consequence, nullity can be invoked only by a party to the treaty at stake.[5]

If one admits a plurality of types of *jus cogens*, as this author does in the present monograph, it stands to reason that the effect of *jus cogens* has to be slightly broadened beyond the concept of absolute nullity. Thus, universal public order *jus cogens* will mainly have the effect of nullity of contrary legal acts. But public interest *jus cogens* will most often not have such a radical effect (which is applicable only where a norm provides for this special effect). Thus, an agreement whereby two litigant States purport to depart from various rules of the Statute

12 *Australian Yearbook of International Law* 38. See also N Ronzitti, 'La disciplina dello *jus cogens* nella conventione di Vienna sul diritto dei trattati' in *Comunicazioni e studi*, vol XV (Milan, 1978) 264ff; J Martensen, '*Ius Cogens* im Völkerrecht—Gibt es bindende Normen des Völkerrechts die durch völkerrechtliche Verträge nicht aufgehoben warden können?', PhD thesis (Hamburg, 1971) 82ff; GB Zotiades, 'Staatsautonomie und die Grenzen der Vertragsfreiheit im Völkerrecht' (1967) 17 *Oesterreichische Zeitschrift für öffentliches Recht* 103.

[3] E Suy, 'The Concept of *Jus Cogens* in Public International Law' in Lagonissi Conference, Carnegie Endowment for International Peace (ed), *The Concept of Jus Cogens in Public International Law: Papers and Proceedings* (Geneva, 1967) 72 (non-invokability at the ICJ suffices); G Gaja, '*Jus Cogens* beyond the Vienna Convention' (1981-III) 172 *Recueil des cours de l'Académie de droit international de La Haye* 281–83 (sometimes illegality rather than invalidity); H Mosler, 'Ius Cogens im Völkerrecht' (1968) 25 *Annuaire suisse de droit international* 21 (non-applicability of agreements contrary to Statutes of International Organizations), 39–40 (generally, considering the uncertainty of nullities in international law); A Miaja de la Muela, 'Ius cogens y ius dispositivum en derecho internacional publico' in *Essays in Honor of L Legaz y Lacambra*, vol II (Zaragoza, 1960) 1149 (the possibility of obtaining invalidation suffices); E Schwelb, 'Some Aspects of International *Jus Cogens* as Formulated by the ILC' (1967) 61 *American Journal of International Law* 959; J Huillier, *Droit international public* (Paris, 1949) 72–73 (nullity or non-opposability); B Conforti, *Diritto internazionale*, 4th edn (Naples, 1992) (non-derogability and priority, not necessarily nullity). Certain authors insist that the essential aspect of *jus cogens* is the limitation of the law-making power of subjects: J Jurt, *Zwingendes Völkerrecht: Ein Beitrag zur lehre vom objektiven Völkerrecht* (Wil (St Gallen), 1933) 24.

[4] J Vidmar, 'Rethinking *Jus Cogens* after Germany v Italy: Back to Article 53?' (2013) 60 *Netherlands International Law Review* 22.

[5] See, eg, M Magallona, 'The Concept of *Jus Cogens* in the Vienna Convention on the Law of Treaties' in J Scott Davidson (ed), *The Law of Treaties* (Aldershot, 2004) 507; W Czaplinski, '*Jus Cogens* and the Law of Treaties' in C Tomuschat and JM Thouvenin (eds), *The Fundamental Rules of the International Legal Order: Jus Cogens and Obligations Erga Omnes* (Leiden/Boston, 2006) 89; A Gomez Robledo, 'Le *jus cogens* international: sa genèse, sa nature, ses fonctions' (1981-III) 172 *Recueil des cours de l'Académie de droit international de La Haye* 150ff. However, it has rightly been stressed that for public order *jus cogens* third States may claim nullity under *erga omnes* rights: JA Frowein, 'Ius Cogens' in R Wolfrum (ed), *The Max Planck Encyclopedia of Public International Law*, vol VI (Oxford, 2012) 445; R Ago in [1966-I] *Yearbook of the ILC*, 828th meeting, § 18. Moreover, international tribunals have never refused to consider the point, even *ex officio*: see eg *Aloeboetoe v Suriname* (1993) 116 ILR 278 (Inter-American Court of Human Rights).

of the International Court of Justice (ICJ) will not be void, but will be deprived of legal effect. Its proper function is to motivate the ICJ to do something or to abstain from doing something contrary to its Statute. Since the Court will refuse to do so, the agreement at stake will not have its intended legal effect. And since its object is limited to the functioning of the Court in a particular procedure, it will remain completely inapplicable and deprived of any meaningful legal effects. This is tantamount to functional nullity. If one considers Article 6/6/6/7 Geneva Conventions I–IV (1949) *jus cogens*, unlawful special agreements, purporting to lower the protections of persons under international humanitarian law, will not have their purported effect. The substantive rules of the Conventions prevail. This prevalence sterilises the contrary content of the special agreement and is again largely tantamount to functional nullity. If one takes the previously mentioned example of the emblem of the UN, an agreement to allow use of the emblem by a private corporation cannot be concluded (or would have to be denounced, if concluded). Here, the peremptory effect is to limit the law-making power of the UN as long as the relevant rules on the protection of the emblem are not changed.

B. Responsibility

Classical developments in *jus cogens* were limited to the law of treaties and to the law of legal acts. A further step was taken when the International Law Commission (ILC) adopted its Articles on State Responsibility (ASR) (2001).[6] *Jus cogens* was here extended beyond the domain of legal acts and their validity. The main question was now the one of 'aggravated' consequences flowing from the breach of a *jus cogens* norm. Breach is now the keyword, not derogation. As we know, Articles 40–41 ASR add some specific legal consequences to those flowing from the breach of each norm of international law when the breach concerns a norm of *jus cogens*.[7] These additional effects are threefold:

— a duty of non-assistance in maintaining the situation created by the breach;[8]
— a duty of non-recognition of the lawfulness of the situation created by the breach of the peremptory norm;[9] and
— a duty to cooperate among States to bring to an end, through lawful means, the breach of the peremptory norm.[10]

[6] J Crawford, *The ILC's Articles on State Responsibility* (Cambridge, 2002); J Crawford, A Pellet and S Olesson (eds), *The Law of State Responsibility* (Oxford, 2010). For the effects of *jus cogens* in the law of State responsibility, see Gaja (n 3) 290ff; Hannikainen (n 1) 249ff, 301ff. Some authors have spoken of the development of a concept of 'objective illegality': see eg AA Cançado Trindade, 'International Law for Humankind: Towards a New Jus Gentium' (2005) 316 *Recueil des cours de l'Académie de droit international de La Haye* 343.

[7] On this legal regime, cf Crawford, Pellet and Olesson (n 6) 405ff. The main criticism in legal doctrine is that the regime is modest in its extension and effects: see eg Verhoeven (n 1) 148. See also the broader study of L Yarwood, *State Accountability under International Law: Holding States Accountable for Breach of 'Jus Cogens' Norms* (London, 2011).

[8] ASR, Art 41, § 2.

[9] ibid.

[10] ibid, Art 41, § 1.

It should be noted that the threshold of the relevant breaches of peremptory norms is raised for the application of Articles 40–41: the breach must be a 'serious breach by a State of an obligation arising under a peremptory norm'.[11] It will also be noted that some of these consequences probably flow from the commission of any unlawful act, such as the duty not to assist in the perpetuation of a breach (as long as it remains an unlawful act and is not, for example, cured by acceptance). It should conversely be noted that the duty of non-recognition has here been extended, since in international practice until 2001 it was applied essentially in the context of a breach of two peremptory norms linked with territorial statuses, that is, the creation of territorial situations through the unlawful use of force and the creation of such situations in violation of the principle of self-determination of peoples.[12] Additionally, *jus cogens* is relevant in the branch of responsibility, in that it limits the availability of circumstances precluding wrongfulness (Article 26 ASR)[13] and the lawfulness of counter-measures (Article 50, § 1, letter d ASR).[14] This is a bundle of positive obligations: not to assist; not to recognise; to actively cooperate; and then a series of objective limitations to available action: limitation on counter-measures, limitations on available circumstances precluding wrongfulness.

These responsibility-related consequences of *jus cogens* norms are, on closer inspection, consequences of universal public order norms. It is unfortunate that the ILC conflated the two notions of *jus cogens* and public policy, even if that is understandable in view of the fact that public order norms have nowhere authoritatively been defined in international law, whereas *jus cogens* has a positive anchor in Articles 53 and 64 VCLT, as well as in the customary international law developed around these provisions. It is evident that the consequences described in the provisions of the ASR fit only universal public order norms, probably the ones the drafters of Articles 53 and 64 envisaged as main examples of *jus cogens*. However, the correct way to put the matter in the light of legal technique is that these public order norms have, because of their public policy status, several legal consequences, which distinguish them from ordinary norms. One of these consequences is the *jus cogens* effect in the context of the validity and the nullity of legal acts; another consequence is the special effects flowing from breach under the rules of State

[11] ibid, Art 40, § 1. On the meaning of this restriction, see Crawford (n 6) 245ff.

[12] See, eg, L Oppenheim, (ed RY Jennings and A Watts), *International Law* 9th edn, vol I (London, 1992) 183ff, with further references. On non-recognition doctrines and *jus cogens*, see also in particular J Dugard, *Recognition and the United Nations* (Cambridge, 1987) 123ff.

[13] 'Nothing in this Chapter precludes the wrongfulness of any act of a State which is not in conformity with an obligation arising under a peremptory norm of general international law.' See also, for example, T Meron, 'International Law in the Age of Human Rights: General Course of Public International Law' (2003) 301 *Recueil des cours de l'Académie de droit international de La Haye* 258.

[14] 'Countermeasures shall not affect: … (d) other obligations under peremptory norms of general international law.' The link between counter-measures and *jus cogens* has long been perceived: see C Focarelli, *Le contromisure nel diritto internazionale* (Milan, 1994) 471ff; LA Sicilianos, *Les réactions décentralisées à l'illicite* (Paris, 1990) 339ff.

responsibility. The use of *jus cogens* instead of public order mistakenly omits an essential intermediary step in legal conceptualisation. This is made evident by the fact that other *jus cogens* norms (according to the inclusive conceptualisation in this monograph) clearly do not trigger such effects. This is the case with public interest *jus cogens* norms, but also even with some peremptory mechanisms which are quite close to a public policy logic, like that of Articles 6/6/6/7 Geneva Convention I–IV (1949). By using the term '*jus cogens*' in this context the risk of confusion is increased. Even under universal public order *jus cogens* norms, it is not absolutely certain that all of them would trigger all the consequences provided for in the ASR. Thus, for example, it remains to be seen to what extent even a serious violation of certain human rights triggers a universal duty of cooperation in order to bring the breach to an end. International practice is not abundant with such universal cooperation, even if serious human rights breaches are very frequent. Thus, either States regularly breach their secondary obligation to cooperate, or the duty under the ASR was drafted in an overly inclusive manner.

C. Boundlessness?

Since the beginning of the twenty-first century, the possible or actual effects of *jus cogens* have exploded in all directions, rather like a seminal Big Bang. Questions obviously remain vis-a-vis the extent to which this constant expansion is a sign of progress and the extent to which it can be properly digested by the system. The most varied effects have been attached to this super-*jus cogens*, some of them in practice, most of them only by various authors. To wit:[15] inapplicability of jurisdictional immunities;[16] assumption of universal jurisdiction (for so-called *jus cogens* crimes);[17] admissibility of retroactivity;[18] various effects in domestic legal orders[19] (such as voidance of amnesties[20] or, in Switzerland, according to Article 139, § 3 of the Swiss Constitution, invalidation of popular initiatives); a duty to

[15] See Focarelli (n 1) 439ff.

[16] See, eg, the stocktaking of A Bianchi, 'Gazing at the Crystal Ball (Again): State Immunity and *Jus Cogens* Beyond Germany v Italy' (2013) 4 *Journal of International Dispute Settlement* 457ff; S Knuchel, 'State Immunity and the Promise of *Jus Cogens*' (2011) 9 *Northwestern University Journal of International Human Rights* 149ff; Orakhelashvili (n 1) 322ff, with further references.

[17] See, eg, C Bassiouni, 'International Crimes: *Jus Cogens* and Obligatio Erga Omnes' (1996) 59 *Law and Contemporary Problems* 63ff; Orakhelashvili (n 1) 288ff.

[18] See the reference in Focarelli (n 1) 441, quoting the *Ferrini* decision (2004) of the Italian Court of Cassation.

[19] Orakhelashvili (n 1) 539ff; A Cassese, 'An Enhanced Role of *Jus Cogens*' in A Cassese (ed), *Realizing Utopia: The Future of International Law* (Oxford, 2012) 167–68; A Paulus, '*Jus Cogens* in a Time of Hegemony and Fragmentation' (2005) 74 *Nordic Journal of International Law* 297 319; ME O'Connell, '*Jus Cogens*: International Law's Higher Ethical Norms' in DE Childress (ed), *The Role of Ethics in International Law* (Cambridge, 2012) 97, 98; and International Criminal Tribunal for the Former Yugoslavia, *Furundzija* case (1998) 121 ILR 260–62 (Trial Chamber).

[20] Orakhelashvili (n 1) 223ff.

exercise diplomatic protection;[21] the creation of a title of jurisdiction,[22] etc. Most of these effects are obtained by deductive reasoning in the sense that they are taken to be inherent in the very notion of *jus cogens*. Consequently, an attentive spirit can locate and deduce them from the concept. It has even been claimed that State practice has less (or no?) weight in matters of *jus cogens*.[23] Such a stance reinforces the space for subjective deductive reasoning according to the varying standards and agendas of every legal operator. The list of effects of *jus cogens* thus becomes potentially unlimited. At any time, a new effect can be 'discovered' in line with the apparent needs of the international society and the vision of the legal operator. Moreover, these effects are not confined to 'nullity'—that is, to a more or less automatic and limited legal effect. Quite the contrary: new *jus cogens* imposes on States a series of positive duties. Thus, for example, the concept of *jus cogens* crimes triggers the duty of States to prosecute the culprits on the basis of universal jurisdiction. An unlimited number of new duties could consequently be created simply by way of deduction from the concept of *jus cogens*, States having to shoulder all the costs and bureaucracy this entails. Note that these duties would not necessarily have to be accepted by State practice or by agreements. They would already be there, waiting to be awakened by a deductive exercise.

The foregoing developments elicit two main questions on the effects of *jus cogens*. The first is the extent to which it is correct to say that the consequences of a breach of *jus cogens* are themselves *jus cogens* (secondary rules as *jus cogens*?). The purpose of this cryptic formulation is to determine the extent to which a breach of *jus cogens* (for example by war crimes) triggers a series of duties, such as the one to exercise jurisdiction, which themselves would have a peremptory character. If true, this would be a remarkable extension of *jus cogens*, going into an overly rich array of corollary positive obligations. The second question concerns the manner in which the effects of *jus cogens* going beyond validity nullity can be determined. Is it true that these effects are inherent in the notion of *jus cogens* so that they can be deduced therefrom? Or are these additional effects, which must be ascertained in State practice (inductive reasoning)? The time has come to turn to these two points.

II. Secondary Rules as *Jus Cogens*?

For some authors,[24] the 'legal effects' of *jus cogens* are themselves peremptory. Thus, all the rules of international law in direct contact with a *jus cogens* provision, in that they constitute a consequence of its breach or are useful to its proper implementation, are peremptory. Let us take some examples.

[21] Verhoeven (n 1) 159. The question was considered by the ILC and also in judicial practice in the *Kaunda* case (2004) 136 *ILR* 463, 503–04 (South Africa Constitutional Court), the judges not agreeing on the issue.

[22] On this issue, Orakhelashvili (n 1) 489ff.

[23] ibid, 301–02.

[24] ibid, 144.

- **Example 1:** if certain prohibitions are *jus cogens* (war crimes, genocide, etc), all the consequences of a breach of such prohibitions are also peremptory,[25] such as the right of victims to have access to justice, their right to get full reparation, their right to see the culprits prosecuted and sentenced, the right not to be frustrated by amnesties, etc.
- **Example 2:** if a certain refugee stream was caused by a breach of a peremptory norm, no validation of any new state of affairs may intervene, and only the full return of all refugees could be a remedy (one may think of the Palestinian refugees). An analogous example can be given in terms of a territorial situation, such as that in Kosovo after 1999.[26]
- **Example 3:** if there is a breach of *jus cogens*, all States have a duty to remedy that breach, for example through the exercise of mandatory civil universal jurisdiction. This civil universal jurisdiction then itself becomes at once mandatory and peremptory.[27]

Jus cogens thus irradiates into an indefinable number of corollary normative propositions. The chain of normative causality potentially stretches very far, all the more since no clear restrictive criterion is indicated. One of the main reasons given for this enlarged reach of *jus cogens* is the necessity of overriding effectiveness of international public order. If the consequences of *jus cogens* were not peremptory, breaches and non-applications of such norms could be deprived of their proper sanctioning effects. States could agree differently and compromise in their regard. By not drawing all the consequences from the breach of these norms, the effectiveness of these overriding norms would itself be called into question. Thus: 'If peremptory norms are to operate as norms, not merely as aspirations, they must generate consequences that are themselves peremptory.'[28] Let us note that some other authors have explicitly rejected such a consequential *jus cogens*.[29]

The theory of 'consequential *jus cogens*' seems to the present writer to be the greatest legal and practical mistake ever made in the context of *jus cogens*. The true position is that the consequential effects are simple norms of customary international law, whose existence must be ascertained in every case. It is possible that some of these norms have attained peremptory status. But this would have to be proved case by case through the ordinary means of legal analysis. It could not be deduced from the notion of *jus cogens* itself. The reasons for this conclusion are as follows.

First, positive international law does not evidence the existence of a rule whereby all the possible consequences flowing (or said to flow) from a *jus cogens* norms are

[25] See the statements of Judge Al-Khasawneh, *Arrest Warrant* case [2002] ICJ Rep 2002 98, § 7: 'The effective combating of grave crimes has arguably assumed a *jus cogens* character', a statement which could hardly be vaguer from a legal point of view.

[26] Orakhelashvili (n 1) 449ff.

[27] ibid, 307ff.

[28] ibid, 580.

[29] U Linderfalk, 'The Creation of *Jus Cogens*: Making Sense of Article 53 of the Vienna Convention' (2011) 71 *Zeitschrift für ausländisches öffentliches Recht und Völkerrecht* 376.

themselves peremptory. Such a rule has neither to be written down in a convention nor is it shown in State practice and *opinio juris*. It is moreover wrong to say that State practice and legal opinion are not of the essence in the context of *jus cogens*. To the extent that this latter concept is given a positive law meaning, and not just the fanciful aura of personal belief, it is clearly the legislator who must be heard when determining the four corners of what is, and what is not, peremptoriness.

Second, the consequential rule completely transforms the reach and thus the very notion of peremptoriness. In its inception, this was a rule on the validity of legal acts. With the consequential rule, *jus cogens* is made the epicentre of an unlimited series of positive obligations drawn from the concept itself and imposed upon States without ascertaining their will. In other words, while *jus cogens* was initially a concept with only negative reach, inhibiting the legal act-making power of States through nullities and non-applicabilities, it here becomes the basis for the postulation of a great number of positive duties which revolutionise both international and municipal legal systems.[30] Especially in human rights law, one may easily imagine the extent of 'affirmative action' which could be made mandatory, and by the same token also peremptory, by a simple blow of more or less illuminated whim. To consider that such revolutionary modifications of the law are accepted as pure deductions from the concept of *jus cogens* in itself is at best intellectually dishonest.

Third, from the point of view of legal technique, secondary rules are entirely separate from primary ones. To transfer a particular quality of a primary rule wholesale to all secondary rules without further ado reveals a fundamental misunderstanding of the legal system. Primary rules may be subject to various nullities or to other specific effects. Secondary rules flowing from the primary ones have their own logic and needs. They must accommodate and harmonise new and sometimes concurrent duties (such as a duty to make reparation and an attempt not to burden a State excessively, for example in the context of war reparations). To jump from a law on nullities to a law on positive action without considering the effectively existing rules and practice is unwarranted.

Fourth, if all secondary rules flowing from the operation of *jus cogens* were peremptory, this would lead to excessive rigidity in the application and administration of the law. No compromises of any type could be concluded, as in our example on the return of refugees. This is not only utterly unrealistic but also unjust. International law needs some flexibility in the highly political matters that are affected by public order norms. It does not need less flexibility here, it needs even more. *Jus cogens* should not hamper it or render it impossible. Such a course would be largely self-defeating. Rather than helping to solve problems, *jus cogens*

[30] Authors frequently stress the fact that *jus cogens* cannot become the basis for wide-ranging affirmative action: see O'Connell (n 19) 80. See also Vidmar (n 4) 24; K Schmalenbach, 'Article 53' in O Dörr and K Schmalenbach (eds), *Vienna Convention on the Law of Treaties: A Commentary* (Heidelberg/Dordrecht/London/New York, 2012) 917; JA Carrillo-Salcedo, 'Droit international et souveraineté des Etats' (1996) 257 *Recueil des cours de l'Académie de droit international de La Haye* 140.

would perpetuate and aggravate them. The equities created by longstanding situations on the ground, and also the very complexities of such situations, have to be taken fully and earnestly into account. Thus, all Palestinian refugees will not be able to return to Israel. That would completely upset this State and make of its current majority almost a minority. There are many sensible compromise solutions that can be explored, such as a partial return with monetary compensation for the others, and resettlement of the latter elsewhere. The same is true of reparation for war crimes. It is not proven that a myriad of claims brought to the fore of internal tribunals would be the better course than overall settlements concluded by governments or set up through international schemes, such as the Iraq Compensation Commission.[31] But if the consequences of *jus cogens* were peremptory, any single human right holder could contest the overall settlement reached by agreement and possibly have it voided as being contrary to consequential *jus cogens*. This would reward extremism as against a constructive spirit and the search for workable solutions. Would there be any gain in such a course? And why should a community notion like *jus cogens* serve the stubborn different drummer rather than the mainstream compromise effort?

Fifth, in response to the argument that a *jus cogens* without consequential peremptoriness would not be effective but simply remain in the realm of aspirations, the following must be said. Nullity is an effect that the legal order may attach to a certain legal act. This nullity has its own, distinctive legal effectiveness. To jump from there to the proposition that a host of affirmative actions have to be taken to go beyond that nullity may enhance effectiveness from a certain point of view, but will add nothing or very little to the effectiveness of nullity itself. One cannot therefore say that a legal order without consequential *jus cogens* does not confer any effectiveness on the notion of *jus cogens*. The legislator has the right to consider sufficient this particular nullity effect, without being prepared to venture further. Moreover, if consequential *jus cogens* is accepted, effectiveness may be enhanced from a certain perspective but a series of other disadvantages for the legal system will ensue. The greatest of these is the tendency to a creeping and complete subversion of the legal system, where consequential duties can be invented at all times and at all corners by all sorts of legal operators. By simple proclamation, they could be made peremptory. How such an anarchical, utterly uncertain and progressively rigid system of law could function remains opaque. Thus, consequential *jus cogens* is the best way to throw international law into dysfunction, discredit, decline and derision. States would tend to take many of its parts significantly less seriously than they do today, since such a law would no longer be 'theirs'. It would be strange indeed that the notion of *jus cogens*, which was framed in order to strengthen international law, should at the end of the day have exactly the opposite effect.

[31] On this commission, see eg RB Lillich (ed), *The United Nations Compensation Commission* (New York, 1995); V Jütte, *Die United Nations Compensation Commission* (Bern/Frankfurt, 1999); JA Crook, 'The United Nations Compensation Commission: A New Structure to Enforce State Responsibility' (1993) 87 *American Journal of International Law* 144ff.

III. What Effects Flow from *Jus Cogens*?

There is one effect which is inherent in the notion of *jus cogens*; indeed, we can trace its influence on the notion of peremptoriness as far back as Antiquity. This is the effect of 'nullity' (or inapplicability) of contrary legal acts, an effect that does not need to be specifically justified. It flows directly from *jus cogens*, with the necessary adaptations according to the type of legal order in which the norms at stake are situated. For the domain of treaties, this effect is regulated in Articles 53 and 64 VCLT. For unilateral legal acts, the effect arises by analogy. Some of these unilateral acts are directly linked to the conventional process and here the analogy rests on solid ground: for example, reservations to a treaty, or to optional clauses for the jurisdiction of the ICJ (the latter being based on the Statute, Article 36, § 2). With unilateral legal acts independent of the treaty process, things become slightly less clear. To what extent can recognition of a State (recognition being a legal act) be considered void if it is made notwithstanding that the State was created by a violation of peremptory norms? Recognition itself is attached at its root to a mere fact: the existence of an entity as a State. This, in itself, is not contrary to a *jus cogens* norm, nor could it be. But if there is a duty of non-recognition, recognition made in its violation could be void. This supposes that the duty of non-recognition is peremptory. The recognition would then be contrary to this *jus cogens* norm and voided by its operation. However, State practice is not crystal clear on this point. Instances of recognition have not been voided with the necessary legal clarity. Conversely, the duty of non-recognition has been upheld as a mandatory duty of international law which might be breached. In other words, the responsibility aspect was made clear, but not the nullity aspect. The question is practically important. According to the view taken, the several instances of recognition of Kosovo after 2008 may be void or not. And many other acts of recognition could then stand or fall. The issue was canvassed here only to show that even in the context of legal acts, all the concrete legal effects of *jus cogens* are far from settled and clear.

Then come all the other actual or potential effects which are regularly attached to the notion of *jus cogens* (see above, I). The correct answer in their regard has been given by C Focarelli in his searching and seminal studies on *jus cogens*.[32] The answer is articulated as follows:

— There can be no deductive approaches to further effects of *jus cogens*—the approach must in this context be fully inductive.
— Thus, it is only through examination of State practice and concomitant legal opinion that it is possible to determine whether a particular effect is accepted or not—all these effects must be tested in practice and do not flow from the notion of peremptoriness itself.

[32] See notably Focarelli (n 1) 439ff, 444ff, 450ff, 455ff.

- These effects, if adopted in practice, become free-standing norms of customary international law (determining for example to what extent there is a right to access to justice for victims of international crimes, whether jurisdictional immunities are to be set aside, or whether universal jurisdiction applies).
- Thus, *jus cogens* is in most cases superfluous, since the effects flow from the customary provision and not from the concept of *jus cogens*. The role of peremptoriness will here most often be promotional, that is, used as an argument in favour of the development of new customary effects said to be attached to *jus cogens* requirements.

If deductive reasoning discounting State practice were allowed, this would mean that any legal operator could usurp a far-reaching, if not boundless, legislative function. Like a magician, he could postulate entirely different new obligations for States. This would be an attempt at law-making in disguise and an advanced exercise in legal conceptualism (*Begriffsjurisprudenz*). In a sort of ontogenetic process, any type of consequence could be drawn from the concept of *jus cogens* as varyingly defined by several legal operators. There would barely be any dogmatic limit to the capacity of *jus cogens* to be a free-standing and never-ending source of law and obligations. All types of effects and consequences could be drawn from there, according to the wishes and imagination of the operator, while bypassing any legislative process. Moreover, it would be possible to sweep away or trump almost every 'disturbing' norm of existing positive law by arguing that it is in conflict with some 'hierarchically' superior *jus cogens* … being inherent in and deducible from another *jus cogens* provision. It is not necessary to delve into the depths of one's imagination to see that such a course would completely upset and subvert the system of international law. Moreover, as already mentioned in the previous subsection, such an exercise would deeply discredit international law in the eyes of its 'customers', States, at a time when it is already difficult to sell to them the duties they have assumed through positive and hard law sources. As has been said with some lucidity, one of the major threats to *jus cogens* is the tendency of some of its most fervent supporters to see it everywhere.[33] By closing the gate to such conceptualist and auto-referential legislative exercises, *jus cogens* can be brought back into the realm of effective and positive international law, rather than illusory international law. The acid test is whether a particular consequence is accepted by rules of positive law, either in the context of general international law or in the context of particular international law. What has been said in the preceding lines should not be taken to mean that the judge has no leeway in interpreting norms and their collisions. He or she may do so and may consequently find some effects of *jus cogens* which are not yet completely settled in practice. He or she then contributes to the development of international law. The point is rather that such a judicial function can only be incidental and limited. The judge may take steps forward in grey areas; but he may not invent entirely new obligations.

[33] A Bianchi, 'Human Rights and the Magic of *Jus Cogens*' (2008) 19 *European Journal of International Law* 506.

If the various effects mentioned in the legal literature are tested against this criterion, it will be seen that some effects are not recognised in positive law, while others are partially recognised, and still others are completely recognised. One example for each category may be given.

— **Example 1** (non-recognised effects): the commission of international crimes does not have the effect of casting away the jurisdictional immunities of the State (ICJ, *Jurisdictional Immunities* (2012)).
— **Example 2** (partially recognised effects): international crimes sometimes lead to mandatory universal jurisdiction (for example the grave breaches regime in the Geneva Conventions) and sometimes to optional universal jurisdiction (for example in the context of genocide).[34]
— **Example 3** (fully recognised effects): the nullity or inapplicability of contrary legal acts, especially treaties (such as Article 53 VCLT); and the consequences of that voidness under article 71 VCLT.

For the rest, there remains a political fight for what we believe to be a better international legal order, and the better effects of peremptory norms.

[34] M Henzelin, *Le principe de l'universalité en droit pénal international* (Basel, 2000).

7

A Blind Spot: Conflicts Between *Jus Cogens* Norms

For most authors, the reduction of *jus cogens* to public order norms entails as a consequence that not much reflection is done on potentially conflicting relationships[1] between such norms. These norms seem to pull in the same direction and all have the same aim, namely the supreme realisation of international community values. For a long time, mentions of this issue were only sporadic and in a context of abstract interrogation. In one important textbook of international law one reads:

> [N]or can a rule of customary international law which conflicts with a rule of *ius cogens* continue to exist or subsequently be created (unless it has the character of *ius cogens*, a possibility which raises questions—to which no firm answer can yet be given—of the relationship between rules of *ius cogens*, and of the legitimacy of an act done in reliance on one rule of *ius cogens* but resulting in a violation of another such rule).[2]

It is not possible to state that the issue is completely lacking in practical interest. With the increase in the number of peremptory norms, the problem will probably become even more prominent. For example, with the discussion on humanitarian intervention in the wake of the Kosovo intervention (1999),[3] and later with the emerging concept of 'responsibility to protect',[4] the conflict between non-use of force and human rights has come to the fore. This conflict is nourished on both sides by norms that are said to be peremptory. Notwithstanding its practical interest, there exist only two studies on this question.[5] The time has perhaps come to consider the issue more closely.

[1] For the sake of simplicity, we shall here take the clearest example of conflict, namely the impossibility of applying both norms at the same time to the same set of facts, to which they formally apply.

[2] L Oppenheim, *International Law* (ed RY Jennings and A Watts), 9th edn, vol I (London, 1992) 8. Other authors have mentioned the problem but have not ventured into a closer analysis. See, eg, J Charpentier, 'Discussion' in Société française pour le droit international (ed), Colloque de Toulouse, *L'élaboration du droit international public* (Paris, 1975) 215 (non-use of force and humanitarian intervention); I Brownlie, *Principles of Public International Law*, 4th edn (Oxford, 1990) 515.

[3] See the literature mentioned in V Lowe and A Tzanakopoulos, 'Humanitarian Intervention' in R Wolfrum (ed), *The Max Planck Encyclopedia of Public International Law*, vol V (Oxford, 2012) 47ff.

[4] See the summing-up of former UN legal advisor N Michel, 'La responsabilité de protéger: une vue d'ensemble assortie d'une perspective Suisse' (2012) 131 *Revue de droit suisse* 5ff.

[5] R Kolb, 'Conflits entre normes de *jus cogens*' in *Essays in Honor of J Salmon* (*Droit du pouvoir, pouvoir du droit*) (Brussels, 2007) 481ff; and JE Christofolo, 'Solving Antinomies between Peremptory Norms in Public International Law', PhD thesis (Geneva, 2014).

As well as theoretical and practical interest, there is also an opportunity to cast new light on the notion of *jus cogens* when considered from a different angle to the usual ones. The question will here be approached from the broad perspective taken by this monograph, with *jus cogens* not limited to public order norms but encompassing public utility *jus cogens* and norms which are logically non-derogable.

Considering this notion of peremptoriness, the conflicts can occur in different sets of relations:

(i) two norms of public order *jus cogens* conflict with one another;
(ii) two norms of public utility *jus cogens* conflict with one another;
(iii) a norm of public order *jus cogens* conflicts with a norm of public utility *jus cogens* or vice versa;
(iv) a norm of public order *jus cogens* conflicts with a logically non-derogable rule or vice versa;
(v) a rule of public utility *jus cogens* conflicts with a logically non-derogable rule or vice versa.

We will ignore other broader conceptualisations, which consider for example that Article 103 of the United Nations Charter (UNC) is a type of *jus cogens*.[6] As is immediately apparent, categories (iv) and (v) are of no practical interest. The very few logically non-derogable norms do not conflict with public order or public utility *jus cogens* norms, and are not expected to do so in the future. Category (iii) may have a certain scope of application, but true conflicts will be almost non-existent. Categories (i) and (ii) make most sense. Let us thus break the analysis down into three sub-sections: first, possible conflicts between public order and public utility *jus cogens*; secondly, conflicts between public utility *jus cogens*; and thirdly, conflicts between public order *jus cogens*.

Before entering into the analysis, it may be useful to emphasise that the issues at stake are not limited as to how to solve such conflicts. In many cases, the gist of the matter lies in the determination of whether there is a conflict at all.[7] This latter point is frequently insufficiently clear in particular cases. As we will see in the following sub-sections, it is often difficult to delineate a conflict between public order norms. The conflict is on many occasions only apparent. If one looks more closely, a series of concrete rules must be found to exist before being able to articulate a clear-cut conflict. However, these concrete rules do not always exist in positive international law. The problem of conflicts between *jus cogens* norms does not thereby disappear. It is at most reduced in scope. The precise meaning of the last sentences will become apparent in what follows.

Finally, it stands to reason that many examples of actual or potential conflicts can be imagined and canvassed. However, only a few will be presented in the narrow compass of this monograph.

[6] See the references in R Kolb, 'L'article 103 de la Charte des Nations Unies' (2013) 367 *Recueil des cours de l'Académie de droit international de La Haye* 86ff.

[7] On conflicts of norms in international law, see in particular J Pauwelyn, *Conflict of Norms in Public International Law* (Cambridge, 2003).

I. Conflicts Between Public Order *Jus Cogens* and Public Utility *Jus Cogens*

Conflicts between normative propositions of these two classes are not common, but they may occur. A classic example is the opposition between the duty to provide remedies for breaches of fundamental norms (notably international crimes) and the jurisdiction of international tribunals, such as the International Court of Justice (ICJ). We may here suppose that both norms have a peremptory aspect: the first would be of public order *jus cogens* (if the rule exists at all) and the second of public utility *jus cogens*, since it is regulated by the Statute of the ICJ (Article 36). The Court cannot depart from the rule of the Statute, even if the parties to the dispute wish to do so by agreement. The problem of the 'conflict' of fundamental norms with the consensual jurisdiction of the ICJ came to the fore in the *East Timor* case (1995). There, the Court refused to trump the rules on its competence in order to give priority to fundamental norms. It expressed the point as follows:

> [T]he Court considers that the *erga omnes* character of a norm and the rule of consent to jurisdiction are two different things. Whatever the nature of the obligations invoked, the Court could not rule on the lawfulness of the conduct of a State when its judgment would imply an evaluation of the lawfulness of the conduct of another State which is not a party to the case.[8]

The Court thus dissociated the two aspects and refused to give a sweeping priority to the public order aspect of the dispute over the requirements of its Statute. This stance has been criticised by some authors.[9] Two positions were thus crystallised in this context: either (i) public order *jus cogens* must impact on the procedural law of the Court by virtue of its superior ('higher law') status; or (ii) the public order *jus cogens* cannot displace the proper integrity of public utility *jus cogens*, at least in the context of the ICJ Statute. The Court and mainstream opinion sustain the second solution.

The true question, however, is whether there is a conflict of norms at all. Certainly, the issue has been presented in this way. But following a meticulous analysis of the respective scopes of application of the two sets of normative propositions, it becomes apparent that these rules do not conflict. Rather, they apply parallel to one another, each in its context. It is in particular not true that the two cannot be simultaneously applied. The legal point is that fundamental norms do not create automatically and by themselves the jurisdiction of any particular organ.

8 [1995] ICJ Rep 102, § 29.

9 C Chinkin, 'The Right to Self-Determination in International Law: Its Development and Future' in P Alston (ed), *People's Rights* (Oxford, 2001) 7ff; C Chinkin, 'The East Timor Case' (1996) 45 *International and Comparative Law Quarterly* 712ff. Contra: H Thirlway, 'The Law and Procedure of the International Court of Justice: Questions of Jurisdiction and Competence, 1954–1989' (1998) 69 *British Yearbook of International Law* 52.

The gist of the matter is consequently that fundamental norms may have *jus cogens* quality (non-derogability, etc) but they do not have as a recognised legal effect the creation of a competence. The latter depends on the constitutive instruments of the various organs. There is thus no real conflict here between *jus cogens* propositions. Such a conflict would only occur if there was a public order rule of international law that required any international organ to assume jurisdiction in respect of such breaches, and if moreover this rule were peremptory. In this case we would have a clear-cut conflict between the described public order *jus cogens* rule and the public utility integrity of the Statute and the rules sustaining the latter. In this case, perhaps, the public order rule would prevail as a matter of contextual interpretation. Compare the different situation under present international law: there are rules of public order which have certain specific consequences, but not one of creating a jurisdiction; and there are separate rules governing the jurisdiction of tribunals. The two sets of rules do not conflict in any meaningful way. Fundamental norms have their ordinary consequences and rules on jurisdiction continue to apply on their own account. This is not even an issue of *limitation* of fundamental norms by rules on jurisdiction. It is rather a matter of *application* of rules on jurisdiction to fundamental norms, to the extent that the latter have not yet carved out an exception in this regard. Further normative developments must first take place before a true conflict can be delineated here.

II. Conflicts Between Public Utility *Jus Cogens* Norms

Assuming that not all norms of the United Nations Charter (UNC) and not all norms of international humanitarian law (IHL) are public order *jus cogens* norms, conflicts that occur between them may be framed, at least in part, as conflicts between public utility *jus cogens*. The latter are legal regimes imbued with mechanisms to preserve a particular normative unity. For the UNC, this non-derogatory regime comes down to the fact that the Charter is the constitutive instrument of an international organisation. Such an instrument is by its statutory nature not derogable into *leges speciales inter partes*. The non-derogable nature of the regime also flows in part from Article 103 UNC,[10] which upholds the unity and priority of the UNC in the context of the obligations of Member States. For IHL, this *jus cogens* regime is plainly situated between public utility (Articles 6/6/6/7 GC I–IV) and public order (fundamental humanitarian rules). Now, true conflicts may occur, especially when the Security Council (SC) adopts binding Chapter VII resolutions. The question is then concretely the extent to which the SC can derogate from IHL in its Chapter VII action. The issue is too complex to be fully pursued here.

[10] On the scope of this provision see Kolb (n 6) 25ff.

The general view on the matter is that the SC must respect international *jus cogens*.[11] But a problem stems from the fact that legal doctrine considers only public order *jus cogens* norms; and that even in this narrow compass, the issue of which norms of IHL are public order *jus cogens* for the SC remains controversial and uncertain. There are different schools of thought in this regard:

(i) Maximalists[12] consider that the UN SC must respect IHL in its entirety; this conclusion is founded mainly on common Article 1 of the GC, the duty to respect IHL 'in all circumstances' being interpreted as extending to the SC.
(ii) Minimalists[13] consider that the SC must respect only the core guarantees of IHL, notably common Article 3 of the four Geneva Conventions.
(iii) Moderates[14] consider that the SC may derogate from a series of IHL norms, but that it cannot do so for IHL public order norms; the latter are all the rules with a humanitarian aim that is, the rules situated in the context of protection of persons and the conduct of hostilities.

There are thus three views on the reach of *jus cogens* with respect to the SC and in consequence three views about the delineation of conflicts between such norms. Manifestly, there is also a series of intermediate views.

At first sight, it might be concluded that the quality of '*jus cogens*' potentially ascribed to the two sides of the equation is of little help. The question would rather turn on the most correct interpretation of the two normative realms: on the one hand the extent of the powers of the SC under Chapter VII, including issues of necessity and proportionality; and on the other hand the differentiation of IHL norms according to their protective importance. Harmonisation between these potentially or actually conflicting normative circles would, on this view, have to be performed largely in the same way as if the two sets of propositions were not labelled as *jus cogens*. Both normative circles are imbued with public interest (and even to some extent public order interests), and both are considered by the legislator to be worthy of being given priority and to be protected in their normative unity. For the UNC regime, this flows from the paramount importance of the maintenance or restoration of peace and security; for IHL it lies in the protection of vulnerable persons. However, *jus cogens* seems all the same to enter the equation

[11] See generally A Peters, 'Article 25' in B Simma, D Erasmus-Khan, G Nolte and A Paulus (eds), *The Charter of the United Nations: A Commentary*, 3rd edn, vol I (Oxford, 2012) 818–19; E de Wet, *The Chapter VII Powers of the United Nations Security Council* (Oxford/Portland, 2004) 187ff; A Tzanakopoulos, *Disobeying the Security Council* (Oxford, 2011) 70–72. As to the case law, see eg the *Yusuf* and the *Kadi* decisions of the European Court of First Instance (2005) 149 ILR 237, 296–97, 230. See also the Swiss Federal Tribunal's practice: *A c Seco*, arrêt du Tribunal fédéral suisse du 22 avril 2008, § 5.4; affaire *Nada c Seco*, arrêt du Tribunal fédéral suisse du 14 novembre 2007, § 5.3.

[12] L Condorelli, 'Le Statut des Forces des Nations Unies et le droit international humanitaire' in C Emanuelli (ed), *Les casques bleus: policiers ou combattants?* (Montreal, 1997) 105–06.

[13] B Tittemore, 'Belligerents in Blue Helmets: Applying International Humanitarian Law to United Nations Peace Operations' (1997) 33 *Stanford Journal of International Law* 105–06.

[14] D Schindler, 'Probleme des humanitären Völkerrechts und der Neutralität im Golfkonflikt 1990/1991' (1991) 1 *Revue suisse de droit international et européen* 12.

through the sweeping phrase according to which the SC cannot ignore, derogate from, violate, etc *jus cogens*. Translated into legal terms, this means that the fundamental nature of UNC law does not reach so far as to allow the brushing aside of other *jus cogens* norms, including those under IHL. The question boils down to how widely or narrowly these other norms are to be defined. As to this crucial question there is no consensus.[15] In short, the conflict, to the extent that it exists, is solved by this meta-rule on the competence of the Council in favour of the 'other *jus cogens* norms'. They limit the competence of the Council and entail the nullity of the operative parts[16] of its resolution contrary to such norms. In still briefer terms, there exists in positive international law a special rule for the solution of this conflict. But the rule indicates only a formal solution, not a substantive one. The latter has to be reached by interpretation in every single case, by determining the proper scope of application of the norms in conflict. In this latter context the label of *jus cogens* is of only limited use. This is true all the more since there is a presumption of validity of resolutions of the SC.[17]

III. Conflicts Between Public Order *Jus Cogens* Norms

We are now reaching the core of the problem. The most salient problems presented by *jus cogens* norm conflicts are situated here.[18] We face clear-cut oppositions or antimonies, with two *dramatis personae* apparently irremediably facing each other. The two most famous examples are the conflict between peremptory non-use of force and peremptory fundamental human rights (such as prohibition of genocide) to be protected if necessary by military intervention, in short the issue of humanitarian intervention; and the right to self-determination of peoples and the prohibition on territorial acquisition through the use of force, in other words the issue of compromise agreements for the settlement of complex territorial issues, such as the Israeli/Palestinian conflict. Clearly, the legal conflicts have to be worked out in a precise way. Moreover, the existence of the relevant norms in positive international law must in the first place be established (since otherwise there could be no conflict). This is what the following paragraphs will attempt to do.

A. 'Humanitarian Intervention'/'Responsibility to Protect'

Simply stated, the antinomy here is between the non-use of force rule, which knows of no exception for human rights, and the active protection of the most

[15] With regard to occupation in Iraq, see eg R Kolb, 'Occupation in Iraq since 2003 and the Powers of the UN Security Council' (2008) 90 *International Review of the Red Cross* 29ff.

[16] If severability is here admitted, contrary to what is suggested for treaties in Art 44, § 5 VCLT.

[17] See notably the *Certain Expenses* Advisory Opinion [1962] ICJ Rep 167ff and the famous Separate Opinion of Morelli at 219ff.

[18] Christofolo (n 5) focuses on these conflicts.

fundamental rights of human persons, for example against the commission of genocide or massacres, if necessary by using a proportionate amount of force.[19] Conflicts between these two norms may occur in different settings. Either the non-use of force rule is a binding prohibition and the human protection rule is a mere legal faculty, which can but must not be exercised by States; or alternatively the norm on human protection is also framed as an internationally recognised duty to act, possibly imbued with peremptory status. In this latter case, a duty to act would directly conflict with a duty to abstain. In reality, there is much doubt as to the existence of a rule *allowing* for the use of force in such situations;[20] even more doubtful is the existence of a rule *requiring* the use of force. Conversely, if the rule on human protection is negated in the sense that it does not encompass a licence or a duty to use force, the antinomy disappears. If we assume for the sake of our argument that some rule on human protection exists in such extreme contexts, either as a faculty or as a duty, how is the antinomy to be solved?

State practice and concomitant legal opinion by the subjects of law have made it possible to determine how that conflict has to be composed in the realm of positive law. The balancing process is as follows. *First*, the overwhelming majority of States (notably the so-called Group of 77) have emphatically rejected the idea that one State or a self-proclaimed coalition of States can intervene militarily in another State without the latter's consent, even if massacres are being perpetrated there.[21] There are many arguments in favour of this position, in particular the fact that in view of the chronic instability of many States and the open-ended spectrum of possible triggering situations, a power to intervene militarily would destabilise the international system and open the gates to subjective, pretexted and power-policy interventions. *Second*, the same overwhelming majority of States accept the recent Chapter VII UNC interpretation which gives the Security Council the power (and morally the duty) to take collective measures in order to prevent, to halt and to remedy such gross human rights violations (today under the banner of the 'Responsibility to Protect').[22] In other words, the faculty or duty

[19] The conflict is well described in C Tomuschat, 'International Law: Ensuring the Survival of Mankind on the Eve of a New Century: General Course of Public International Law' (1999) 281 *Recueil des cours de l'Académie de droit international de La Haye* 218ff.

[20] See the solid arguments of O Corten, *Le droit contre la guerre* (Paris, 2008) 801ff. Contra, postulating a duty of assistance: FR Tesón, *Humanitarian Intervention: An Inquiry into Law and Morality*, 2nd edn (New York, 1997). Military intervention is then limited to an *extrema ratio*: see eg the position of the Dutch Government in (2003) 34 *Netherlands Yearbook of International Law* 285, 290, 292.

[21] Ministerial Declaration of the Meeting of Foreign Ministers of the Group of 77, New York, 24 September 1999, www.g77.org/Docs/decl1999.html. See also the World Summit Outcome Document 2005: UN Doc A/60/L.1, Resolution of 24 October 2005, §§ 138–39. See C Focarelli, 'La dottrina della "responsabilità di proteggere" e l'intervento umanitario' (2008) 91 *Rivista di diritto internazionale* 317ff.

[22] This evolution started in the 1990s: M Zambelli, *La constatation des situations de l'article 39 de la Charte des Nations Unies par le Conseil de sécurité* (Basel/Geneva, 2003) 286ff, 326ff. See now C Stahn, 'Responsibility to Protect: Political Rhetoric or Emerging Legal Norm?' (2007) 101 *American Journal of International Law* 99ff; C Verlage, *Responsibility to Protect: Ein neuer Ansatz im Völkerrecht zur Verhinderung von Völkermord, Kriegsverbrechen und Verbrechen gegen die Menschlichkeit* (Tübingen, 2008); AJ Bellamy, *A Responsibility to Protect: The Global Effort to End Mass Atrocities* (Cambridge, 2009);

to act is transferred from the plane of States taken individually to the plane of the organised community acting through its 'executive' organ, the UN SC (or theoretically, with the 'Uniting for Peace' Resolution 377 of 1950, through the UN General Assembly). It will be noted that this balancing process has been performed by the 'legislator', that is, States, and not by a judge. The two imperatives are taken into account and harmonised through an interpretation which upholds the non-use of force rule and acknowledges at the same time the necessity to act. The solution is found along the lines of differentiating the actors called to deal with the humanitarian urgency. The situation where the Security Council is unable or unwilling to act, notably because of some veto, clearly still looms. But even in such cases, the law of the UN provides for some means of collective redress, such as the Dean Acheson Resolution (Uniting for Peace)—even if that resolution has largely been idle for many years. It is therefore possible to say that the human protection rule has carved out from the non-use of force rule a power of the SC to act, thereby pushing back the non-intervention in internal affairs rule; conversely the non-use of force rule has carved out from the human protection rule the anarchic right of unilateral intervention. Whether that is the most sensible method of harmonising the two sets of rules is up for discussion. But it is the method States have chosen, and it thus reflects the positive law of the day.

Summing up this first example, it can be seen that the *jus cogens* nature of the two norms has not played any direct role in the balancing process, but perhaps for the care with which it has to be conducted in view of the importance of the legal positions at stake. This is hardly surprising. If both norms to be balanced are public order (*jus cogens*) norms, this quality cannot determine the outcome. In particular, any hierarchical arguments are unavailable. It might be otherwise only if legal doctrine or international practice devises some hierarchy *within and among* public order norms, which is not the case to date and is hardly imaginable in the near future. Since such a prioritisation rule does not exist, the peremptory or public order quality disappears in the equation, exactly as constants can be bracketed out in mathematics. It is thus the substance of the rules that directly interacts. A solution has to be found by way of a harmonising legal interpretation. Any good ideas regarding the most reasonable conciliation of concurrent legal positions will be rewarded by legal emulation. In municipal law, the process is exactly the same. Thus, when tribunals consider conflicts between constitutional norms or between different human rights norms (which under municipal law are clearly *jus cogens*),

A Rausch, *Responsibility to Protect: Eine juristische Betrachtung* (Frankfurt, 2011); I Winkelmann, 'Responsibility to Protect' in R Wolfrum (ed), *The Max Planck Encyclopedia of Public International Law*, vol VIII (Oxford, 2012) 965ff; WA Knight and F Egerton (eds), *Handbook on the Responsibility to Protect* (London, 2012); J Genser and I Cotler (eds), *The Responsibility to Protect: The Promise of Stopping Mass Atrocities in our Time* (New York, 2012); Michel (n 4) 5ff; M Labonte, *Human Rights and Humanitarian Norms, Strategic Framing, and Intervention: Lessons from the Responsibility to Protect* (London, 2013); G Zyberi (ed), *An Institutional Approach to the Responsibility to Protect* (Cambridge, 2013); C Sampford and RC Thakur (eds), *Responsibility to Protect and Sovereignty* (Farnham, 2013); L Glanville, *Sovereignty and the Responsibility to Protect* (Chicago/London, 2014).

the point is not to derive some answer from their peremptory character. The gist of the matter lies rather in balancing the competing legal positions and finding a way out of the quagmire through sensitive and sensible interpretive solutions. This is the case, for example, in the construction of anti-terrorist legislation and competing legislation as to the protection of the personal data of citizens. Neither normative realm is *jus dispositivum* and both have to be actively harmonised regarding their various points of friction and antinomy.

B. Non-Recognition of Territorial Situations Obtained by Force and Self-Determination of Peoples

The main situation to be considered here is a clash between a territorial situation obtained by force (such as the Palestinian occupied territories as the outcome of the 1967 War) and the possibility of the people enjoying self-determination, here the Palestinians, to accept some form of compromise on the final territorial status through an agreement with the occupying power. Note that the initial use of force need not be unlawful; it may have occurred in self-defence. What is unlawful is to annex or to keep hold of territories acquired by warfare.[23] Thus, in the search for a peaceful solution, it has been envisaged that a part of the Palestinian occupied territory could be ceded to Israel as a concession towards a final peace agreement.[24] If these territorial cessions are not significant in number and extension—but serve to provide reasonable answers to situations created on the ground in the now almost 50 years of occupation—it would be foolish to rule them out sweepingly and rigidly. However, a conflict of *jus cogens* positions might occur here: could it be said that any agreement whose content is based on some compromise regarding territory unlawfully acquired as a consequence of the use of force must be considered void (to the extent that the non-use of force rule with its peremptory character extends that far)?

In order to construe this question as a matter of conflicting *jus cogens*, the following interpretation is necessary. On the one hand, the peremptory non-use of force rule has to be regarded as reaching to a prohibition on any territorial

[23] The rule against annexation flows from both the non-use of force and the self-determination rules. See Oppenheim (n 2) vol I pt 2 698ff; R Hofmann, 'Annexation' in R Wolfrum (ed), *The Max Planck Encyclopedia of Public International Law*, vol I (Oxford, 2012) 408ff, with many further references.

[24] Agreements concluded between occupied peoples and occupying powers, such as the Oslo Agreements between the Palestinians and Israel, also pose some problems with regard to peremptory rules of the law of occupation, notably under Art 47 GC IV. Here too some interpretive flexibility is necessary: see R Kolb, 'Etude sur l'occupation et sur l'article 47 de la Convention de Genève IV de 1949 relative à la protection des personnes civiles en temps de guerre: le degré de l'intangibilité des droits en territoire occupé' (2002) 10 *Annuaire africain de droit international* 267ff. A stricter position is taken by J Quigley, 'The PLO-Israeli Interim Agreements and the Geneva Civilians Convention' in S Bowen (ed), *Human Rights, Self-Determination and Political Change in the Occupied Palestinian Territories* (The Hague/Boston/London, 1997) 25ff, in a very interesting study.

disposition if that would *indirectly* condone the acquisition of that territory by force. Some degree of indirect reach is indeed necessary here, since legally the acquisition of the territory by the former occupier would be based directly on the later agreement and only indirectly on the former use of force. But if the agreement is considered void because of some 'fruit of the poisonous tree' doctrine, the peremptory status of the norm extends to all consequential dispositions of the territory. The situation can be cured only by full and integral restitution of the territory to the lawful owner. Does the international norm against territorial statuses obtained by force extend that far? The issue is not clear cut, but we may assume such a reach here for the sake of our argument. On the other hand, the self-determination of peoples would have to be construed as containing some positive rights of the peoples at stake, in this context the right to determine their territorial status in order to reach a peace agreement according to their free will. If this rule is accepted and considered peremptory, then the people with the right to self-determination has a non-censurable right to dispose of this matter according to its free and uninfluenced will. If both hypotheses are made, a conflict between peremptory norms appears. How, then, is this to be solved?

In this case, there is no international practice which can give a positive law answer by the 'legislator', as was the case with the so-called humanitarian intervention analysed above. This is understandable: we are dealing here with a series of particular territorial situations which are quite different on the facts. If harmonisation had to be achieved, the principle of proportionality would have to play a fundamental role. The proper scope of each of the principles and rules in conflict should be limited as little as possible; the attempt should be to leave to each of them the greatest possible scope. Concretely, the balancing process should be based on the following elements:[25]

- The agreement must provide for a final and workable peace, with the mutual recognition of both peoples.
- The territorial adjustments must be quantitatively and qualitatively 'non-meaningful', that is, minimal; they should be geared mainly towards the solution of practical problems and take into account of equities on the ground.
- There should be an overall consultative process of the Palestinian people in the exercise of its right of self-determination.
- There should be support for this compromise regime on the part of the international community through the UN (external control).

These criteria do not reflect any existing positive law. But they are useful rationalisations of what would be required for a sensible solution. These criteria would have to be implemented in the international political process.

[25] See Christofolo (n 5) 324.

It will be noted that once again the public order character (and *jus cogens* character) of the norms at stake has played no definable role in the solution of the conflict. The polestar of the balancing process has been the effort to maintain as much as possible of the two concurrent legal positions, under the aegis of the principles of necessity and proportionality. Once again, if the conflict is between public order norms the public order quality cannot itself tilt the balance, since its weight is placed on both sides. It is therefore through a complex interpretive process—which is the core of all legal activity—that a solution has first to be found, then devised and finally realised, always to the extent feasible. The process then links to, and indeed harks back to, international politics.

8

Conclusion

To conclude this study, the main results reached may be briefly recalled and the most significant elements of the notion of *jus cogens* summed up.

First, there can be no doubt as to the necessity of the notion of *jus cogens* in a fully fledged legal order whose development has moved beyond the most primitive stages.[1] Even lock, stock and barrel positivists such as Guggenheim and Marek[2] lucidly admitted this fact without much ado. In a developed and complex society, it is necessary to have articulated legal tools in order to achieve various desired legislative results. One of them—and a legitimate one—is to maintain the normative unity of legal regimes.

Second, the gist of *jus cogens* lies in the protection of the unity of general legal regimes *ratione personarum* against their splitting up into a series of special laws applicable on a priority basis between some parties. Conversely, it is doubtful to try to identify *jus cogens* with public order norms. The latter norms exist, but

[1] AD McNair, *The Law of Treaties* (Oxford, 1961) 213–14: 'It is difficult to imagine any society, whether of individuals or of States, whose law sets no limit whatever to freedom of contract. In every civilized community there are some rules of law and some principles of morality which individuals are not permitted by law to ignore or to modify by their agreements'; HB Reimann, *Jus Cogens im Völkerrecht* (Zurich, 1971) 41; J Jurt, *Zwingendes Völkerrecht: Ein Beitrag zur lehre vom objektiven Völkerrecht* (Wil (St Gallen), 1933) 91ff; M Schweitzer, 'Ius Cogens im Völkerrecht' (1971) 15 *Archiv des Völkerrechts* 197, 202; G Zotiades, 'Staatsautonomie und die Grenzen der Vertragsfreiheit im Völkerrecht' (1967) 17 *Oesterreichische Zeitschrift für öffentliches Recht* 90, 111; A Miaja de la Muela, 'Ius cogens y ius dispositivum en derecho internacional publico' in *Essays in Honor of L Legaz y Lacambra*, vol II (Zaragoza, 1960) 1121, 1126 (a purely dispositive legal order would amount to a series of pieces of advice rather than to a system of rules); EP Nicoloudis, *La nullité de jus cogens et le développement contemporain du droit international public* (Athens, 1974) 37; A Gomez Robledo, 'Le *jus cogens* international: sa genèse, sa nature, ses fonctions' (1981-III) 172 *Recueil des cours de l'Académie de droit international de La Haye* 9, 204ff; MM Magallona, 'The Concept of *Jus Cogens* in the Vienna Convention on the Law of Treaties' in J Scott Davidson (ed), *The Law of Treaties* (Aldershot, 2004) 495; Z Drnas De Clément, 'Las normas imperativas de derecho internacional general (*jus cogens*). Dimension sustancial' in Z Drnas de Clément (ed), *Estudios de derecho internacional en homenja al professor EJ Rey Caro*, vol I (Cordoba, 2002) 647, 663; L Haopei, '*Jus Cogens* and International law' in S Yee and W Tieya (eds), *International Law in the Post-Cold War World: Essays in Memory of Li Haopei* (London, 2001) 521; D Carreau, *Droit international*, 4th edn (Paris, 1994) 72; JA Barberis, 'Le concept de "traité international" et ses limites' (1984) 30 *Annuaire français de droit international* 263.

[2] P Guggenheim and K Marek, 'Verträge, Völkerrechtliche' in K Strupp and HJ Schlochauer (eds), *Wörterbuch des Völkerrechts*, 2nd edn, vol III (Berlin, 1962) 532: no legal order can be composed only of dispositive norms.

jus cogens is just one technical consequence of their need for normative unity. The damaging identification between the two has closed the door to other types of *jus cogens*, namely that based on simple public utility or interest. There are thus two basic types of non-derogable or *jus cogens* norms: public order *jus cogens* and public utility *jus cogens*. Both converge in terms of legal technique (maintenance of the unity of the legal regime, ruling out of the *lex specialis* rule) but differ as to policy aspects (fundamental norms/ordinary norms).

Third, *jus cogens* is a part of positive international law and is subject to the rules of functioning of this legal order as well as to its legal environment. In this complexion, it must be seen as an operational concept of law and not as a vehicle for subjective manipulation towards ideological ends or as a grandiloquent receptacle of lofty ideas. The latter, to the extent they are cherished, must be mainly brought to bear in the political process and in the struggle for *lex ferenda*.

Fourth, the best avenue is to give a fairly restrictive reading of public order *jus cogens*. That it exists and to some extent has managed to limit all too insolent positivism ('States may agree on any object whatsoever') is true. But the victory should not be pushed too far, lest it transform itself into a Pyrrhic one. The subjects of law, especially States, with their sovereignty and beliefs, must be able to live in peace with the concept and its ramifications. That this concept opposes some resistance to some misplaced intention of some State(s) is entirely in order. But if the notion is pushed too far, it will backfire. The danger of a 'do-gooder' *jus cogens* is that it may discredit the concept entirely and allow power politics to exact an all too easy revenge. The same problem does not appear for public utility *jus cogens*, where the legal technique aspect is at its peak. Here, the concept of *jus cogens* finds a significant room, which is entirely neglected by mainstream thinkers, obsessed as they are with the 'fundamental values' discourse.

Fifth, the notion of *jus cogens* raises some important and highly complex problems of construction and administration of the international legal system and its norms. Practice and writings have not yet adequately explored, and even less found reasonable answers to, all the lingering problems in this area. The question of the length of the link of causality between a breach of *jus cogens* norms and subsequent events, and the concomitant interrogation as to the concrete reach of peremptory duties, is one such question. We may here recall the current territorial status of Kosovo and its more or less direct link with the unlawful use of force in 1999. Such difficult issues will need to be explored more fully if the concept of public order *jus cogens* is to gain more weight in international affairs. Critics of peremptory norms have voiced concerns in this regard which deserve to be taken very seriously.

Overall, when the notion of *jus cogens* is on the whole perceived more than is the case today as a simple legal technique and not as a dramatic (or threatening) magic, when it thus starts its descent over the horizon of the most heated scholarly debates, an important leap forward will have been made and the notion will have gained maturity. However, it will never come full circle to the obscure quietness of its beginnings before 1969. A notion that insolently interrogates and opposes arrogant State power can never live a quiet life in serene skies. Clouds and storms are inseparable from various aspects of public order peremptory law; these are and will remain the most visible side of the concept, even if public utility *jus cogens* is statistically more frequent. However, is that not one reason to be fascinated by a notion which is at once combating Antigone in public policy and administering Penelope in legal technique?

SELECT BIBLIOGRAPHY

This bibliography contains only books and articles on the notion of *jus cogens*. The extremely large corpus of studies on the notion of peremptory law explains the limitation of this bibliography to those books and articles which deal with *jus cogens* in general, to the exclusion of the many studies dealing with sectorial aspects of peremptory norms, such as *jus cogens* and State immunities or *jus cogens* and environmental law. The reader will find such additional references, where necessary, in the footnotes. For further bibliographic references, see www.ppl.nl, under 'catalogue'.

Books and Theses

Cançado Trindade, AA, 'Jus Cogens: The Determination and the Gradual Expansion of its Material Content in Contemporary International Case Law' in *XXXV Curso de derecho internacional organizado por el Comite Juridico Interamericano* (2008) (Washington, DC, 2009).

Casado Raigon, R, *Notas sobre el ius cogens internacional* (Cordoba, 1999).

Christofolo, JE, 'Solving Antinomies between Peremptory Norms in Public International Law', PhD thesis (Geneva, 2014).

Diaconu, I, *Contribution à une étude sur les norms imperatives en droit international (jus cogens)* (Geneva/Bucharest, 1971).

Fröhlich, M, 'Die Sittlichkeit in völkerrechtlichen Verträgen', PhD thesis (Zurich, 1924).

Hannikainen, L, *Peremptory Norms (Jus Cogens) in International Law: Historical Development, Criteria, Present Status* (Helsinki, 1988).

Jacovides, AJ, *Treaties Conflicting with Peremptory Norms of International Law and the Zurich/London-Agreements* (Nicosia, 1966).

Jurt, J, *Zwingendes Völkerrecht: Ein Beitrag zur lehre vom objektiven Völkerrecht* (Wil (St Gallen), 1933).

Kadelbach, S, *Zwingendes Völkerrecht* (Berlin, 1992).

Knuchel, S, *Jus Cogens: Identification and Enforcement of Peremptory Norms* (Zurich, 2015).

Kolb, R, *Théorie du jus cogens international* (Paris, 2001).

Koloma, EJB, 'Kritische Analyse bürgerlicher Auffassungen über das ius cogens im Völkerrecht der Gegenwart', PhD thesis (Leipzig, 1981).

Lagonissi Conference, Carnegie Endowment for International Peace (ed), *The Concept of Jus Cogens in Public International Law: Papers and Proceedings* (Geneva, 1967).

Maia, C, 'Le concept de jus cogens en droit international public', PhD thesis (University of Bourgogne, 2006).

Martensen, J, '*Ius Cogens* im Völkerrecht — Gibt es bindende Normen des Völkerrechts die durch völkerrechtliche Verträge nicht aufgehoben warden können?', PhD thesis (Hamburg, 1971).

Nicoloudis, EP, *La nullité de jus cogens et le développement contemporain du droit international public* (Athens, 1974).
Orakhelashvili, A, *Peremptory Norms in International Law* (Oxford, 2006).
Pastor Ridruejo, JA, *La determinación del contenido del ius cogens* (Madrid, 1972).
Reimann, HB, *Jus Cogens im Völkerrecht* (Zurich, 1971) 41.
Rivier, R, 'Droit impératif et juridiction internationale', PhD thesis (Paris II, 2001).
Rozakis, C, The Concept of Jus Cogens in the Law of Treaties (Amsterdam/New York/ Oxford, 1976).
Sztucki, J, *Jus Cogens and the Vienna Convention on the Law of Treaties: A Critical Appraisal* (Vienna/New York, 1974).
Zotiades, GB, *To anakastikon diethnes demosion dikaion* [The peremptory international law] (Thessaloniki, 1968).

Articles and Book Chapters

Aberkane, A, 'La règle du jus cogens international: son rôle dans le droit international' (1970) 7 *Revue Algérienne de Sciences Juridiques, Economiques et Politiques* 9.
Alexidse, L, 'Legal Nature of *Jus Cogens* in Contemporary International Law' (1981-III) 172 *Recueil des cours de l'Académie de droit international de La Haye* 219.
Barberis, JA, 'La liberté de traiter des états et le *jus cogens*' (1970) 30 *Zeitschrift für ausländisches öffentliches Recht und Völkerrecht* 44.
Barnidge, R, 'Questioning the Legitimacy of *Jus Cogens* in the Global Legal Order' (2008) 38 *Israel Yearbook on Human Rights* 199.
Bernardini, A, 'Qualche riflessione su norme internazionali di *jus cogens* e giurisdizione della corte nella Convenzione di Vienna sul diritto dei trattati' (1975) XIV *Comunicazioni e studi* 81.
Bernstorff, J von, 'Kerngehaltsschutz durch den UN-Menschenrechtsausschuss und den EGMR' (2011) 50 *Der Staat* 165.
Bianchi, A, 'Human Rights and the Magic of *Jus Cogens*' (2008) 19 *European Journal of International Law* 491.
Byers, M, 'Conceptualizing the Relationship between Jus Cogens and Erga Omnes Rules' (1997) 66 *Nordic Journal of International Law* 211.
Caicedo Perdomo, JJ, 'La teoria del ius cogens en derecho internacional a la luz de la Convencion de Viena sobre el derecho de los tratados' (1975) 206/07 *Revista de Academia colombiana de jurisprudencia* 259.
Cançado Trindade, AA, 'The Expansion of the Matrial Scope of Jus Cogens: The Contribution of the Inter-American Court of Human Rights' in *Essays in Honor of C Rozakis* (Brussels, 2011) 27.
Cannizzaro, E, 'Peremptory Law-Making' in *Essays in Honor of J Klabbers* (London/New York, 2014) 261.
Cassese, A, 'An Enhanced Role of *Jus Cogens*' in A Cassese (ed), *Realizing Utopia: The Future of International Law* (Oxford, 2012) 158.
Chaumont, C, 'Mort et transfiguration du *jus cogens*' in *Essays in Honor of PF Gonidec* (Paris, 1985) 469.
Christenson, GA, '*Jus Cogens*: Guarding Interests Fundamental to International Society' (1988) 28 *Virginia Journal of International Law* 585.

Christenson, GA, 'The World Court and Jus Cogens' (1987) 81 *American Journal of International Law* 93.

Conklin, WE, 'The Peremptory Norms of the International Community' (2012) 23 *European Journal of International Law* 837.

Criddle, EJ and E Fox-Decent, 'A Fiduciary Theory of Jus Cogens' (2009) 134 *Yale Journal of International Law* 331.

Czaplinski, W, '*Jus Cogens* and the Law of Treaties' in C Tomuschat and JM Thouvenin (eds), *The Fundamental Rules of the International Legal Order: Jus Cogens and Obligations Erga Omnes* (Leiden/Boston, 2006) 83.

d'Amato, A, 'It's a Bird, it's a Plane, it's Jus Cogens' (1990/91) 6 *Connecticut Journal of International Law* 2.

Danilenko, GM, 'International Jus Cogens: Issues of Law-Making' (1991) 2 *European Journal of International Law* 42.

Decaux, E, 'Le jus cogens — les faiblesses d'une idée-force?' (1997) 3 *Observateur des Nations Unies* 13.

Drnas de Clément, Z, 'Las normas imperativas de derecho internacional general (*jus cogens*): dimension sustancial' in Z Drnas de Clément (ed), *Estudios de derecho internacional en homenja al professor EJ Rey Caro*, vol I (Cordoba, 2002) 647.

Dubois, D, 'The Authority of Peremptory Norms in International Law: State Consent or Natural Law?' (2009) 78 *Nordic Journal of International Law* 133.

Espaliu Berdud, C, 'Refolexiones en torno a la presencia del *jus cogens* en el derecho internacional contemporaneo' in R Casado Raigon and I Gallego Dominguez (eds), *Personalidad y capacidad juridicas*, t I (Cordoba, 2005) 419.

Fahmi, AM, 'Peremptory Norms as General Rules on International Law' (1971) 22 *Oesterreichische Zeitschrift für öffentliches Recht* 383.

Ferrer Sanchis, PA, 'Los conceptos "ius cogens" y "ius dispositivum" y la labor de la Comisión de derecho internacional' (1968) 21 *Revista española de derecho internacional* 763.

Focarelli, C, 'Promotional *Jus Cogens*: A Critical Appraisal of *Jus Cogens*' Legal Effects' (2008) 77 *Nordic Journal of International Law* 429.

Fois, P, 'La funzione degli accordi di codificazione nella formazione dello jus cogens' in *Essays in Honor of R Ago*, vol I (Milan, 1987) 287.

Ford, CA, 'Adjudicating Jus Cogens' (1994) 13 *Wisconsin International Law Journal* 145.

Frowein, JA, 'Ius Cogens' in R Wolfrum (ed), *The Max Planck Encyclopedia of Public International Law*, vol VI (Oxford, 2012) 443.

Gaja, G, '*Jus Cogens* beyond the Vienna Convention' (1981-III) 172 *Recueil des cours de l'Académie de droit international de La Haye* 271.

Geamanu, G, 'Jus cogens en droit international contemporain' (1967) 11 *Revue roumaine d'études internationales* 87.

Glaser, E, 'International Peremptory Law (Jus Cogens)' (1973) 17 *Revue Roumaine d'études internationales* 57.

Glennon, M, 'De l'absurdité du droit impératif (jus cogens)' (2006) 110 *Revue générale de droit international public* 529.

Glennon, MJ, 'Peremptory Nonsense' in *Human Rights, Democracy and the Rule of Law: Essays in Honor of L Wildhaber* (Zurich/Baden-Baden, 2007) 1265.

Gomez Robledo, A, 'Ius cogens y ius natural' (1985) 17 *Boletin mexicano de derecho comparado* 515.

Gomez Robledo, A, 'Le *jus cogens* international: sa genèse, sa nature, ses fonctions' (1981-III) 172 *Recueil des cours de l'Académie de droit international de La Haye* 9.

Grandino Rodas, J, 'Jus cogens em direito internacional' (1974) 69 *Revista de faculdad de direito da Universidad São Paulo* 125.

Grosse, L, 'Racines historiques et fondements contemporains des normes impératives (*jus cogens*) dans la théorie et la pratique du droit international' (1995) 73 *Revue de droit international, de sciences diplomatiques et politiques* 225.

Haimbaugh, GD, 'Jus Cogens: Root and Branch (An Inventory)' (1987) 3 *Touro Law Review* 203.

Hameed, A, 'Unravelling The Mystery of Jus Cogens in International Law' (2014) 85 *British Yearbook of International Law* 1.

Haopei, L, '*Jus Cogens* and International Law' in S Yee and W Tieya (eds), *International Law in the Post-Cold War World: Essays in Memory of Li Haopei* (London, 2001) 499.

Hartmann, G, 'Gewohnheitsrecht und ius cogens im Völkerrecht' (1978) 10 *Juristische Arbeitsblätter* 81.

Hartmann, G, 'Internationales ius cogens?' (1983) 11 *Demokratie und Recht* 390.

Heydte, FA von der, 'Die Erscheinungsformen des zwischenstaatlichen Rechts; *jus cogens* und *jus dispositivum* im Völkerrecht' (1932) 16 *Zeitschrift für Völkerrecht* 469.

Heydte, FA von der, 'Glossen zu einer Theorie der allgemeinen Rechtsgrundsätze' (1933) 33 *Die Friedenswarte* 297.

Hoogh, AJJ de, 'The Relationship between Jus Cogens, Obligations Erga Omnes and International Crimes: Peremptory Norms in Perspective' (1991) 42 *Oesterreichische Zeitschrift für öffentliches Recht* 183.

Hossain, K, 'Jus Cogens and Obligations under the UN Charter' (2005) 3 *Santa Clara Journal of International Law* 72.

Jaenicke, G, 'Zur Frage des internationalen Ordre Public' in *Berichte der Deutschen Gesellschaft für Völkerrecht*, vol 7 (Karlsruhe, 1967) 77.

Janis, MW, 'The Nature of *Jus Cogens*' (1983) 3 *Connecticut Journal of International Law* 359.

Janis, MW, 'The Nature of *Jus Cogens*' in L May and J Brown (eds), *Philosophy of Law: Classic and Contemporary Readings* (Chichester, 2010) 184.

Kadelbach, S, '*Jus Cogens*, Obligations Erga Omnes and other Rules: The Identification of Fundamental Norms' in C Tomuschat and JM Thouvenin (eds), *The Fundamental Rules of the International Legal Order, Jus Cogens and Obligations Erga Omnes* (Leiden/Boston, 2006) 21.

Knuchel, S, 'General Principles: The Surest Path for the Formation of *Jus Cogens*?' in S Besson and P Pichonnaz (eds), *Les principes en droit européen* (Paris/Geneva, 2011) 121.

Knuchel, S, 'Words, Words, Words … Where are the Values? Assessing the International Judge and *Jus Cogens*' in S Besson and A Ziegler (eds), *The Judge in European and International Law* (Paris/Geneva/Zurich/Basel, 2013) 87.

Kolb, R, 'Conflits entre normes de *jus cogens*' in *Essays in Honor of J Salmon (Droit du pouvoir, pouvoir du droit)* (Brussels, 2007) 481.

Kolb, R, '*Jus cogens*, intangibilité, intransgressibilité, dérogation "positive" et "negative"' (2005) 109 *Revue générale de droit international public* 305.

Kolb, R, 'La détermination du concept de *jus cogens*' (2014) 118 *Revue générale de droit international public* 5.

Kolb, R, 'Nullité, inapplicabilité ou inexistence d'une norme coutumière contraire au *jus cogens* universel?' (2013) 117 *Revue générale de droit international public* 281.

Kolb, R, 'Observations sur l'évolution du concept de *jus cogens*' (2009) 113 *Revue générale de droit international public* 837.

Kolb, R, 'The Formal Source of Ius Cogens in Public International Law' (1998) 53 *Zeitschrift für öffentliches Recht* 69.

Kolb, R, 'Théorie du ius cogens international' (2003) 36 *Revue belge de droit international* 5.

Kreca, M, 'Some General Reflections on the Main Features of *Jus Cogens* as a Notion of International Public Law' in *Essays in Honor of W Abendroth* (Frankfurt/New York, 1982) 27.

Laghmani, S, 'Le jus cogens et la cohérence de l'ordre juridique international' in *Les droits de l'homme: une nouvelle coherence pour le droit international? Rencontre à la mémoire de D Jazi* (Paris, 2008) 65.

Leonetti, AJ, 'Interprétation des traités et règles impératives du droit international général (*jus cogens*)' (1973) 24 *Oesterreichische Zeitschrift für öffentliches Recht* 91.

Linderfalk, U, 'Normative Conflict and the Fuzziness of International Ius Cogens' (2009) 69 *Zeitschrift für ausländisches öffentliches Recht und Völkerrecht* 961.

Linderfalk, U, 'The Creation of *Jus Cogens*: Making Sense of Article 53 of the Vienna Convention' (2011) 71 *Zeitschrift für ausländisches öffentliches Recht und Völkerrecht* 359.

Linderfalk, U, 'The Effect of Jus Cogens Norms: Whoever Opened Pandora's Box, Did You Ever Think About the Consequences?' (2007) 18 *European Journal of International Law* 853.

Linderfalk, U, 'The Source of *Jus Cogens* Obligations: How Legal Positivism Copes with Peremptory Norms' (2013) 82 *Nordic Journal of International Law* 369.

Linderfalk, U, 'What is So Special about *Jus Cogens*? On the Difference between the Ordinary and the Peremptory International Law' (2012) 14 *International Community Law Review* 3.

MacDonald, RSJ, 'Fundamental Norms in Contemporary International Law' (1987) 25 *Canadian Yearbook of International Law* 115.

Magallona, M, 'The Concept of Jus Cogens in the Vienna Convention on the law of Treaties' (1976) 51 *Philippine Law Journal* 521.

Magallona, M, 'The Concept of *Jus Cogens* in the Vienna Convention on the Law of Treaties' in J Scott Davidson (ed), *The Law of Treaties* (Aldershot, 2004) 495.

Maia, C, 'Le juge international au cœur du dévoilement du droit impératif: entre nécessité et prudence' (2005) 83 *Revue de droit international, de sciences diplomatiques et politiques* 1.

Maia, C, 'Le jus cogens dans la jurisprudence de la Cour interaméricaine des droits de l'homme' in L Hennebel and H Tigroudja (eds), *Le particularisme interaméricain des droits de l'homme* (Paris, 2009) 273.

Mann, FA, 'The Doctrine of *Jus Cogens* in International Law' in *Essays in Honor of U Scheuner* (Berlin, 1973) 399.

Marek, K, 'Contribution à l'étude du *jus cogens* en droit international' in *Essays in Honor of P Guggenheim* (Geneva, 1968) 426.

Marin Lopez, A, 'Las normas imperativas en derecho internacional' in *Essays in Honor of L Sela Sempil*, vol I (Oviedo, 1970) 61.

Miaja de la Muela, A, 'Ius cogens y ius dispositivum en derecho internacional publico' in *Essays in Honor of L Legaz y Lacambra*, vol II (Zaragoza, 1960) 1121.

Molina Orantes, A, 'El ius cogens en el derecho internacional codificado — su problematica' in *Essays in Honor of L Sela Sempil*, vol I (Oviedo, 1970) 81.

Morelli, G, 'A proposito di norme internazionali cogenti' (1968) 51 *Rivista di diritto internazionale* 108.

Morelli, G, 'Norme c.d. fondamentali e norme cogenti' (1981) 64 *Rivista di diritto internazionale* 509.

Morelli, G, 'Norme dispositive e diritto internazionale' (1932) 11 *Rivista di diritto internazionale* 388 and 483.

Mosler, H, 'Ius Cogens im Völkerrecht' (1968) 25 *Annuaire suisse de droit international* 9.

Münch, F, 'Bemerkungen zum ius cogens' in *Essays in Honor of H Mosler* (Berlin/Heidelberg/New York, 1983) 617.

Nageswar Rao, V, '*Jus Cogens* and the Vienna Convention on the Law of Treaties' (1974) 14 *Indian Journal of International Law* 362.

Nahlik, SE, 'Jus Cogens and the Codified Law of Treaties' (1973) 17 *Revista de ciencia y tecnica juridicas* 85.

Nieto-Navia, R, 'International Peremptory Norms (*Jus Cogens*) and International Humanitarian Law' in LC Vorah (ed), *Man's Inhumanity to Man: Essays in Honour of A Cassese* (The Hague/London/New York, 2003) 595.

Nigro, R, 'Lo jus cogens nella prassi internazionale più recente' in C Focarelli (ed), *Le nuove frontiere del diritto internazionale* (Perugia, 2008) 119.

Nisot, J, 'Le concept de *jus cogens* envisage par rapport au droit international' (1968) 4 *Revue belge de droit international* 1.

Nisot, J, 'Le jus cogens et la Convention de Vienne sur les traités' (1972) 76 *Revue générale de droit international public* 692.

O'Connell, ME, '*Jus Cogens*: International Law's Higher Ethical Norms' in DE Childress (ed), *The Role of Ethics in International Law* (Cambridge, 2012) 78.

Onuf, N and RK Birney, 'Peremptory Norms of International Law: their Source, their Function and Future' (1974) 4 *Denver Journal of International Law and Policy* 187.

Paul, V, 'The Legal Consequences of Conflict between a Treaty and an Imperative Norm of General Intrenational Law (Jus Cogens)' (1971) 21 *Oesterreichische Zeitschrift für öffentliches Recht* 19.

Paulus, A, '*Jus Cogens* in a Time of Hegemony and Fragmentation' (2005) 74 *Nordic Journal of International Law* 297.

Perez Gonzales, M, 'Los gobiernos y el ius cogens: las normas imperativas del derecho internacional en la Sexta Comision' in *Essays in Honor of L Sela Sempil*, vol I (Oviedo, 1970) 105.

Perrin, G, 'La nécessité et les dangers du *jus cogens*' in *Essays in Honor of J Pictet* (Geneva, 1984) 751.

Puceiro Ripoll, R, 'Desarrollos actuales del ius cogens: el fantasma rompe su hechizo' (1974) 3 *Revista uruguaya de derecho internacional* 49.

Puceiro Ripoll, R, 'Las normas de *jus cogens* en el campo del derecho internacional contemporaneo' in H Arbuet-Vignali and R Puceiro Ripoll (eds), *Derecho internacional publico, Breviarrio*, vol 1 (Montevideo, 2010) 49.

Radnitzky, E, 'Dispositives Völkerrecht' (1914) 1 *Oesterreichische Zeitschrift für öffentliches Recht* 656.

Riesenfeld, SA, 'Jus Dispositivum and Jus Cogens in International Law: In the Light of a Recent Decision of the German Supreme Constitutional Court' (1966) 60 *American Journal of International Law* 511.

Riphagen, W, 'From Soft Law to Jus Cogens and Back' (1987) 17 *Victoria University of Wellington Law Review* 81.

Rolin, H, 'Vers un ordre public réellement international' in *Essays in Honor of J Basdevant* (Paris, 1960) 441.

Ronzitti, N, 'La disciplina dello *jus cogens* nella conventione di Vienna sul diritto dei trattati' in *Comunicazioni e studi*, vol XV (Milan, 1978) 241.

Ronzitti, N, 'Trattati contrary a norme imparetive del diritto internazionale' in *Essays in Honor of G Sperduti* (Milan, 1984) 209.

Rosenstock, R, 'Peremptory Norms: Maybe Even Less Metaphysical and Worrysome' (1975) 5 *Denver Journal of International Law and Policy* 167.

Ruiz Fabri, H, 'Enhancing the Rhetoric of Jus Cogens' (2012) 23 *European Journal of International Law* 1049.

Rumpf, H, 'Zur Lehre von den zwingenden Völkerrechtsnormen' in *Essays in Honor of B Meissner* (Berlin, 1985) 561.

Saladin, P, 'Völkerrechtliches ius cogens und schweizerisches Landesrecht' in G Jenny and W Kälin (eds), *Die schweizerische Rechtsordnung in ihren internationalen Bezügen* (Bern, 1988) 67.

Sarkar, S, 'International Jus Cogens and its Bearing on Treaty-Making of States' (1969) 6 *Law Quarterly: Journal of the Indian Law Institute* 88.

Scheuner, U, 'Conflict of Treaty Provisions with a Peremptory Norm of General International Law' (1969) 29 *Zeitschrift für ausländisches öffentliches Recht und Völkerrecht* 28.

Scheuner, U, 'Conflict of Treaty Provisions with a Peremptory Norm of General International Law and its Consequences' (1967) 27 *Zeitschrift für ausländisches öffentliches Recht und Völkerrecht* 520.

Schmahl, S, 'An Example of *Jus Cogens*: The Status of Prisoners of War' in C Tomuschat and JM Thouvenin (eds), *The Fundamental Rules of the International Legal Order, Jus Cogens and Obligations Erga Omnes* (Leiden/Boston, 2006) 41.

Schwarzenberger, G, 'International Ius Cogens?' (1964/65) 43 *Texas Law Review* 455.

Schwarzenberger, G, 'The Problem of International Public Policy' (1965) 18 *Current Legal Problems* 191.

Schweitzer, M, 'Ius Cogens im Völkerrecht' (1971) 15 *Archiv des Völkerrechts* 197.

Schwelb, E, 'Some Aspects of International *Jus Cogens* as Formulated by the ILC' (1967) 61 *American Journal of International Law* 946.

Stephan, PB, 'The Political Economy of *Jus Cogens*' (2011) 44 *Vanderbilt Journal of Transnational Law* 1073.

Tavernier, P, 'L'identification des règles fondamentales: un problème résolu?' in C Tomuschat and JM Thouvenin (eds), *The Fundamental Rules of the International Legal Order: Jus Cogens and Obligations Erga Omnes* (Leiden/Boston, 2006) 1.

Terz, P, 'Zum jus cogens im demokratischen Völkerrecht' (1978) 27 *Staat und Recht* 617.

Tunkin, GI, 'Jus Cogens in Contemporary International Law' (1971) 1 *University of Toledo Law Review* 107.

Turpel, ME and Sands, P, 'Peremptory International Law and Sovereignty: Some Questions' (1988) 3 *Connecticut Journal of International Law* 364.

Uibopuu, HJ, 'Neue Wendung im sowjetischen Jus Cogens Konzept' (1971) 15 *Recht in Ost und West* 135.

Verdross, A, 'Anfechtbare und nichtige Staatsverträge' (1935) 15 *Oesterreichische Zeitschrift für öffentliches Recht* 289.

Verdross, A, 'Der Grundsatz "pacta sunt servanda" und die Grenzen der guten Sitten im Völkerrecht' (1936) 16 *Oesterreichische Zeitschrift für öffentliches Recht* 79.

Verdross, A, 'Heilige und unsittliche Staatsverträge' (1935/36) 2 *Völkerbund und Völkerrecht* 164.

Verdross, A, 'Jus Dispositivum und Jus Cogens in International Law' (1966) 60 *American Journal of International Law* 55.

Verdross, A, 'Trattati contra bonos mores' (1937) 29 *Rivista di diritto internazionale* 3.

Verdross, A, 'Forbidden Treaties in International Law' (1937) *31 American Journal of International Law* 571.

Verhoeven, J, 'Sur les "bons" et les "mauvais" emplois du *jus cogens*' (2008) 5 *Anuario brasileiro de direito internacional* 133.

Vidmar, J, 'Rethinking *Jus Cogens* after Germany v Italy: Back to Article 53?' (2013) 60 *Netherlands International Law Review* 1.

Virally, M, 'Réflexions sur le *jus cogens*' (1966) 12 *Annuaire français de droit international* 5.

Visscher, P de, 'Positivisme et jus cogens' (1971) 75 *Revue générale de droit international public* 5.

Weckel, P, 'Un exemple remarquable d'application du *jus cogens*, le statut de prisonnier de guerre' in C Tomuschat and JM Thouvenin (eds), *The Fundamental Rules of the International Legal Order, Jus Cogens and Obligations Erga Omnes* (Leiden/Boston, 2006) 69.

Weisburd, AM, 'The Emptiness of the Concept of *Jus Cogens*, as Illustrated by the War in Bosnia-Herzegovina' (1995) 17 *Michigan Journal of International Law* 1.

Whiteman, MM, 'Jus Cogens in International Law, With a Proposed List' (1977) 7 *Georgia Journal of International and Comparative Law* 609.

Wolfke, K, '*Jus Cogens* in International Law' (1974) 6 *Polish Yearbook of International Law* 145.

Yasseen, MK, 'Réflexions sur la détermination du "*jus cogen* s"' in Société française pour le droit international, *L'élaboration du droit international* (Paris, 1975) 204.

Zemanek, K, 'The Metamorphosis of *Jus Cogens*: From an Institution of Treaty Law to the Bedrock of the International Legal Order?' in E Cannizzaro (ed), *The Law of Treaties Beyond the Vienna Convention* (Oxford, 2010) 381.

Zotiades, GB, 'Staatsautonomie und die Grenzen der Vertragsfreiheit im Völkerrecht' (1967) 17 *Oesterreichische Zeitschrift für öffentliches Recht* 90.

INDEX

Abrogation
abrogation of customary rules, 70–72
modification of *jus cogens*, 100
see also **Modification of *jus cogens***
norm creation and abrogation, 31
termination of legal norm, 2
Absolute obligations
absolute nullity, 105
concept of *jus cogens*, 8, 12, 14, 30, 76, 80, 86, 97–100
see also **Concept of *jus cogens***
moral absolutes, 30
Agreements
see also **International treaties**
agreements between belligerents, 61
bilateral agreements, 99–100
see also **Bilateral agreements**
compromise agreements, 25–27
conflicting clauses, 61
conflicting treaties, 40–42
derogation by agreement, 70
essential elements, 60
incompatible agreements, 41–42
international agreements, 20, 32, 40, 47
international humanitarian law (IHL), 81–83
jus cogens norms, 60–61
jus cogens superveniens, 61
later derogatory agreements, 58
legal acts, 60–61
see also **Legal acts**
partial agreements, 56
peace agreements, 125
sources of international law, 89
sources of *jus cogens*, 91
see also **Sources of *jus cogens***
submission agreements, 51–52
unlawful special agreements, 106
void *contra bonos mores*, 60
Anti-terrorist measures
balancing of rights, 124
Armed conflicts
agreements between belligerents, 61
international humanitarian law (IHL), 81
see also **International humanitarian law (IHL)**
international law, 47
self-defence, 74
Bibliography
articles and book chapters, 131–37
books and theses, 130–31
Bilateral agreements
absence of general law, 99
absence of international practice, 100
contrary acts, 99
inter se derogation, 99–100
jus cogens norms, 99
lex posterior rule, 99
Boundlessness
admissibility of retroactivity, 108
breaches of *jus cogens*, 108–9
deductive reasoning, 109, 113–14
effects beyond validity/nullity, 109
exercise of diplomatic protection, 109
imposition of positive duties, 109
inductive reasoning, 109, 113
jurisdictional immunities, 108
super-*jus cogens*, 108
universal jurisdiction, 108
unlimited new duties, 109
voidance of amnesties, 108
Bouquet of arguments
creation of practical problems, 28–29
derogation from old norms, 27
development of customary international law, 27–28
excessive problems created, 27–28
Glennon's arguments, 27–28
identification of *jus cogens* norms, 27–28
international legal order
incompatibility, 27–28
moralisation, 27–28
State rejection, 27–28
subjectivism, 27
validity of treaties, 28–29
Breach of *jus cogens* norms
effects, 128
fundamental norms, 118–19
public order norms, 118–19
public utility norms, 118–19

Cançado Trinidade
new *jus gentium*, 42
protecting human values, 42
role of *jus cogens*, 42

Chaumont, C
Maoist ideology, 43
right of self-determination, 43
right to revolution, 43
Concept of *jus cogens*
absolute obligations, 8, 12, 14, 30, 76, 80, 86, 97–100
breach of *jus cogens* norms, 128
causality link, 128
contextual nature, 45
differences in scope, 7–10
doctrinal debates, 7
fundamental norms of international law, 7
hierarchical theories, 86
hierarchically neutral, 34
international *jus cogens*, 4–7
see also **International *jus cogens***
legal consequences, 45
legal technique, 40, 45–46, 76, 80, 97–98, 107, 128–29
see also **Legal technique theory**
legislative dimension, 39
limitation of law-making power, 4
logical *jus cogens*, 56–58
see also **Logical *jus cogens***
municipal *jus cogens*, 4–8
necessity of *jus cogens*, 127
non-derogability, 2–4, 8–10, 31, 34, 39, 45–46, 49–51, 56–58, 67
see also **Derogation**
non-fragmentation, 9–10, 13, 17, 34, 37, 39, 49, 65
norm left in tact, 2–4
nullity of contrary norms, 41
see also **Nullity**
peremptoriness, 1–2, 7–9, 12, 26, 29, 34–35, 37, 41, 46, 48, 50, 128
see also **Peremptoriness**
positive international law, 128
positive law, 32, 45–46, 69
protection of overriding interests, 10
protection of unity, 127–28
public function, 5
public interest, 7–8, 55
public legislation, 2–3
public order *jus cogens*, 3–6, 8–10, 45–48, 127–29
see also **Public order *jus cogens***
public utility *jus cogens*, 49–51, 55–56, 128
see also **Public utility *jus cogens***
public policy norms, 34
quality of norm at stake, 2–3, 9
regional *jus cogens*, 45
relative *jus cogens*, 37, 42, 45–46
sovereignty issues, 6–7
special substantive norms, 9
State power, 129
universal nature, 37
variable/multiple nature, 45
voiding effect, 3–5
Conflict of successive treaties
see **Rules of horizontal collision**
Conflicts between *jus cogens* norms
actual or potential conflicts, 117
existence of conflict, 117–19
fundamental norms, 118–19
human rights protection, 116
non-derogable rules, 117, 119
non-use of force rule (NUFR), 116
see also **Non-use of force rule (NUFR)**
peremptory norms, 116–17
public order *jus cogens*, 116–19, 121–26
see also **Public order *jus cogens***
public utility *jus cogens*, 117–21
see also **Public utility *jus cogens***
relevance, 116–17
responsibility to protect, 116
Consequential *jus cogens*
effects of *jus cogens*, 88, 110–12
Contract law
contractual engagements, 18–19
validity, 19
Customary international law
abrogation of customary rules, 70–72
access to justice, 66, 68, 70, 87, 95
autonomous norms, 12
conflicting norms, 65–67, 70
derogation by agreement, 70
extinction of norm, 72
general customary law norms, 65, 68–69
hierarchical superior norms, 67
immunity rules, 66, 68, 70, 87, 95
imperative norms, 70
incompatible norms, 69
international tribunals, 66
jus cogens norms, 64–67, 69
lex specialis, 71
lex superior, 70
modification of *jus cogens*, 69, 100
see also **Modification of *jus cogens***
non-imperative customary laws, 69
non-peremptory norms, 70
norms taking precedence, 64–66, 70
nullity, 65, 67–69, 114
see also **Nullity**
particular customary law norms, 65
peremptory norms, 67– 71
practice and legal opinion, 68–70
proper normative conflict, 87
see also **Proper normative conflict**
public order norms, 70
regional and bilateral custom, 65, 71–72
self-defence, 74

sources of *jus cogens*, 90, 93, 95
see also **Sources of *jus cogens***
State practice, 66, 70
voidness of norms, 64–65, 69

Definitional issues
see also **Concept of *jus cogens***
classes of definitions, 10–12
definition by effect, 39
non-derogability, 10–11
norm accepted as general law, 39
rules of hierarchical superior status, 11–12
starting hypothesis, 1
Derogation
abrogation distinguished, 2
bilateral agreements, 99–100
binary concept, 4
conflicts between *jus cogens* norms, 117, 119
see also **Conflicts between *jus cogens* norms**
derogation by agreement, 70
derogation clauses
absolute obligations, 78
contemporary influences, 79
customary law, 80
fair trial provisions, 79
human rights treaties, 77–78, 80
ICCPR provisions, 77, 79
international human rights law, 80
lex specialis, 80
municipal law, 77–78, 80
necessary and proportionate limitations, 78
non-derogable rights, 78–80
non-discrimination, 77–78
norms of same legal order, 78
peremptory human rights, 78–80
self-exemption, 77
state of emergency, 78–80
temporary suspension, 78, 80
derogation from old norms, 27
international community, 32
international humanitarian law (IHL), 76, 79, 82, 119–21
see also **International humanitarian law (IHL)**
international treaties, 49
later derogatory agreements, 58
law of occupation, 86
see also **Law of occupation**
negative derogations, 82
non-derogability, 2–4, 8–11, 24, 31, 34, 39, 45–46, 49–51, 56–58, 67
non-use of force rule (NUFR), 75
see also **Non-use of force rule (NUFR)**
norm left in tact, 2–4
nullity, 104
see also **Nullity**
proper normative conflict, 86–88
see also **Proper normative conflict**
regional *jus cogens*, 97–99
see also **Regional *jus cogens***
Differentiation of *jus cogens*/legal subjects
international organisations, 85
inter-State level, 85
law of occupation, 86
see also **Law of occupation**
non-use of force rule (NUFR), 85–86
see also **Non-use of force rule (NUFR)**
relative differences, 85

Effects of *jus cogens*
boundlessness, 108–9, 113–14
see also **Boundlessness**
chain of normative causality, 110
consequential *jus cogens*, 88, 110–12
corollary normative propositions, 110
effects beyond validity/nullity, 109
extension of possible effects, 104–109
international public order, 110
legal technique theory, 39
see also **Legal technique theory**
nullity, 104–6, 112–15
see also **Nullity**
peremptoriness, 109–12
see also **Peremptoriness**
primary rules, 111
rendered ineffective, 25
responsibility, 106–8
see also **Responsibility**
scope of action, 104
secondary rules, 111
subversive reach, 104
voiding effect, 3–5
Environmental protection
international community, 32
international law, 46
Extension of *jus cogens*
customary international law, 64–71
see also **Customary international law**
general principles of law, 72
see also **General principles of law**
legal acts, 58–59, 61–65, 68–69
see also **Legal acts**
legal facts, 59, 68–69
see also **Legal facts**
unilateral legal acts, 61–64
see also **Unilateral legal acts**
Extent of peremptoriness
see also **Peremptoriness**
international humanitarian law (IHL), 75–76, 79, 81–84
see also **International humanitarian law (IHL)**
non-use of force rule (NUFR), 73–75
see also **Non-use of force rule (NUFR)**

normative exceptions, 76
reach of peremptory duties, 128
subject-matter ontology, 73

Functions of *jus cogens*
absolute obligation, 8, 12, 14, 30, 76, 80, 86, 97–100
contractual *jus cogens*, 13
educating State practice, 12
human right protection, 13
see also **Human rights law**
judicial *jus cogens*, 13
legal reform, 12
legislative context, 12, 14
limitation of power, 13
main functions, 12
non-fragmentation, 9–10, 13, 17
policy aspects, 12
political analysis, 13
political-legal shift, 14
preventive function, 13
promotional role, 12, 14
public function, 5
relativizing sovereignty, 13–14
role in positive law, 12, 14
safeguarding human values, 13
sanction of nullity, 13
see also **Nullity**
sanctioning ***jus cogens***, 13
shield and sword, 13–14

General principles of law
conflict with *jus cogens* norms, 72
derogation, 72
international law, 72
municipal law, 72
sources of *jus cogens*, 91, 93–94, 96
see also **Sources of *jus cogens***
Geneva Conventions
customary law, 94
international humanitarian law (IHL), 79, 81–84, 93–94, 106
see also **International humanitarian law (IHL)**
jus cogens norms, 81–82
non-discrimination rule, 83
occupied territories, 79
peremptory techniques, 99
prisoners of war, 81–84
see also **Prisoners of war**
prosecutions for breaches, 83
protection, 6, 79, 81–84, 94, 106
repatriation provisions, 81
rights and guarantees, 79
unlawful special agreements, 106
Genocide
prohibition of genocide, 46, 85, 87, 94, 121–22

Horizontal collision rules
see **Rules of horizontal collision**
Human rights law
balancing of rights, 124
derogation clauses, 77–80
see also **Derogation**
fair trial, 79
fundamental human rights, 121–22
human rights protection, 32, 37, 116
human rights treaties, 77–78, 80
human rights violations, 108
ICCPR provisions, 77, 79
international human rights law, 80
international law, 46
necessity and proportionality, 78
non-discrimination, 77–78
peremptory human rights, 78–80
state of emergency, 78–80
temporary suspension, 78, 80
Humanitarian intervention
see also **International humanitarian law (IHL)**
balancing of norms, 123–24, 126
duty to act, 122–23
fundamental human rights, 122
hierarchy of norms, 123
Kosovo, 116
see also **Kosovo**
necessity to act, 123
non-use of force rule (NUFR), 121, 123
see also **Non-use of force rule (NUFR)**
proportionate force, 122
public order *jus cogens*, 121–24
see also **Public order *jus cogens***
responsibility to protect, 122
State practice, 122
unilateral intervention, 123
United Nations Security Council powers, 122

Institutional critique (Schwarzenberger)
absence of authority, 16–17
centralised enforcement, 17
international governance, 16–17
judicial institution, 16–18
public order norms, 16–17
public order organs, 16–17
International Committee of the Red Cross (ICRC)
treatment of prisoners of war, 84
see also **Prisoners of war**
International community
constitutional norms, 32
derogation, 32
environmental protection, 32, 46
fundamental values, 32, 37–38
human rights protection, 32, 37
see also **Human rights law**

international humanitarian law (IHL), 32
see also **International humanitarian law (IHL)**
international peace, 32
international public order, 33
international relations, 33–34
self-determination of peoples, 32
see also **Self-determination of peoples**
International constitutional law theory
international legal order, 38
legal foundation, 38–39
minimum conditions of existence, 38
objections, 38–39
plurality of theories, 38
structural principles, 38
substantive principles, 38
International Court of Justice (ICJ)
advisory opinions, 52–53
consultation, 52
equality between parties, 52
interpretative role, 53
jurisdiction, 50, 118–19
operation, 50
procedural issues, 6, 51–52
Statute of the International Court of Justice
amendment, 51
departure from rules, 105–6
form of *jus cogens*, 93
imperative nature, 51
non-derogation, 50–51
peremptory norms, 49–50
public utility *jus cogens*, 118
regional customary law, 99
submission agreements, 51–52
subordinating binding character of judgment, 53–54
International humanitarian law (IHL)
see also **Humanitarian intervention**
armed conflicts, 81
basic rights, 82
concomitant duties or charges, 82
conflict between norms, 119
derogation, 76, 79, 82, 119–21
diminishing of rights, 82
fundamental humanitarian rules, 119
Geneva Conventions, 79, 81–84, 93–94, 106
see also **Geneva Conventions**
guarantees, 75–76, 79
international crimes, 81
jus cogens norms, 75–76, 81–82
necessities of war, 75–76
normative exceptions, 76
occupied territories, 79
peremptoriness
conventional, 82
peculiar, 81
unidirectional, 82
prisoners of war
see **Prisoners of war**
protection, 32, 46, 79, 81, 120
public order norms, 119
public utility norms, 119
special agreements, 81–83
International *jus cogens* (legal construction)
concept, 4–7
differentiation of *jus cogens*/legal subjects, 85–86
see also **Differentiation of *jus cogens*/legal subjects**
extension of *jus cogens*, 58–72
see also **Extension of *jus cogens***
extent of peremptoriness
see **Extent of peremptoriness**
human rights law, 77–80
see also **Human rights law**
international humanitarian law (IHL), 81–85
see also **International humanitarian law (IHL)**
legal acts, 59
see also **Legal acts**
logical *jus cogens*, 56–58
see also **Logical *jus cogens***
proper normative conflict, 86–88
see also **Proper normative conflict**
public order *jus cogens*, 46–47
see also **Public order *jus cogens***
public utility *jus cogens*, 49—51, 55–58
see also **Public utility *jus cogens***
relativity of *jus cogens*, 45–46
International law
access to justice, 95
agreement between States, 32, 40, 46
armed conflicts, 47
compromise agreements, 25–27
conventional international law, 20
coordinative character, 40
cross-cultural application, 25
customary international law, 12, 20, 64–72
see also **Customary international law**
decentralisation, 5, 16, 19, 21
dynamics of international law, 12
environmental protection, 32, 46
fundamental norms, 7, 46–47
general international law, 56, 72
genocide, 46, 85, 87, 94, 121–22
human rights protection, 46
see also **Human rights law**
imperativeness, 6–7
inherently non-hierarchical, 21
international agreements, 20
international governance, 16–17
international humanitarian law (IHL), 46
see also **International humanitarian law (IHL)**
international legislator, 21

jurisdictional immunities, 95
jus ad bellum, 47
jus in bello, 47
law of occupation, 47, 86
see also **Law of occupation**
law-creating entities, 18, 20–21
law-subjected entities, 18, 20–21
legal acts/legal consequences, 20
legal nature, 16
legal technique analysis, 47
see also **Legal technique theory**
leges generals/leges speciales, 21
non-use of force rule (NUFR), 46, 61
see also **Non-use of force rule (NUFR)**
nullity of norms, 20
see also **Nullity**
objective laws, 19–20
overlapping norms, 21
partial agreements, 56
political compromises, 21
positive norms, 30
primitivism, 22
public order norms, 9
rigid norms, 26
self-defence, 74
see also **Self-defence**
self-determination of peoples, 46, 61, 85
see also **Self-determination of peoples**
soft law standards, 21
sources of *jus cogens*, 91–92
see also **Sources of *jus cogens***
sources of law
agreements, 89
customary law, 89
general principles of law, 89
resolutions of international organisations, 89
unilateral acts of States, 89
sovereignty issues, 6–7, 20
State immunity, 5, 66, 68, 70, 87, 95
State responsibility, 5
super-norms, 21, 25
Western values, 25
will of States, 21, 28, 30
International organisations
constitutive treaties, 49, 53
differentiation of *jus cogens*, 85
resolutions, 89
sources of international law, 89
International society
decentralised nature, 5, 16, 19, 21, 56, 104
International treaties
see also **Vienna Convention on the Law of Treaties (VCLT)**
agreement between States, 32, 40
conflict of successive treaties, 40–42
see also **Rules of horizontal collision**
conflicting clauses, 61
constitutive treaties, 49, 53
contrary to *jus cogens* norms, 60
incompatible treaties, 41–42
integral treaties, 41, 49
international organisations, 49
limitation of State powers, 40–41
modification of *jus cogens*, 101
see also **Modification of *jus cogens***
multilateral treaties, 90, 93–96, 101
non-derogation, 49
public law theory, 32
see also **Public law theory**
quasi-universal treaties, 90, 93–96
sources of *jus cogens*, 90–91, 93–96
see also **Sources of *jus cogens***
validity, 28–29
violations, 29
International tribunals
administration of justice, 54
conflict between norms, 118
customary international law, 66
judicial integrity, 54
jurisdiction, 118
public interest, 54

Jus dispositivum
lex specialis, 2–3
see also ***Lex specialis***
non-peremptory laws, 2
peremptory laws distinguished, 1–2

Kosovo
declaration of independence, 48
humanitarian intervention, 116
see also **Humanitarian intervention**
international recognition, 48, 73, 113
territorial status, 48, 73, 110, 128
treaty violations, 29
use of force, 28, 48

Law of occupation
derogability, 86
differentiation of *jus cogens*, 86
international humanitarian law (IHL), 79
see also **International humanitarian law (IHL)**
international law, 47, 86
jus cogens rules, 86
Palestinian conflict, 121, 124
see also **Palestinian conflict**
rights and guarantees, 79
territorial administrations, 86
territory obtained by force, 124–25
see also **Territory obtained by force**
unlawful occupation, 47

Legal acts
acts of will, 59, 68
agreements, 60–61
see also **Agreements**
international *jus cogens*, 58–59
legal consequences, 20
legality or illegality, 59
normative effects, 59, 68
obligations and rights, 59, 68
unilateral legal acts, 61–64
see also **Unilateral legal acts**
validity or nullity, 58–59, 65, 69, 112–13
Legal facts
intentions, 59
legal consequences, 68–69
legal effects, 59
legal order, 68
material facts, 59
Legal technique theory
concept of *jus cogens*, 40, 45–46, 76, 80, 97–98, 107, 128–29
effects of *jus cogens*, 39
international law, 47
non-derogability, 39
peremptoriness, 40
public order *jus cogens*, 47
see also **Public order *jus cogens***
regional *jus cogens*, 97–98
see also **Regional *jus cogens***
reinstating a global dimension, 40
sources of *jus cogens*, 89
see also **Sources of *jus cogens***
Legislation
non-fragmentation, 7, 9
public interest, 7–8
unity of legal regime, 7–8
Lex specialis
choice of law, 2
customary international law, 71
derogation clauses, 80
dispositive norms, 3
modification of *jus cogens*, 100
see also **Modification of *jus cogens***
public order theory, 35
see also **Public order theory**
public utility *jus cogens*, 56
see also **Public utility *jus cogens***
regional *jus cogens*, 98–99
see also **Regional *jus cogens***
special legal rules, 2–3
Logical *jus cogens*
good faith, 56–57
later derogatory agreements, 58
non-derogability, 56–58
pacta sunt servanda, 56–58
peremptoriness, 57–58
Military necessity clause
destruction of private property, 76
international humanitarian law (IHL), 76, 79
see also **International humanitarian law (IHL)**
Modification of *jus cogens*
abrogation, 100
contrary material acts, 101–2
customary international law, 69, 101
lex specialis, 100
multilateral treaty, 101
non-modifiability, 102
norms having peremptory character, 100–1
new treaty norms, 101–2
norms in parallel application, 100
objective norms, 100
parallelism of form, 100–1, 103
subsequent norms/general international law, 100–1, 103
Vienna Convention on the Law of Treaties (VCLT), 100–1, 103
see also **Vienna Convention on the Law of Treaties (VCLT)**
Municipal *jus cogens*
concept, 4–8

Natural law theory
form and content of norms, 31
issues of substance, 31
law-creation process, 31
legal uncertainty, 31
limitation of subjectivism, 31
limitation on States, 30–31
misconceptions and weaknesses, 31
modification of norms, 32
moral absolutes, 30
norm creation and abrogation, 31
norms part of legal order, 31
objections, 31–32
technical insufficiency, 31
Western values, 31
will of States, 30
Negationism
adversarial arguments, 15–16
bouquet of arguments, 27–29
see also **Bouquet of arguments**
institutional critique, 16–18
see also **Institutional critique (Schwarzenberger)**
political argument, 25–27
see also **Political argument**
positive law argument, 23
see also **Positive law argument**
pragmatic argument, 23–24
see also **Pragmatic argument**
structural arguments, 18–22
see also **Structural arguments**

Non-use of force rule (NUFR)
binding prohibition, 122
conflicts between *jus cogens* norms, 116
see also **Conflicts between *jus cogens* norms**
derogation, 75
differentiation of ***jus cogens***, 85–86
exceptions, 98–99
humanitarian intervention, 121, 123
see also **Humanitarian intervention**
international law, 46, 61
intervention in third State, 74–75
invitation to undertake military action, 74, 85
lawfulness/unlawfulness, 85–86
peremptoriness, 73–75
see also **Peremptoriness**
prohibition of aggression, 74
public order *jus cogens*, 121
see also **Public order *jus cogens***
scope of prohibition, 74
self-defence, 74, 85
see also **Self-defence**
territory obtained by force, 124–25
see also **Territory obtained by force**
UN Security Council authorisation, 74, 85

Nullity
absence of effect, 105
absolute nullity, 105
contrary legal acts, 105, 113
customary international law, 65, 67–69, 114
deductive reasoning, 109, 113–14
derogatory acts, 104
effect of nullity, 86, 112, 115
fully recognised effects, 115
functional nullity, 106
impeachment of contrary norm, 105
imposition of new obligations, 114
inapplicability, 105
inductive approach, 109, 113
international *jus cogens*, 104
international law, 20
judicial interpretation of norms, 114
legal acts, 58–59, 65, 69, 112–13
non-opposability, 105
non-prevalence, 105
non-recognised effects, 115
nullity of contrary norms, 25, 41
partially recognised effects, 115
peremptoriness, 113–15
see also **Peremptoriness**
prohibition on concluding agreements, 105
public interest *jus cogens*, 105
public order *jus cogens*, 105
see also **Public order *jus cogens***
public utility *jus cogens*, 56, 58
see also **Public utility *jus cogens***
sanction of nullity, 13
State recognition, 113
State practice, 113–14
unilateral legal acts, 61–64

Occupation
see **Law of occupation**

Palestinian conflict
Israeli/Palestinian conflict, 121
refugees, 25, 110–12
self-determination of peoples, 124–25
territorial issues, 121, 124

Peremptoriness
chain of causality, 73
concept, 7–9, 12, 26, 29, 34–35, 37, 41, 46, 48, 50
customary international law, 67–71
see also **Customary international law**
effects of *jus cogens*, 109–12
see also **Effects of *jus cogens***
extent of peremptoriness
see **Extent of peremptoriness**
international humanitarian law (IHL)
conventional peremptoriness, 82
peculiar peremptoriness, 81
unidirectional peremptoriness, 82
international law, 73
legal technique theory, 40
see also **Legal technique theory**
logical *jus cogens*, 57–58
see also **Logical *jus cogens***
non-derogability, 2–4, 8–10, 31, 34
nullity, 113–15
see also **Nullity**
public order *jus cogens*, 118
public utility *jus cogens*, 118
proper normative conflict, 87–88
see also **Proper normative conflict**
reach of peremptory duties, 128
regional *jus cogens*, 97–99
see also **Regional *jus cogens***
treaty provisions, 7–9, 34, 37, 41, 60
unilateral legal acts, 63

Political argument
compromise agreements, 25–27
danger for international law, 25–26
jus cogens rendered ineffective, 25
nullity of contrary norms, 25
political manipulation, 25–27

Positive law argument
denial of positive law basis, 23
derogatory norms, 23
existence of *jus cogens*, 23

Pragmatic argument
international criminal law, 23

international humanitarian law (IHL), 24
see also **International humanitarian law (IHL)**
jus cogens superfluous, 24
non-derogability, 24
Sur's arguments, 23–24
uselessness of *jus cogens*, 23–24

Prisoners of war
advantaged and disadvantaged prisoners, 82–85
detention on land requirement, 84
favourable treatment, 83
non-discrimination, 83
receipt of correspondence, 83
Red Cross treatment, 84
rights, 82
semi-liberty, 82–83
special agreements, 82–83
unhealthy or dangerous labour conditions, 84

Proper normative conflict
access to justice, 87
customary international law, 87
see also **Customary international law**
derogation, 86–88
derogatory norms, 86
effect of nullity, 86
general norms, 86
hierarchical theories, 86–87
jurisdictional immunities, 87
objective norms, 87–88
peremptory norms, 87–88
positive obligations, 87
procedural/substantive norms distinguished, 87

Public interest *jus cogens*
nullity, 105

Public order *jus cogens*
see also **Public order theory**
administration, 48
breach of fundamental norms, 118–19
concept of *jus cogens*, 3–6, 8–10, 127–29
conflict with public utility norms, 118
conflicts between *jus cogens* norms, 116–19, 121–26
see also **Conflicts between *jus cogens* norms**
direct/indirect infringements, 48
fundamental human rights, 121
fundamental norms, 46
humanitarian intervention, 121–24
see also **Humanitarian intervention**
International Court of Justice (ICJ), 118–19
see also **International Court of Justice (ICJ)**
international humanitarian law (IHL), 119
see also **International humanitarian law (IHL)**
international law, 9
international tribunal jurisdiction, 118
judicial pronouncements, 47
jus ad bellum, 47
jus in bello, 47
legal certainty, 48
legal technique analysis, 47
see also **Legal technique theory**
non-derogability, 46
non-use of force rule (NUFR), 121
see also **Non-use of force rule (NUFR)**
nullity, 105
see also **Nullity**
peremptory norms, 118
public policy *jus cogens*, 94–95, 99
regional public policies, 94
responsibility, 107–8
see also **Responsibility**
self-determination of peoples, 121, 124–26
see also **Self-determination of peoples**
setting norms aside, 48
sources of *jus cogens*, 94
see also **Sources of *jus cogens***
State practice, 47
structural arguments, 22
see also **Structural arguments**
suspension of norms, 48
universal public policy, 94

Public order theory
agreements between States, 32
constitutional norms, 32
hierarchy of norms, 34–37
international community, 32–38
see also **International community**
international public order, 33
international relations, 33–34
lex generalis/lex specialis, 35
lex superior/lex inferior, 35–36
non-derogability, 34
objections, 34–37
predominant theory, 32
protecting superior values, 33
power relations, 34
raison d'Etat, 33
regional dimension, 37
restriction of *jus cogens*, 34
treaty law, 32
universal application, 37

Public policy
common interest norms, 5–6
jus cogens distinguished, 9
material sources, 9
non-derogability, 9
non-fragmentation, 7
private international law, 3–4
public policy *jus cogens*, 94–95, 99
public policy norms, 8–9
regional public policy, 94
universal public policy, 94

Public utility *jus cogens*
breach of fundamental norms, 118–19
common interests, 49, 56
concept of *jus cogens*, 128–29
conflict with public order norms, 118
conflicts between *jus cogens* norms, 117–121
see also **Conflicts between *jus cogens* norms**
constitutive treaties, 49, 53
decentralised power, 56
integral treaties, 49
International Court of Justice (ICJ), 49–51, 118–19
see also **International Court of Justice (ICJ)**
international humanitarian law (IHL), 119
see also **International humanitarian law (IHL)**
international tribunal jurisdiction, 118
lex specialis, 56
local statutes (*jus proprium*), 56
non-derogability, 56
non-fragmentation, 49
normative unity, 119
nullity, 56, 58
see also **Nullity**
peremptory norms, 118
public interest, 55
relations between sources of law, 56
Roman law influences, 55–56
see also **Roman law**
sources of *jus cogens*, 93
see also **Sources of *jus cogens***

Refugees
Palestinian conflict, 25, 110–12
see also **Palestinian conflict**
Regional *jus cogens*
conceptions of democracy, 98
existence, 97
Inter-American Commission on Human Rights, 96
legal technique, 97–98
lex specialis, 98–99
objections, 97–98
peremptoriness, 97–99
protection against derogation, 97–99
Responsibility
aggravated consequences, 106
breaches of *jus cogens* norms, 106–7
circumstances precluding wrongfulness, 107
duty of non-assistance, 106–7
duty of non-recognition, 106–7, 113
duty to cooperate, 106–8
human rights violations, 108
limitation on counter-measures, 107
public order norms, 107–8
State responsibility, 108
unlawful acts, 107
Roman law
ius civile
public order, 56
subjective obligations, 56
jus privatum, 55 (subjective legal acts), 55
jus publicum (objective laws), 55–56
utilitas publica, 55–56
utilitas singulorum, 55
Rules of horizontal collision
conflicting treaties, 40–42
horizontal conflicts, 40–42
integral treaties, 41
limitation of State powers, 40–41
peremptoriness, 41
positivistic basis, 40
relative *jus cogens*, 42

Self-defence
collective self-defence, 74
customary international law, 74
non-use of force rule (NUFR), 74, 85
see also **Non-use of force rule (NUFR)**
territory obtained by force, 124
see also **Territory obtained by force**
Self-determination of peoples
balancing of norms, 125–26
consultative process, 125
international community, 32, 125
international law, 46, 61, 85
non-censurable right, 125
Palestinian conflict, 124–25
see also **Palestinian conflict**
peace agreements, 125
positive rights, 125
proportionality, 125–26
public order *jus cogens*, 121, 124–26
see also **Public order *jus cogens***
right of self-determination, 43
territorial status, 125
United Nations role, 85
Sources of *jus cogens*
agreements, 91
differing doctrinal positions, 89–92
general customary law, 90, 93, 95
general international law, 91
general principles of law, 91, 93–94, 96
international treaties, 91
legal technique, 89
multilateral/quasi-universal treaties, 90, 93–96
particular international law, 89, 94
public utility *jus cogens*, 93
public order *jus cogens*, 94
sources of international law, 91–92
sui generis sources, 92
treaties and general principles, 92
universal customary law, 93

Vienna Convention on the Law of Treaties (VCLT), 89, 92–93
see also **Vienna Convention on the Law of Treaties (VCLT)**

Sovereignty
acquisition of sovereignty, 20
international law, 6–7, 20
relativizing sovereignty, 13–14

State immunity
immunity rules, 66, 68, 70, 87, 95
jus cogens violations, 5

Structural arguments
contractual engagements, 18–19
descriptive not normative, 22
differentiation of norms, 21–22
hierarchical arguments, 21–22
international law, 19–20, 22
law-creators, 18, 20–21
law-subjected entities, 18, 20–21
legislative norms, 18
municipal law, 18–19
objective laws, 18–19
public order *jus cogens*, 22
State authority, 18
subjective legal acts, 18–19
Weil's criticisms, 22, 24

Territory obtained by force
agreement with occupying power, 124–25
conflict of norms, 124
non-use of force rule (NUFR), 124–25
see also **Non-use of force rule (NUFR)**
proportionality, 125–26
restitution of territory, 125
self-defence, 124
territorial cessions, 124
unlawful annexation, 124
workable peace, 125

Treaties
see **International treaties**

Unilateral legal acts
see also **Legal acts**
a fortiori reasoning, 61
consent to jurisdiction, 64
counter-measures, 64
curtailment of privileges, 64
duty of non-recognition, 63–64
expressions of will, 63
jus cogens applicable, 61–62
legal unilateral acts, 62–63
material unilateral acts, 62
normative effects, 63
normative unilateral acts, 63–64
nullity, 61–64
peremptoriness, 63
reciprocity, 64
recognition, 63
State responsibility, 64

United Nations
jus post bellum administrations, 85
self-determination of peoples, 85

United Nations Charter
conflicts between norms, 119
Member States' obligations, 119
non-derogability, 119, 121

United Nations Security Council
derogation form norms, 119–21
use of force, 74, 85–86, 122

Universal developments
regional experiences, 37

Use of force
see also **Non-use of force rule (NUFR)**
humanitarian intervention, 121–23
Kosovo, 28, 48
see also **Kosovo**
proportionate force, 122
State practice, 122
territory obtained by force, 124–25
see also **Territory obtained by force**
unlawful force, 128
UN Security Council authorisation, 74, 85–86, 122

Vienna Convention on the Law of Treaties (VCLT)
conflicting clauses, 61
customary international law, 9
general international law norms, 89, 92–93
incompatible agreements, 41–42
jus cogens superveniens, 61
modification of norms, 100–1, 103
norms changed by legislation, 71
norms subject to change, 32
nullity, 105
see also **Nullity**
peremptory norms, 7–9, 31, 58, 60
see also **Peremptoriness**
public order norms, 57
public policy, 9
source of *jus cogens*, 89, 92–93
see also **Sources of *jus cogens***
treaties contrary to *jus cogens* norms, 60
universal customary law, 93
universal general principles of law, 93

Wengler, W
active/passive legitimation, 43
erges omnes interests, 43–44
integral legal regimes, 43
sanction of law, 43–44

www.ingramcontent.com/pod-product-compliance
Ingram Content Group UK Ltd.
Pitfield, Milton Keynes, MK11 3LW, UK
UKHW020145290926
15471UKWH00004B/712